TIMOL

A QUEST FOR JUSTICE

Imtiaz Cajee

publishers

First published in 2005 by STE Publishers
4th Floor, Sunnyside Ridge, Sunnyside Office Park,
32 Princess of Wales Terrace,
Parktown, 2143,
Johannesburg, South Africa

First published February 2005

© Photographs as credited
Cover photograph of Johannesburg Central (formerly John Vorster Square)
by Peter McKenzie.
This is the building where Ahmed Timol died. An open window in the picture is reminiscent of the window through which Timol allegedly "jumped".

Extract used in Chapter 9, Inquest are from *No One To Blame* by George Bizos, David Phillip Publishers Cape Town, 1998

ISBN 1-919855-40-8

Editor:	Tony Heard
Editorial Consultant:	Ronald Suresh Roberts
Copy Editor:	Barbara Ludman
Proofreader:	Michael Collins
Indexer:	Mirie Van Rooyen
Cover design:	Adam Rumball
Typesetting:	Mad Cow Studio

Set in 10 on 12 pt Minion

Printed and bound by Creda Communications Cape Town

For further information about Ahmed Timol visit our website at
www.ste.co.za/timol/

DEDICATION

To my beloved Uncle Ahmed who will always remain an inspiration in my life,

and all detainees who died in South African police detention,

and all detainees who have been tortured by the apartheid police.

ACKNOWLEDGEMENTS

Minister Essop Pahad and his wife Meg for always making time for me and supporting me.

Tony Heard for always advising me and encouraging me. Ronald Suresh Roberts for bringing a fresh intellectual mind to bear on the draft.

Salim Essop for reliving his horrendous torture in detention and contributing to the writing of this book.

Salim Gabba (also known as Commentary and Commie), my cousins Nazrene Cajee (Sujee) and Fatima Cajee (Omar), my family and Commissioner Ray Lalla.

My fellow Moroka Swallows supporter Sifiso Ndlovu for assisting me in the initial phases of the writing of this book.

The Kholvad Madressa for making a donation towards the publication of the book, and finally

My love, my wife Kay, for her patience and her grasp of the importance of this book to me.

CONTENTS

FOREWORD

BY PRESIDENT THABO MBEKI

Any good dictionary will refresh your grasp of what is really meant by that much over-used term, "comrade." I myself have just consulted a dictionary, which reminds me that a comrade is an intimate friend or associate. We are accustomed to making, almost automatically, the move from the simple word "comrade" to its revolutionary sense, "comrade-in-arms." My point however is that Ahmed was each and both of these, taken separately as well as together.

Ahmed Timol was my comrade not in only in the broad and diffuse sense that we shared an allegiance to a humane political movement that was determined to overthrow injustice, in that we were comrades-in-arms, but we were also comrades, quite literally. He and I went to receive political training in Moscow in the Sixties. We had the same teachers in the same institution. We ate the same food. We made the same friends, acquaintances and contacts. We shivered alike in that cold foreign place and were warmed by the same revolutionary yearnings.

So now when I glance again at my dictionary, it is fitting and proper that it explains to me that the word "comrade" comes from the early French *comrade* which signified a member of a group sleeping in the same room, a roommate, a companion. This sense of the word originates, in turn, from the Old Spanish word *cámara* which means room. And one can trace this sense of a shared room further back through the Latin. So Ahmed and I shared a room, but a large one. His room was an entire country and not only that, but the world even beyond South African borders, throughout which he also sought justice.

Ahmed himself noted certain ironies in an autobiography that he once wrote, upon which the author of this book is able to draw. Ahmed wrote: "It is indeed a tragic history of our families that my forefathers were once colonial subjects of the British Raj in India and my father both a subject of British Imperialists in India and now a victim of South African colonialists and racialism." There was further irony in the fact that Ahmed's life started as the world began to galvanise itself successfully against the racial tyranny of Hitler and ended as the apartheid juggernaut, feeding on the same dark forces as Nazism, reached its height of repression in South Africa in 1971. He was himself the light in a darkening room. As someone says in this book, he ought never to have existed. The apartheid regime had banned us a decade earlier and had brutally set out to break and torture our scattered comrades. They believed that they had broken the back of the underground. And then they found Ahmed. *Mayibuye!* They performed upon his body a macabre dance, a *danse macabre* of exorcism through violence. It was their own neurosis that spoke through every blow, because in him our revolutionary spirit was made flesh and they simply could not believe it. He was and remained, even after his death, the spectre that was haunting South Africa.

That was at the high tide of apartheid, when every single institution in South Africa, from the tiniest municipality to Parliament, had been finally rid, by the white nationalists, of the remnants of people of colour who in some provinces had enjoyed a precarious place by grace and favour of a paternalistic "English" colonial era. This had been one of the most grimly systematic bleaching operations in history. And yet, the atmosphere of apparent racial control, of white *baasskap*, was misleading. The times were already turning; soon to be followed by strikes, urban protest, freedom for neighbouring countries, sanctions and disinvestment, unprecedented world mobilisation of opposition, and guerrilla warfare. All these forces, and others, combined with growing white doubt to bring the whole edifice crashing down in 1990-94.

You will read in this book that Ahmed was Muslim but never sectarian: he sought national unity across the class, caste and religious divides of his own community. You will further read that he was communist without ever abandoning his religious piety. And you will read how his revolutionary discipline never overtook his joy in simple things. I want to emphasise very strongly that Ahmed was, apart from all this, a great Africanist in the most profound sense. Just as Dr Dadoo expanded the non-racial ethos that is the hallmark of our liberation movement, just as Dr Dadoo lifted the gaze of his community to behold its African realities, so too did Ahmed Timol expand upon and enact, in his own flesh and with his own blood, the great lengths to which the Indian community in South Africa could and would go in order to assert and claim its proper birthright in this place: Ahmed belongs in a high place amidst the pantheon of great African indigenous leadership not only in this country but across the diaspora. As is so often the case, the challenges that we face are not unprecedented and we are able to learn from the prior experience of others in nationalist struggles elsewhere. The vision of Dr Dadoo during our struggle for liberation was, for instance, strikingly similar to the vision of the great West Indian historian and prime minister, Eric Williams, whose book, *Capitalism and Slavery*, pioneered a new understanding of the end of the slave trade a century and a half after the end of the successful revolution of Haitian slaves. In his speech marking the independence of his country, Williams directly addressed the great diversity of his country in the cause of national unity:

> *There can be no Mother India for those whose ancestors come from India. There can be no Mother Africa for those of African origin. There can be no Mother England and no dual loyalties. There can be no Mother China even if one could agree as to which China is the mother; and there can be no Mother Syria and no Mother Lebanon. A nation, like an individual, can have only one mother and Mother cannot discriminate between her children.*

This is the wisdom that we too apply, in our own quest for a single South Africa. And still, as late as 2003, it was possible to read, in the pages of a business newspaper, a column by a notoriously disaffected columnist who has long ridiculed our goals of national unity in the international press. He has long – and wrongly – warned the world that a free South Africa would quickly descend into tribal warfare, particularly in KwaZulu-Natal. This voice turned, during 2003, to try an assault on the longstanding unity between Indians and Africans in this country. Thus the columnist castigated what he chose to call "our Asian countrymen" as though South Africans of Asian ancestry can occupy no indigenous place in our revolutionary pantheon and even in our democratic government. Such men cannot read this book without hanging their heads in shame. Sadly, it is too much to ask for remorse.

These are weighty matters. And yet this book, despite its sombre subject and its analytical seriousness, succeeds in bringing out the bliss that drove the man Ahmed Timol. The author himself correctly quotes CLR James. This great historian of the Haitian revolution, in all its tragedy and triumph, is also the author of a blissful and classic essay concerning cricket, *Beyond A Boundary*. In this essay James saw the beginnings of "the West Indian renaissance not only in cricket, but in politics, in history and in writing." The author is himself to be commended for the labour of this book, which is in itself a further sign of the African renaissance in our own time. In his very first line he writes that "Ahmed Timol is one of the most celebrated official murder victims of apartheid South Africa." When I first read that I paused over the word "celebrated". Was this word not somehow wrong? I know that the writer meant this word in the sense of "famous" or "well known". But the other meanings – the festival overtones of the word "celebrated" – at first seemed out of place. And yet I see that Ahmed's nephew is quite right. Because we do finally celebrate, in the most festive sense, the courage and humanity of this extraordinary African.

NOTE BY A FRIEND

BY ESSOP PAHAD, MINISTER IN THE PRESIDENCY

The preparation of this book on Ahmed Timol has been a most painful experience for many people. Our fallen comrade's family and friends, those who collaborated with Imtiaz Cajee on aspects of the book, will have felt the acute distress that the loss of a person of this calibre, commitment and sensitivity must mean. My wife, Meg, and I have shared in this pain. Every year in spring, as the falling lilac jacaranda blossoms dust the streets of Pretoria, one is reminded of Ahmed's official killing in October 1971. It was more than a generation ago. Yet the memories are graphic – indelibly poignant.

President Mbeki has spoken of the twin meanings of "comrade": the sense of friendship and the separate, if allied, sense of revolutionary solidarity. I want to focus on the first part. Ahmed Timol was one of my closest friends in those days in Roodepoort when apartheid was the reality of our lives and things looked so desolate. Ahmed bought me my first overcoat before I left for exile. I used this coat for years when I was in London. To say that there was warmth between us is no mere metaphor.

I remember him having a very dry sense of humour. Ahmed was not gregarious, not a person you could sit with and who would rattle off a whole lot of jokes or narrate funny stories. I picture him with a bit of a smile that at times was little more than a slight up-turn at the corners of his mouth. I can still picture him sort of twitching up all neat and tidy. I will remember him for his kind-heartedness. Ahmed found it difficult to say unpleasant things about somebody, even about that despicable principal Lorghat of Roodepoort High School. When Ahmed referred to Lorghat, he never spoke in a vicious or aggressive manner. This was his approach to having a better understanding of people. I am not sure if this is always the correct approach. He would speak critically but non-aggressively in his dislike of people.

Ahmed had to help in building the underground structures of the South African Communist Party as well as the African National Congress. In addition he would do underground writing. The idea was for Ahmed to do underground writing in South Africa, and to write for the *African Communist*. He was allegedly arrested for the possession of pamphlets and he was killed in the pursuit of free speech, for his role as an underground educator – the fact that education had to proceed in an underground manner itself illustrates the hideousness of those times.

The case of Ahmed Timol shows that in pursuit of the war of ideas the apartheid regime went beyond banning literature and silencing persons through banning orders which amounted to what we called "civil death". Ahmed's death was not metaphorical. He was grotesquely killed. The international calls for sanctions including academic boycott naturally followed, as in the following resolution passed by a teachers' group in London: "The North London National Union of Teachers deplores the death of Mr Ahmed Timol, formerly a member of the NUT, and demands that the South African government make an official public inquiry into the circumstances of his death. It also demands the release of other political detainees in South Africa. Furthermore it recommends that the National Executive of the NUT instructs its members to uphold the academic boycott of South Africa."

Ahmed died a wretched death at the tender age of 29. In his short life, he had accumulated knowledge that many do not store up in a lifetime. He was rigorous and informed, politically and theoretically, and showed acute insight into South African politics and international affairs, and an exemplary commitment to our national liberation cause. Ahmed, though given glimpses of a freer and better life by travelling extensively abroad, was robbed of the opportunity to blossom to the full. He never had time to use the potential that we, his friends, knew existed in him. The movement for national liberation remained strong, and will continue to be strong in our hard-won democracy, because of people like Ahmed Timol.

And as we join in expressing thanks to a hero of the nation, the nagging questions remain. How, exactly, did he come to plunge 10 storeys to his death while in the exclusive care of the Security Police? What treatment was meted out to him by his interrogators in his last days on earth? How can a system be so cruel as to ignore the reality of evidence and find, outrageously, that someone who would never commit suicide did just this? Overwhelmingly, we are driven to ask: what should be done with those who, if still living, participated in whatever way in this martyrdom in John Vorster Square police headquarters? No one came forward to seek amnesty before the Truth and Reconciliation Commission for this death. Should the matter end there? The author has meticulously and faithfully recorded all there is to help us as a democratic nation to answer such questions.

Ahmed Timol's family and friends, notably his nephew and the author of this book, Imtiaz Cajee, have done a public service in making this study of his life possible.

When I originally saw the gangling young man of earnest disposition who wished to undertake the mammoth task of a biography of his uncle who was such a famous and courageous South African figure, I was naturally sceptical. But as the years went by I was to discover how dedicated, focused and meticulous Imtiaz Cajee was to be. This book is the result.

I say thank you to my Roodepoort friend, who is forever young.

CHRONOLOGY

born in Breyten, then Transvaal, 3 November 1941

arrives with parents in Roodepoort, 1949 (aged eight)

family moves to Balfour, 1955

returns to Roodepoort, 1956 (aged 15)

school in Roodepoort, finishes education at Johannesburg Indian High School

senior certificate with matric exemption, 1959 (aged 18)

works as bookkeeper, Johannesburg, 1960

enrols at Transvaal Indian College (Fordsburg), 1961-1963 (also referred to in the text as 'the Training Institute for Indian Teachers'; 'Teacher's Training College' and 'Johannesburg Training Institute for Indian Teachers).

death of detainee Suliman "Babla" Saloojee, September 1964

Essop and Aziz Pahad go into exile, December 1964

teacher at Roodepoort Indian High School, 1964-1966

Dynamos Soccer Festival, 1965

visits Mecca, December 1966 (aged 25)

in London, 1967-1968

political training for nine months, 1969 (aged 28)

returns to South Africa, February 1970.

underground for 18 months, 1970-1971.

death in detention, 27 October 1971 (aged 29)

ANC's Ahmed Timol Unit named, 1987

Truth and Reconciliation Commission, 1996-2003

renaming of school: Nelson Mandela's remarks, 29 March 1999

book in memory of Ahmed Timol, 2005

IN DETENTION

He fell from the ninth floor
He hanged himself
He slipped on a piece of soap while
washing
He hanged himself
He slipped on a piece of soap while
washing
He fell from the ninth floor
He hanged himself while washing
He slipped from the ninth floor
He hung from the ninth floor
He slipped on the ninth floor while
washing
He fell from a piece of soap while
slipping
He hung from the ninth floor
He washed from the ninth floor while
slipping
He hung from a piece of soap while
washing

Chris van Wyk, 1979

THE LONG DROP

Look down
From a headlong-height
Into a long drop
And know Babla died.

The long drop
A helpless fall
They said he jumped.

"That one?
He left by the window"
They casually boast
Grinning into pain.

A man does not fall
Like stone
There is blinding light
At the centre of an explosion

Transfixed
The murderers stand
Above the abyss

**By ANC Khumalo, pen-name of Ronnie
Kasrils, written in London 1971**

"*Murder, in view of the testimony given, is excluded and even considering it is
ludicrous ... To accept anything other than that the deceased jumped out of the
window and fell to the ground can only be seen as ludicrous.*"
**JJL de Villiers, presiding magistrate at the inquest
into the death of Ahmed Timol**

"*The police used clever techniques in methods of torture preventing any blame put
on them for marks that occurred on injured detainees.*"
**Professor I Simpson, assessor at the inquest,
interviewed by the author on 1 April, 2004**

INTRODUCTION

Ahmed Timol is one of the most celebrated official murder victims of apartheid South Africa – in the grim company of Looksmart Solwandle Ngudle, Joseph Mdluli, Dr Hoosen Haffejee, Steve Biko, Neil Aggett, the Imam Haron and so many others. The technique of "defenestration" – being teasingly dangled and sometimes dropped, by accident or on purpose, from a high police window – was immortalised in his own death. So was the chilling term that the Security Police would use to mock his fate: "Indians can't fly", as George Bizos has grimly noted. This was, evidently, the timbre of their humour. My uncle plunged 10 storeys to the ground at Johannesburg's notorious John Vorster Square, named after apartheid's worst securocrat, the man who introduced the torture laws as justice minister in 1963 and then went on to become apartheid's prime minister, as he was when my uncle died.

The death was in itself not enough for them. They turned even our collective grief into a new tool of torture. Years later, after my uncle's death had inscribed itself in the collective memory of the anti-apartheid movement, detainees at John Vorster Square were taunted with my uncle's death. Gerald Sizani from Orlando East, Soweto, was nearly 14 years old when Ahmed Timol died. Gerald was a product of the June 1976 uprising and was detained by the Security Police in late 1976. The police were not really looking for him, but for his brother Zweli. Gerald narrates: "They took me to the 10th floor of John Vorster Square at approximately 2 am. An English-speaking policeman by the name of Captain Cronwright and his bullies were interrogating me. I refused to co-operate with them. They asked me if I had heard of Ahmed Timol. They told me that I was stubborn like Ahmed Timol and that they had thrown Timol out of the window.

"They then took me to the window and I was told that this was called 'Timol Heights'. I was held by my feet and dangled outside the window. I closed my eyes, sure that I was dead. They would then pull me up again. This happened in broad daylight. They managed to find Zweli and I was released at approximately 1 pm the next afternoon. Then Zweli was severely beaten and assaulted, which damaged him permanently. To this day he has relapses of mental disturbance."

჻჻჻

There is no point giving this book to you, the reader, as a dispassionate or clinical account of my uncle's death. I am not a coroner. Such an approach would merely heap new crudities upon the old indignities that my family had already suffered.

"Ahmed took great delight in his mother," says Aysha, my own mother and Ahmed's sister. "He hugged and held Hawa and often told her how special she was.

He would call out to her like an infant, lovingly telling her: 'You are my mother.' Particularly after Eid prayers, he used to hug her (*bhete*)." Ahmed's favourite book was *Mother* by the Russian novelist Maxim Gorky.

I myself hardly need to emphasise that I loved and revered my uncle and his mother. Every day Hawa made samoosas and a variety of Indian delights for her son Ahmed's lunch. During meals, Ahmed wanted no one to complain about the food. After eating they could tell Hawa what was not right, but they could not say anything at the table as this would hurt Hawa. In any case, "Hawa always cooked his favourites," says Aysha. Indian delights: that is exactly the phrase Hawa chose to describe the food that she cooked for him; it is the phrase that my own mother uses. I use it too.

It captures the absolute affection that is invested in the preparation of food among us. The first chapter of Arundhati Roy's novel *The God of Small Things* is called "Paradise, Pickles and Preserves". And if you read VS Naipaul's *Between Father and Son: Family Letters*[1] you will find this master of darkness, cynicism and pessimism writing home from New York lines such as: "I was about to go to a restaurant for a meal when I remembered that I had a whole baked chicken with me – my darling mother looks after her children with all the poor little love she can dispose of."

Perhaps you will understand what it meant when the food taken to Ahmed in detention never reached him – or worse, as recounted by fellow detainee Indres Moodley: "My wife had sent me food in a flask. When I received the food, the flask was crushed with glass particles in the food. I could not eat the food." This was not only a minor inconvenience but an emotional blow to match the physical ones.

To gauge the scale of it, you might also notice the other mind-games with which this food-trick was coupled. Indres told me: "They would phone my wife and tell her that my body was lying in a ditch somewhere. She would drive and go looking for me. She was pregnant at the time. They even told me that they would put my wife in a cell and a policeman would rape her."

Torture was not only physical violence but a deliberate attack on the basic dignity and security of our domestic arrangements, on the fabric of our families' lives. After Ahmed's death the Security Police made serious attempts to recruit his brother, Mohammed, as an informer. They tried to enlist his parents, my own grandmother and grandfather, to persuade Mohammed. Ahmed's body was not enough; they also wanted my family's soul.

Early every morning the aroma of the food defiantly swept the entire building where the Timols lived. Hawa sliced and peeled fruit for Ahmed daily. "Ahmed would take off for school with a three-minute egg, with salt and pepper and fresh orange juice made by Hawa," recalls my mother. I have often shared the joke with Jewish comrades, of whom there were many, that long before the Jewish Mother there was Ahmed's Mother. That was Hawa. Last year I personally telephoned one of my uncle's captors, Johannes Hendrik Gloy, merely seeking conversation, straining to detect some sense of remorse in him. But the man brazenly attacked Hawa. He said that all her talk of torture was "a bunch of lies". Allah be praised that I never had to report those words to Hawa; she has safely passed away. He can no longer reach her; cannot have her soul.

So I write this book for my mother's mother, notorious "liar" that she was, as Gloy would say.

చి చి చి

I have called this book *A Quest for Justice*. I wanted, if not specific retribution, at least to put right some lingering sense of a wrong committed against my uncle, my family, my country, myself. Immediately after my uncle's death the African National Congress correctly promised, in its official statement, to "avenge" Ahmed's murder and I am, even now, not willing to let go of that word, despite all the colourful talk of "reconciliation" that surrounds such subjects as these.

But any question of vengeance was overtaken, during the writing process, by a more pressing need. It dawned upon me that I wanted to know my uncle. I hope that the reader will want to know him as well. I was five years old when he died and this book is my own act of reclaiming him whom I only almost had. I still have his Beethoven LPs which brought him calm and rest. The *Ninth Symphony* has the most tattered jacket; it must have been my uncle's favourite. But however much I played and re-played his music to myself in old boyish hope, Ahmed never appeared. I had no Aladdin's lamp, but I kept rubbing away.

The process of reclaiming him in fact long pre-dated the idea of a book. I began on my own many years ago, with the hoard of faint memories that I cherish ... of sitting with Uncle Ahmed in Amina Desai's yellow Anglia, the very car in which he was to be arrested shortly before his murder. Uncle Ahmed often took me to Amina's house and I remember her white cat – but all its playfulness is overwhelmed, for me, by the grim recollection, after his death, of coming from Standerton to Roodepoort with my mother in the middle of the night. We were sitting huddled in the small kitchen and the family were whispering to one another. There was the ritual knock on the door. White policemen entered. Later, Uncle Ahmed's body was placed outside the flat in Roodepoort and people filed past. My granny, the dead hero's mother, was standing at the flat balcony. These glimpses are indelibly vivid in my mind.

During the years that followed I would go to the cemetery and visit Uncle Ahmed's grave with my grandfather. I would return to the flat and report back to my granny. She would inquire if I had prayed for my uncle.

These in full are the combined, precious and only personal memories with which I began the journey recorded in this book, to know and reclaim my Uncle Ahmed in the fullness and roundness of his personality, going beyond the grim fixture in my mind of his martyrdom (a word I use literally: he was a martyr) and the immensity of my grief. In 1996 I began to collect documents about Ahmed's life and death as an act of remembrance and also to ensure that I could be of assistance, if necessary, as our democratic country began the process of re-visiting its past. There was, as yet, no idea of a book.

In these acts of remembrance and research I found that my uncle was a colourful character. He would have continued to humour all my childish questions; he always genuinely had time for children. Although his wardrobe had little clothing he was always impeccably dressed. Ahmed's sister Aysha would often tease him, saying that his moustache made him look like a farmer. Ahmed would go to the bathroom and shave off his moustache and then show his clean face to Aysha, asking how he now looked. He wore stovepipe trousers and checked jackets. His high sartorial standards slipped only slightly in the Bohemian London of the Sixties, where he could also be spotted watching television soap operas during breaks from his prescribed readings in sociology. He was a strong swimmer, an energetic soccer administrator and an outstanding cricketer.

The swimming was recreational, for his own relaxation and good health, and he often took me with him to the Roodepoort Club for a dowsing. Yasmin Pahad, (now ministers) Essop and Aziz's niece, remembers Ahmed taking her to the Fulham indoor pool as a seven-year-old in London. "My strokes were terrible and Ahmed taught me to swim properly. Up to today, when I swim (which is very often), I still keep my hands and fingers exactly the way he taught me, but I think he'd be disgusted to know that I don't breathe properly!"

As a soccer player my dear uncle was entirely meritless and never pretended otherwise: his administrative role in soccer was also used as a cover for his political activities. As an administrator of a soccer league he had good reason for the frenetic travel that every busy revolutionary requires. His close comrades Aziz and Essop Pahad even called their soccer team "the Dynamos", after the famous Moscow Dynamos squad, but the Security Branch remained too slow to know. In a soccer brochure written by Ahmed he quotes Indian prime minister Nehru: "Success only comes to those who act bravely and boldly and never to the timid."

It was as a cricketer, however, that Ahmed had genuinely professional talents and might have gone all the way to stardom had he inhabited quieter times. It was here that his temperament was most naturally expressed. As CLR James asked in *Beyond a Boundary* (1963), his path-breaking essay on the anti-colonial politics of cricket: "What do they know of cricket, who only cricket know?"

Michael Manley, the great socialist prime minister of Jamaica, was himself inspired by James when he summed up the importance of cricket as a co-operative endeavour among West Indians: cricket was "a constant reminder, to a people of otherwise wayward insularity, of the value of collaboration"[2]. What better metaphor for Ahmed's own constant efforts to break down elements of the sectarian insularity of politics and religion within the Indian community, for his efforts to break down the divides that were meant to keep Indians and Africans (let alone whites) apart for the purposes of apartheid; for his status as an internationalist, whose work within South Africa was always informed by a world view that looked beyond the water's edge.

My Uncle Haroon remembers his brother as not an argumentative type. If someone said something to him that he did not like he would simply laugh and walk away. However, on matters of principle Ahmed always defied; his profound humanity was far more than mere sentimentality. He was never a pacifist even though he supported the Campaign for Nuclear Disarmament during his time in London.

Uncle Ahmed had a fine sense of the tragic and he well knew that the Good Cause could never win automatically or unassisted. It needed its own men in uniform to contest against the hard men of apartheid. It is fitting then that after his death there was the Ahmed Timol unit of Umkhonto we Sizwe that operated around Johannesburg from 1987. Two of its members, Yusuf Akhalwaya and Prakash Napier, themselves died on 11 December 1989 in the line of duty.

After Ahmed's death, Nassim Pahad told the *Rand Daily Mail*: "Ahmed was the man who in any discussion of politics would say: 'Politics is for politicians. It is our job to be humane in our dealings with others.' You see, it's strange that a man who was forever repeating these sentiments should die in police custody." (29 October 1971).

Mohammed Bhabha (who lives in Canada) tells of the time when his cousin, Ahmed Bhabha, was in detention. "One day my aunt asked us to sprinkle holy water on the path leading from the office to the cells so that the hearts of Special Branch interrogators would be softened when they came and they would not harm my cousin. While I refused, Timol agreed to do it. It was quite a sight to see him performing the task. The policemen walked ahead of us. My aunt and I followed behind. Timol brought up the rear. He held the bottle in his left hand and with his right hand he sprinkled the holy water on the path and on both sides while at the same time anxiously reciting some prayers."

My uncle, Ahmed Timol, was a Muslim of the most profoundly humane kind. His particular brand of fundamentalism, however, was never theological and always humanist. He was no kind of zealot except in the causes of anti-racism and anti-apartheid and such values were hardly zealotry, merely common sense and elementary decency. Underneath his political ideology and religious beliefs Ahmed merely sought a South Africa made safe for schoolteachers such as he himself was; a South Africa that could live up to every child's basic idea of fairness – racial fairness and economic fairness. His ambitions were as simple and as humane as that. In 1999, in Azaadville, Nelson Mandela fittingly dedicated a school to his memory and renamed it after him.

He was a fundamentalist in the cause of common sense; he mingled the pious and the practical. He never left the house in the morning without reading Yaseen (a verse from the Quran), yet he never wore a "topee" (hat) for fear of upsetting his hairstyle; he wore a handkerchief instead. Ahmed always told Aysha (my mother) to keep her heart clean. He used precisely those simple, commonplace words for virtue. "Allah does not like it when the heart is dirty," he would say.

Ahmed was exceptionally well dressed on a Friday, the holy day in the Muslim calendar. In summer, he would bathe twice a day, Aysha recalls. "He was always very neat and tidy. He insisted that new shirts first had to be washed before being worn, since there must be no creases on the shirt. The label on the back of his shirt had to be removed as it left a "mark" on his body. Ahmed always brought his friends home for lunch on Fridays after returning from prayers. Whenever Ahmed entered the flat he first went to the bathroom to comb his hair – never a strand out of place, that was his harmless ambition. But after the torturers had done with him, one of his eyes had rolled loose from its socket and his bush of black hair was pulled out and lay strewn on the cell floor.

Ahmed argued frequently and fervently that apartheid was a heresy against Islam. He refused to choose between Communism and Islam, thus showing that the idea of the "Godless Communist" was a figment of apartheid's own demonology. As the life of an anti-apartheid militant and Muslim, Ahmed Timol's story is of central importance now, in ways he could not have foreseen. His life underlines the profound humanism of political Islam in a divisive time when violent Christian fundamentalism is trespassing upon Iraq (George W Bush has explicitly called his war against terrorism a "Crusade") and when vicious so-called Islamic fundamentalists are dragging the name of a great religion through the mud.

Ahmed Timol's *jihad* was against racism and social and economic inequality.

 srsrsr

Ahmed had a remarkable way of communicating not only with his comrades and pupils but also with children. My Auntie Zubeida, Ahmed's sister, recalls that when my mother Aysha was in hospital giving birth to my sister Amina in February 1971, eight months before his death, I would cry for my mother. Uncle Ahmed would explain to me that my mother had gone to hospital and that I was going to get a brother or a sister. If it was a brother I was going to play cricket with him and if it were a sister I would have to look after her. "Ma (Hawa) would ask Ahmed how he could speak to a young boy in this manner. Uncle Ahmed would respond by saying that he had to explain to the boy what was going on," says Zubeida.

When I was attending Stanwest Secondary School in Standerton the thoughts of Uncle Ahmed, the teacher, always came to my mind. I had participated in a two-day school boycott in the 1980s. I was just entering high school and was the youngest protester. I failed to comprehend why teachers at the school were afraid of making a political stand against the apartheid regime. Students, teachers, workers and the majority of the oppressed people in the country were revolting against the white government. Yet in Standerton, where I grew up, I saw people were afraid even to mention the names ANC or Nelson Mandela or participate in any form of political discussion.

I had read Nelson Mandela's collected speeches, *No Easy Walk to Freedom*, from which these historic words, uttered when he was on trial for his life, stuck in my mind: "I have fought against white domination and I have fought against black domination. I have cherished the ideal of a democratic and free society in which all persons live together in harmony with equal opportunities. It is an ideal which I hope to live for and to achieve. But if needs be, it is an ideal for which I am prepared to die." There is no doubt that this was also the credo of Ahmed Timol, a person who was such an inspiration to me in my own life.

A few years later when I was more senior in the same high school, in the 1980s when I was old enough to begin to feel almost like a peer of the fallen Ahmed, I made a speech in school about the role of Indians in South Africa. The speech focused on people like Dr Dadoo, Ahmed Kathrada and other political activists who were regarded as so-called "terrorists" by the regime at the time.

A teacher at the school, who was a police reservist and an active supporter of the racist apartheid regime, informed my father about my speech. My father threatened to send me to India if I continued with these political speeches. He commented that the family had suffered enough and that I thought that I was "clever".

This was his means of protecting me and urging me away from politics which had been the cause of so much pain. My hero, my uncle Ahmed, had in his day turned a deaf ear to those who would tone down his political activities. My mother at no stage ever found any political literature in Ahmed's clothes when she did the washing. "If I had found any papers or notes in Ahmed's clothes I would have immediately informed my parents," she said. But as Ahmed's political consciousness persisted his parents learned to take a more accepting, if nervous, attitude towards their son's commitments.

Ahmed constantly made the students aware of resistance to oppression in other countries. Friends in London remember Ahmed having a picture in his bedroom of Ho Chi Minh, the Vietnamese anti-imperialist who became an icon of the struggle against colonial violence as he led the struggle against the American invaders in the Vietnam War. Ho Chi Minh remains the eternal spiritual leader of the current Vietnamese communist regime and a hero beyond ideology. He was a seasoned revolutionary who perfected the art of guerrilla warfare.

Ahmed had a keen and early interest in Palestine and the PLO struggle long before this had become the cause célèbre that it is today. Ahmed was in the Middle East just before the outbreak of the Seven-Day War in 1967, the event that singularly politicised the Palestinian intellectual Edward Said and marked the definite birth of Palestinian nationalism as an articulate force in world affairs. It was in this year that the voice of Yasser Arafat was first heard in the West when Gianciocomo Feltrinelli, the Italian publishing magnate and communist, interviewed him.

Ahmed was intellectually and emotionally galvanised by the experience of this war, as was Said himself. Salim Gabba (also known as Commentary and Commie) clearly remembers once walking behind Ahmed and Nassim Pahad (brother of Essop and Aziz) in 1971, shortly after the Palestine Liberation Organisation was expelled from Jordan. Ahmed was disappointed with King Hussein of Jordan for evicting the PLO. Ahmed was an early adherent of the Palestinians' global movement for justice which is so powerful today. As with his anti-apartheid commitment, which claimed his life, his commitment to justice in the Middle East was more courageous and forward-looking than fashionable. He displayed a mind and a moral sensibility well in advance of his personal youth and his political era.

జ్ఞజ్ఞజ్ఞ

I moved to Johannesburg from Standerton eight months before the ANC was unbanned in February 1990, a time of protest marches across the country. The joy of a new political dawn mingled with the pangs of historical remembrance. At one protest march a memorandum was handed to a government official at John

Vorster Square police station. I was among the approximately 100 000 protesters who sat on the road as Jay Naidoo addressed the masses. I stared at this massive blue building and counted the number of floors. I identified the fateful 10th one from which, it was said, Ahmed Timol's body fell in 1971. I was angry at this totemic place. Even as a young boy coming to the city with my parents and family I could never pass John Vorster, seen distantly from the N1 (North) highway, without a confusion of emotions: sadness but primarily rebellion and a desperate thirst to understand the facts of Uncle Ahmed's ordeal there. A solitary ordeal, so at odds with his nature as a team player and collaborator, a violent ordeal, so unlike his own tenderness – an alleged "suicide" that could not have been.

Meg Shorrock, who knew Ahmed in London, and subsequently married Essop Pahad, a cabinet minister in the democratic South African government, says: "I saw Ahmed as one of the gentlest persons I ever met, and how could this have happened to him? It was so unfair that someone who had never hurt anybody at all, neither mentally or physically or even with his words, could be the victim of such brutal and horrendous treatment." Meg recalls how, in a lighter moment, on one occasion in London everybody jumped on top of Timol and tickled him. He cried out, urging them to stop. "If there was one person in the universe whom you could not bear the thought of anybody hurting, then it would be Timol."

It was unbearable to consider – and worse to be forced merely to speculate – upon my uncle's journey from being tickled to tortured to death.

Soon after I arrived in Johannesburg I started working at Pick 'n Pay in Steeledale, Johannesburg South. My eagerness to actively participate in politics led me towards the ANC branch in Mayfair. It was here that I made contact with various comrades of the struggle such as Fazel Randera, Cas Coovadia, Nassim Pahad, Dr Yussuf Saloojee and Ronnie Kaka (only later did I establish that they stayed with Ahmed in London), Mohammed Valli Moosa (minister of environment and tourism from 1999 to 2004) and others. These were dynamic and exciting times politically as various structures of the now unbanned liberation movements were forced to consolidate and prepare for the 1994 elections under the banner of the ANC. I recall Comrade Valli and I putting up posters in the streets of Mayfair and Fordsburg calling on supporters to attend public meetings.

The threat of violence was real. Domestic workers attending ANC meetings were under threat of attack from Inkatha supporters. Train massacres were common occurrences in South Africa and ANC supporters were dying. It was my association with David Robb at the ANC meetings that directed me towards the Alexandra Health Centre and University Clinic (Alex Clinic). The clinic was founded in 1929 and has been delivering comprehensive primary healthcare services in Alexandra to over 200 000 patients a year who are living in appalling conditions in the one square mile in the heart of the financial centre of Johannesburg.

I commenced working there in June 1991. It was at the epicentre of the hostel wars in which innocent residents of Alex were set upon by Inkatha hostel-dwellers whose violence was often fomented by the dying apartheid state.

David habitually collected me in his car during the middle of the night to go to the clinic where the flood of casualties overwhelmed the night staff. It was impossible to call in reinforcements as nurses had to depend on public transport. The police and the army would not enter the township as they felt it was not safe. The ambulance personnel in their armoured cars would collect injured or dead persons and bring them to the entrance of the clinic. David and I would assist them to move the bodies on to the trolleys and then into the casualty ward. The injured would have limbs cut off, blood pouring out, stab and gunshot wounds.

There was a perception created in the media that this was senseless "black on black violence". This was however not true. Who was ultimately responsible for the violence? It was very evident that there was collusion between the security forces and the hostel-dwellers. There was a constant supply of arms to the hostel-dwellers. The disclosure by Eugene de Kock of providing arms caches to Phillip Powell of the Inkatha Freedom Party (IFP) confirms this. The mainstream media could have done more to politicise the atrocities. David and I took the responsibility of distributing press releases to the media quoting the number of fatalities that had occurred due to the continuing violence that had engulfed the Alexandra township.

After witnessing the atrocities, committed in front of my own eyes during broad daylight and the darkness of the night, I would return to my comfortable and safe abode in Johannesburg only to find that this human tragedy was not fully reported by the media. (The full story of Alex was never told at the Truth and Reconciliation Commission and a book has to be written about the histories of the Alex Clinic and Alexandra.)

I had never witnessed anything like this in my entire life. It deepened the stock of mental images upon which my imagination involuntarily drew in those recurring moments when my mind returned to my uncle, to the body of my uncle and what that body had gone through before its famous fall. These images rested in my own mind with the images of care, fastidiousness and sartorial presence that I knew had expressed Ahmed's own sense of self. Ahmed told nieces and nephews to look after their teeth as they could never buy their teeth back, and he told them to see a dentist regularly. Then he had been tortured, butchered and high-dropped. The brutal manner of his death could not have been more strikingly distinct from the healing ethos of his life.

卐卐卐

I always wondered: "If only I had been older when this happened. I could have supported my grandmother and grandfather. I could have avenged his death." I regularly questioned my grandmother, Hawa Timol, about Ahmed's life. Most importantly, I sat with her and went over and over the last time she saw him alive and what had happened after his arrest. She would tell me the details again and again, wondering why I seemed so eager to find out about my uncle. I would sit attentively and listen to her.

Hawa's own personal grief did not make her turn inward but outward, it placed her in communion with the families of other torture victims. She would ask me why people always referred to Ahmed and not to Babla Saloojee who had died in a similar fashion in 1964.

ﺣﺣﺣ

The Promotion of National Unity and Reconciliation Act 34 of 1995 provided the opportunity for South Africans to understand the gross human rights violations committed during the political conflicts of the apartheid period and for perpetrators of gross human rights to apply for amnesty. The Truth and Reconciliation Commission (TRC), the body given the major responsibility of implementing the Act, encouraged the many thousands of our people who had locked away their indignities, suffering and losses for so long to come forward – within the framework developed by the TRC and with the understanding that the TRC could provide answers to the senseless death of Ahmed Timol and many others.

The Act placed the emphasis less on retribution and more on finding out the facts and seeking the truth from perpetrators in exchange for the acknowledgement and granting of amnesty from prosecution. This last aspect in particular was controversial. Some thought that it created the environment for the re-victimisation of victims of gross human rights violations who would be made to watch as the perpetrators were granted amnesty instead of prosecution through the due process of law. Most of the oppressors escaped all consequences. But just as Hawa Timol always asked more about Babla Saloojee than her own son, so too our democratic government, generous in victory, had decided that the mass legacy of apartheid was the priority and that divisive acts of vengeance would be self-indulgent. None would have understood this better than Ahmed Timol himself. I too was prepared to give the TRC the benefit of the doubt.

My family tried and initially failed to interest Hawa Timol in testifying. She did not want to relive it. I made a personal effort to persuade her and eventually she consented. She agreed to make a statement to the TRC and when approached to personally testify at a public hearing, she agreed. She did so on 30 April 1996 (Case Number GO/0173). Her husband, who had painfully and bravely endured all during the inquest on Ahmed, was sadly no longer at her side. Haji Timol had passed away in August 1981, coincidentally as with his beloved son, during the Holy Month of Ramadan (Islamic Calendar). He had slipped into a coma whilst performing his prayers at home.

Vice-chairperson of the TRC Dr Alex Boraine opened the proceedings: "The name Ahmed Timol is very, very well known, not only in Gauteng but throughout South Africa. Many of us sitting on the panel remember him and what happened to him and to your family as though it was yesterday. You have come to tell us your story about what happened."

My grandmother relived the pain and agony of losing her son: "It is 25 years now and I will not forget what happened." Professor Piet Meiring, a former NGK theologian who served as a committee member of the Human Rights Committee (on the recommendation of the TRC chairperson, Archbishop Desmond Tutu) made the following notes as he sat and listened to her: "It is a moving sight! The small elderly woman who looks much older than her 76 years struggles with her headphones. Her two sons have to help her. She asks whether she could testify in Gujurati. She wipes her tears. She looks very frail ... and very brave. When she first starts talking, it is like a tap being opened."

I attended the hearing and felt partly responsible for the intensity of my grandmother's experience on the day. I felt that it was worthwhile, however, because the process would now take its course. Our private conversations over the years would now find public acknowledgment, as had been promised. Soon after her testimony my grandmother's health deteriorated and, after a lengthy illness, she passed away in May 1997 without ever finding out how and under what circumstances her son had died.

I met with Piers Pigou, the TRC investigator of the Timol case, in 2001. I established that Piers had made contact with Joao Anastacio Rodrigues, who was in the room when Ahmed allegedly jumped. They had had a meeting but Rodrigues insisted on seeing a lawyer before making any commitments. Unfortunately Piers resigned before the completion of the investigation and the matter of Rodrigues was never followed up.

In the TRC Timol file, which I have seen pursuant to the freedom of information laws, there is a note to the effect that Rodrigues should be subpoenaed. This never happened. In this very important and elementary sense the TRC failed my uncle through sheer bureaucratic oversight, as well as my grandmother who reluctantly exposed herself to the pain of revisiting these matters in public. It also failed South African history, and owes us some explanation.

The TRC, for our family, had become an enormous disappointment. The expectation had been created that a full and proper investigation would take place besides the appeal to the perpetrators to apply for amnesty. The TRC by law had the power to subpoena persons who could provide information about any gross human rights violation being investigated – this could be done in an open hearing or in an *in camera* hearing. As far as we are aware the TRC failed to subpoena any of the members of the Security Police who were allegedly responsible for the arrest and detention, torture and death of Ahmed. I feel that if this had been done the police could have at least given their version of the story, not in an apartheid inquest court, but in a free and democratic South Africa.

There are many arguments about the nature of the TRC's final report. Some people question whether it was excessively harsh towards the liberation movement, or else unduly lenient in failing to condemn the systematic socio-economic legacy of apartheid. Others wonder why it leant over backwards to accommodate PW Botha and then simply failed to follow through with its subpoena; or why FW de Klerk was able to delay things and in fact was able to prevent the TRC from altering its finding about his role in gross human rights violations in the final report. These are important questions that historians and others will correctly debate for years into the future. My own concern about the TRC process, however, is far more basic and personal and, in my opinion, unanswerable. Why did the presiding commissioners who spoke about the importance of the Timol case then fail, through sheer bureaucratic negligence, to subpoena the perpetrators and call them to account? If the case was admittedly of major importance why was it allowed to falter in its small steps?

While my grandmother was testifying, Joao Anastacio Rodrigues, Johannes Hendrik Gloy, Johannes Zacharia van Niekerk and all the others simply continued with their normal lives, unperturbed by their role in Ahmed's death. They must have seen footage of my grandmother's testimony on the local television and followed coverage in the media. They have been allowed to persist in their impunity. Today they live in leisure on the basis of pensions provided from the funds of a democratic government. In the middle of their interrogation of Ahmed, they had once been interrupted when Rodrigues brought them their monthly apartheid pay-cheques. Violence was by definition their career.

Conducting my own investigation, I established that two of the individuals responsible for Ahmed's death had died (Brigadier John Pattle and Captain Bean) after my grandmother's testimony in 1997. Not so Johannes Hendrik Gloy, who was enjoying his retirement.

Gloy was born on 7 July 1938. He had joined the police force in 1957 as a constable. In 1960 he became a sergeant; 1963 a warrant officer; 1965 a lieutenant; 1969 a captain and after Ahmed's death Gloy was promoted to major in the South African Police in 1972. His superiors must have been happy with Gloy's performance as his rise in the police force continued. In 1977 Gloy became a lieutenant-colonel; a colonel in 1982; a brigadier in 1985 and in 1991 Gloy was a major-general in the SAP. He was found to be medically unfit a year later and left the police force in 1992.

I had established Gloy's contact details and was preparing to set up a meeting with him. I wanted to hear his side of the story. Why did he become a policeman? What were his views on communism and the ANC? What was his immediate reaction when he met Uncle Ahmed for the first time? Was this the first time that he had interrogated a communist? What did he think of Uncle Ahmed at the time? Why did he think that Uncle Ahmed jumped? How did Uncle Ahmed get the earlier marks and bruises on his body? I wanted to ask him if he remembered Uncle Ahmed's body. How did he respond after hearing that Uncle Ahmed had jumped? How did he deal with the publicity in the press? How did his family cope? Was he happy about the negotiated settlement in the country? My intention was to meet former Captain Johannes Hendrik Gloy over a cup of coffee and listen to his side of the story. Maybe there would be a slight possibility that he would tell me what really happened.

On the evening of 27 September 2002 I mustered up the courage to phone Gloy in Pretoria. I explained to him who I was and my relation to Ahmed. Gloy was familiar with the name and immediately questioned me on the whereabouts of my grandparents and Ahmed's siblings. I provided him with all the necessary details and informed him that I was aware that he had been in the room when Ahmed had "jumped". Gloy denied that he had been in the room and said that he was outside the room. (The official version had it that Rodrigues had been alone with my uncle.) Gloy instructed me to read the inquest findings to establish what really happened. I proposed a meeting and Gloy responded that I should call him to make an appointment. The conversation took place in Afrikaans.

I was relieved and quite surprised that I had succeeded in speaking to Gloy in a dignified manner without losing my cool.

I called Gloy on 28 October 2002 (exactly 31 years and one day after Ahmed's death) to make an appointment for us to meet. Gloy had now decided that he no longer wanted to meet me as his health was not good, he had Parkinson's disease, and he was not prepared to meet me without his lawyer being present. I told him that I had no problem with that. I reminded him that I had been a five-year-old boy when this happened and all that I wanted was to conduct an interview with him. Gloy responded that he was not the senior man in the case; Van Wyk (former lieutenant-colonel) and the station commander were, and he wanted to know why I was targeting him. I once again appealed to him, saying that this matter was very important to me. I reminded him that it had been 31 years since my uncle had died. I informed Gloy that I had not intended pursuing the legal route but had no alternative.

Gloy told me that I had no option but to read the inquest findings and that interviewing him was not going to help me in any way. He added: "Look here, the case is closed. With the advice of my lawyer, the case is closed."

I pleaded with Gloy to listen to my story but he was not interested. I asked him to understand my side of the story. He said that my uncle had been dead for more than 30 years and that I should speak to someone who had been more senior on the case who would be prepared to speak to me. He continued: "Get the court records and you will see what happened. The reason that I am reluctant is that the mother and the father had made allegations that this man was tortured, which was not true, because their own doctor that they called up to testify, denied this. In other words, the mother and father had come to court with a bunch of lies." Gloy concluded: "This is all on record. It is a pity that the mother and father are now dead. They could have provided more information on this."

After concluding this remarkable but inconclusive telephone discussion with him, I realised that Gloy was not prepared at all to meet me. I realised that he was arrogant and that he felt no remorse about what had happened. I had upset him. Despite all my pleading to resolve this matter with a meeting, with his lawyer present, Gloy had no intention of meeting me. I realised that I was going to get no information from him.

My last conversation with Gloy was on 21 November 2002. I informed him that I had the court records in my possession; I had obtained the names of all persons involved in the Timol case; I had obtained statements made by all policemen; I had obtained his own notes that he had made during the interrogation of Ahmed; I had confirmation that Brigadier Pattle and Captain Bean were now deceased. Gloy confirmed that his former colleagues were deceased.

I told him that I was following up with Van Niekerk and Rodrigues and that the family lawyer had instructed me that we had a good case as no one had applied for amnesty during the TRC process. Gloy argued that it was not necessary for anyone to apply for amnesty as the courts had already made a decision. I informed Gloy that the decision was made by an apartheid court of law.

Gloy was now agitated and became more aggressive. He insisted that I had no case. I asked him if he had seen my uncle's body. And I told him that my uncle had been murdered. This really made him angry. He threatened to take action against me and warned me not to contact him again. I once again tried to persuade him to meet me for an amicable resolution or even just a chat about the matter. But he said he had made up his mind and he was not prepared to meet me.

This was the last conversation that I had with him.

1 VS Naipaul, *Between Father and Son: Family Letters*, (London: Little Brown, 1999).
2 Michael Manley, quoted by Jervis Anderson, "Two Giants of Literary Cricketism", *The New York Times Book Review*.

Frequently mentioned names

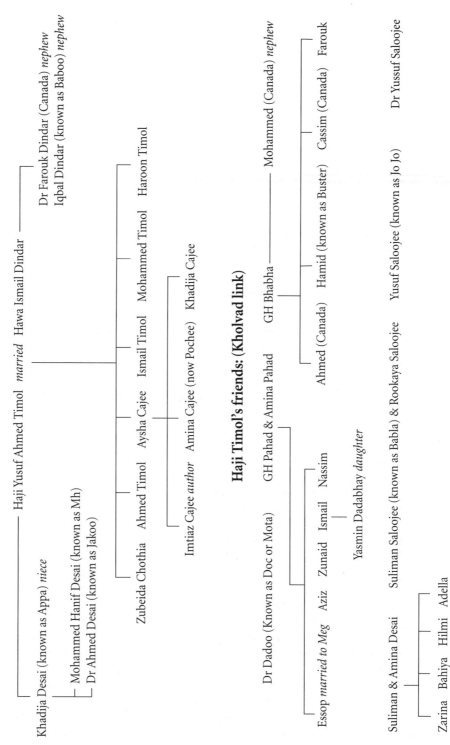

Khadija Desai (known as Appa) *niece*

Mohammed Hanif Desai (known as Mh)
Dr Ahmed Desai (known as Jakoo)

Haji Yusuf Ahmed Timol *married* Hawa Ismail Dindar

Dr Farouk Dindar (Canada) *nephew*
Iqbal Dindar (known as Baboo) *nephew*

Zubeida Chothia Ahmed Timol Aysha Cajee Ismail Timol Mohammed Timol Haroon Timol

Imtiaz Cajee *author* Amina Cajee (now Pochee) Khadija Cajee

Haji Timol's friends: (Kholvad link)

Dr Dadoo (Known as Doc or Mota)

GH Pahad & Amina Pahad

Essop *married to Meg* Aziz Zunaid Ismail Nassim

Yasmin Dadabhay *daughter*

GH Bhabha

Ahmed (Canada) Hamid (known as Buster)

Mohammed (Canada) *nephew*

Cassim (Canada) Farouk

Suliman Saloojee (known as Babla) & Rookaya Saloojee Yusuf Saloojee (known as Jo Jo) Dr Yussuf Saloojee

Suliman & Amina Desai

Zarina Bahiya Hilmi Adella

27

1

EARLY DAYS
Family, Kholvad and Roodepoort

Haji Yusuf Ahmed Timol, Ahmed Timol's father, first came to South Africa in 1918 at the age of 12. Based in Heidelberg, in the Eastern Transvaal (now Mpumalanga), he travelled constantly between India and South Africa, initially for education. There were limited schooling opportunities for Indians available in those days and obtaining a matric certificate was an achievement equivalent to obtaining a BSc degree today.

He was fortunate; he enrolled at the prestigious Aligarh Muslim University (AMU), southeast of Delhi, and matriculated in 1927. AMU was known more as a movement than an academic institution. Founded as the Mohammedan Anglo Oriental College at Aligarh in 1875 by Sir Sayed Ahmed Khan, this university was representative of upwardly mobile middle class Indian Muslims and had a significant impact on Muslim politics in India.

Disagreeing with the fundamentalist ideology of Dar-ul-Uloom (abode of Islamic learning), founded in 1866 at Deoband, Khan was of the view that Muslims needed western education as well as Islamic knowledge. Accordingly he set up the institution to impart both. He wanted to prepare the Muslim mind to change the failed mediaeval system of education which had not met the material and intellectual needs of the community.

Haji Timol forged bonds at AMU with colleagues he would count among his closest friends in the decades to come. Among them was was one of South Africa's foremost political leaders, the legendary activist Dr Yusuf Dadoo, who was also from the village of Kholvad.

Kholvad is situated 15 km from Surat in Gujarat on the banks of the Tapi River (see map on Page 37). At the time of the Mogul dynasty, which made a significant contribution to the development of India before British rule, Surat was the centre of trade, with its influence extending to the Arabian Peninsula and elsewhere. It was also the centre of Hajj pilgrimage from the earliest period of the Islamic presence in India.

In 1883, in what was termed the Pre-Migration Period, the Kholvad community, like all others in British India, was a colony of poor and struggling peasants. They were self-educated subsistence farmers and sought trading opportunities in South Africa with news of the discovery of gold on the Witwatersrand. A number of young men braved the treacherous journey by sea, some coming via Mauritius, and arrived in the Transvaal (now Gauteng) in 1883. Many other Kholvadians followed, forming a sizeable community living and trading in the rural areas.

People originating in Kholvad were a close-knit community, choosing to remain cohesive among themselves even while engaging the wider community within which they maintained a distinctive identity. Hence the use of the term "Kholvadians" to describe them, a term that grew in left-wing discourse in South Africa.

The Kholvadians, like many other similar communities, ensured that their children would be educated. Much of this was done in India. Impetus was given to religious and secular education by the establishment of a madressa for Islamic education and a school in Kholvad. The Madressa Anjuman Islamia of Kholvad came into formal existence in Vrededorp (Fietas, as it was popularly known) and continues to function to this day. The objectives were, inter alia: "To provide for the education of children and to conduct an educational institution at Kholvad." Ahmed Timol, as well as thousands of students from all over the country, benefited from the bursary scheme offered by the Kholvad Madressa.

The tradition of Kholvadian self-help expressed by the madressas is legendary. In 1935, at a time when the world was grappling with its worst depression, "the South African (Kholvad) Committee decided to introduce electricity in Kholvad, and to this end a collection was made which enabled the Kholvad Electricity Supply Commission to be established in the village. It was the first village in India to have established such a public utility without the aid and assistance of a government body." (Source: the Madressa Anjuman Islamia of Kholvad 80th Anniversary Brochure).

Kholvadians looked after their own in South Africa as well. The Kholvad Hostel was established in Johannesburg in the early 1900s for the then princely sum of £2 000. A property at 27 Market Street was purchased, consisting of three shops and a double-storey building with a restaurant on the ground floor. Three rooms were set aside for the convenience of visitors from country towns and those newly arrived from India.

The hostel provided boarding and lodging facilities for children from all over the Transvaal (which today includes Gauteng, North West, Limpopo and Mpumalanga provinces) who would otherwise not have been able to pursue both secular and religious education. It was also during this period that the principle of granting scholarships to suitable pupils for higher education was successfully put into effect. The club at Kholvad House also came into being and provided for lodging and the social requirements of visitors from country towns and districts.

In 1933, at the age of 25, Haji Timol married Hawa Ismail Dindar, aged 16, in Kholvad. The marriage was arranged between the families. At that time it was customary for South African Gujarati men to seek wives from their village of origin in India. Hawa had been born in South Africa but her family was from Kholvad. Her father, Ismail Dindar, had come to South Africa in the second decade of the century. He had gone to live in Breyten in the Eastern Transvaal (now Mpumalanga province) where he opened small retail shops. Once he became sufficiently settled in his new country he called over his large family from India.

Haji Timol worked in Breyten from 1934 to 1949, receiving a partnership in Ismail Dindar's business. Haji Timol managed the main store, called Amod and Ismail, in Breyten, and was apparently a very efficient manager; he was the backbone of the business and partly responsible for its success. The workers respected him and he had a commanding presence, exuding authority.

There was an important railway junction in Breyten at that time, and the coal mines in the region were profitable. Coming to Africa by ship from India, landing at Lourenço Marques (now Maputo) in Mozambique, passengers would board a train which stopped at the junction in Breyten and many men would find employment at the Kholvadian family businesses in the Transvaal. For example, the Dindar family in Ermelo, the Bhabha family in Carolina, the Chotia family in Vlakpoort, the Dadabhay family in Vereeniging and the Kaka family in Lichtenberg.

Business in Breyten went well and Ismail Dindar prospered to a degree, expanding the businesses elsewhere. He had managed to establish his retail business despite restrictive government legislation.

Why was he able to thrive in colonial South Africa more than in colonial India? Many years later, Ahmed Timol himself explained: "Firstly, because of the favourable economic conditions in the country that suited such retail enterprises. Secondly, and most importantly, the arrival of Gandhi in South Africa who immediately initiated resistance campaigns to improve the lot of the Indians in the country. These organised pressure campaigns yielded a response from the government that was now forced to grant some trading concessions to Indians."

Ahmed's father exemplified the tight links that always exist between politics and economics. Ahmed himself wrote: "It is indeed a tragic history of our families that my forefathers were once colonial subjects of the British Raj in India and my father both a subject of British Imperialists in India and now a victim of South African colonialists and racialism."

༄༄༄

Ahmed Timol was born on 3 November 1941 in Breyten. There were two sisters, Zubeida and Aysha, and three brothers, Ismail, Mohammed and Haroon. But there was early tragedy. Two babies had died at birth before Ahmed was born, and another, Fatima, died subsequently, aged nine months. Having lost three children in infancy, Hawa gave her remaining children everything she could. The family were tightly knit, caring and affectionate, though not too "political". Haji Timol was a supporter of the Indian Congress under the leadership of people such as Dr Yusuf Dadoo, Goolam Pahad, Molvi Cachalia and others. In addition he was a very close friend of Dr Dadoo and Goolam Pahad.

As there were no primary schools in the vicinity at that time, Ahmed and the others were given classes at home. This was similar to a nursery school. Moulauna Bhayat, who came from India, gave madressa lessons in the mornings before going at 10 am to do the bookkeeping at the Dindar/Timol business in Breyten.

COMING TO ROODEPOORT

In 1949, Haji Timol moved his family to Roodepoort, the gold-mining area of fast-growing Johannesburg. The family lived on Gustav Street, initially in a rented house, and later in a three-room rented flat. Khadija Desai (also known as Appa), Haji Timol's niece, made arrangements for the house to be ready when they arrived from Breyten. Appa was always a very helpful and dependable individual.

Ahmed was eight years old when the family arrived in Roodepoort. More than a decade later he would write: "This was at a time of rapid post-war industrial and manufacturing expansion bringing in its wake the inevitable growth in their numbers of industrial workers and their concentration in urban areas. Settling in Roodepoort was a good move made by my father. For here there were now new opportunities which did not exist in the rural areas such as school for which I was just ready and also coming into contact with boys of different interests and social backgrounds and thus no longer under the protective shelter and atmosphere characteristic of all joint-family systems."

Haji Timol was a wholesaler specialising in rice with GH (Goolam Hussein) Bhabha, a fellow Kholvadian who was also active in the running of the Kholvad Madressa. A tribute to Bhabha is found in the Kholvad Madressa's 62nd annual report: "Mr Bhabha was a legendary figure within the realms of the Kholvad Madressa and from the humble position as a member of the Board of Management, he rose to occupy the highest position in 1959. He served the Madressa in the position of secretary for about 25 years and was a loyal and dedicated Kholvadian.

"Patriotic and sincere to the core, this man whose coat lapel featured a fresh flower daily, was a true servant of the Madressa. Goolam Bhabha and Kholvad – the words are almost synonymous. He lived and breathed his native Kholvad, for whom he was ever willing to fight and for whose interests his own were abandoned. Firm and resolute, he would defy anyone who tried to belittle Kholvad and its inhabitants, yet at heart, he was simple and forgiving. Kholvad had not seen the likes of such a man nor is it likely to see one in the foreseeable future."

Ahmed would play on the swings at the place which SM (Suliman Mohammed) and Amina Desai had at 12 Harold Street, Roodepoort, when he was still in the grades. The families were very closely bonded during those times. It was to this house that Ahmed would return in later years as an underground operative of the banned South African Communist Party.

۞۞۞

Roodepoort, as the *Star* of 27 August 1997 pointed out, had its beginnings in 1886 when the farms Vogelstruisfontein, Paardekraal and Roodepoort were declared public diggings under an Act known as the Gold Law. It was not long before tents and corrugated iron buildings sprang up around the diggings.

Four small townships emerged around the mining camps, and bearded diggers started telling strangers that they were from Maraisburg, Roodepoort, Florida or Hamburg.

The Durban-Roodepoort Gold Mining Company was the first mine to commence operations in the district, and when this proved a success the population called for the establishment of a town.

In 1896 Leander Starr Jameson, confidant of Cecil John Rhodes, led a band of men in a raid in an attempt to provoke an uprising by *uitlanders* – or foreigners, mostly British – against the Boers. The infamous Jameson Raid was unsuccessful; Jameson was ambushed and captured on the farm Vlakfontein near Roodepoort, ironically raising an apron belonging to a "non-white" domestic worker as a surrender flag.

This raid, which was a key factor in decades of mistrust between Boer and Brit, led to full-scale war, and the young Mahatma Gandhi set a humanitarian example to the world by providing stretcher-bearers. By May 1900 many mines on the Witwatersrand were forced to close and provisionally placed under British military rule. So although the protagonists claim the war did not directly concern Indians and Africans it certainly had a direct bearing on their economic circumstances because of the disruption of the mines.

During 1892 the first Indian family, the Nallas, settled in Maraisburg close to Roodepoort. This was followed by the arrival of the Khan, Ally, Asvat, Hassan and Cajee families only a few weeks after the Jameson Raid. The Gold Law of 1885 made special provision for Indian trading rights in Roodepoort.

The earliest Indian families lived and traded in the Station Street area. Later settlers established themselves to the southwest of the central area, on ground adjacent to the Durban Deep Gold Mine Compound, which became fondly known as the "Lappies" (Afrikaans for cloth – in order to describe the patchwork/colourful look of the area).

Indian businessmen located their shops in central areas along busy transit routes and at transportation termini, e.g. railway stations. This traditional settlement pattern of the Indian community in South Africa can be seen in numerous cities.

The official declaration by the Union government at the Imperial Conference in 1918 stating that Indians were part of the population provided a feeling of security for the Indian community. The following year an Act of Parliament permanently safeguarded the rights of the Indian community to trade in any section of Roodepoort. The De Lange Commission further confirmed this in 1921.

However, in 1923 the first ominous sign of the racial storm to come appeared when the municipality served notices on all the Indian traders in Station Street to vacate their premises, but this was immediately rescinded. It was merely a matter of conflict delayed.

In 1927 the first prayer room was opened in Station Street, on the Essack property, followed by the first madressa in Rosslyn Street in the Ally family's yard. For sporting events the town's Curry Street sportsground was made available to the Indian community. In 1953 Roodepoort became the first town in the Transvaal to open a nursery school for all sections of the Indian community.

Despite the discriminatory policies and legislation of the time a harmonious community developed with deep roots in the area, and it was this relatively stable pre-1948 environment which formed the backdrop to Ahmed Timol's earliest years. This pride of ownership and feeling of belonging became self-evident in the environmental quality of Lappies, which prompted the town clerk, a Mr Sadie, to remark that Lappies had become the "Parktown" of Roodepoort.

That was the case up to the period immediately following World War II. Things were far from ideal and Indians, together with other "non-whites" throughout South Africa, suffered many deprivations. But Indians had enjoyed a measure of local security in Roodepoort. The dignity of the Indian community was dealt a vicious blow when, after the accession to power of the National Party in 1948, the government set about implementing systematic segregation in South Africa.

The Group Areas Board, the body set up by statute to separate living areas, began to take evidence in the Roodepoort area in November 1956. The board completed its findings in November 1963, and declared most of the larger Roodepoort municipality, including the Indian trading area of Station Street, a white group area. Lappies remained a section where Indian business could be conducted but subject to control. These offensive racial measures were not lost on the young Timol who was able to see at first hand the disruption caused by the juggernaut of apartheid on established Indian life.

He had some direct, violent experience of it too. When attending high school Ahmed and his close friend Yusuf "Jo Jo" Saloojee (currently South African Ambassador in Iran), whom he had met in Lake Chrissie, near the Swaziland border, had a few direct confrontations with racism in Roodepoort for no reason at all. Jo Jo recalls: "One particular evening when Mohammed Bhabha (now in Canada), Ahmed and myself were taking a walk in central Roodepoort a car approached with four white drunk policemen as occupants. They wanted to know what we were doing in the street and referred to us as 'coolies'. Ahmed responded: 'Jou ma is 'n koelie.' ('Your mother is a koelie.') The policemen then jumped out of the car and beat us up. After the beatings Ahmed responded by saying that we should not ignore this incident and we marched off to the police station to lay a charge against the policemen. At the police station we were beaten up again by the policemen as well as being racially and verbally abused.

"Ahmed was still determined to pursue this matter and wanted to lay charges against the policemen in a court of law. Ahmed wanted to defy. It took a lot of persuasion from elders in the community for Ahmed to forget about this incident. Ahmed would state: 'We will fight them and get them one day, even if it means with our lives. It is better for us to fight these bastards, rather than living like this.'"

༺༺༺

In addition to his rice business Haji Timol also sold khaki material at a small shop in Market Street, Johannesburg. As this did not prosper the family moved in 1955 to Balfour in the southeastern Transvaal, where Haji Timol opened a bicycle shop.

Ahmed's friends in Roodepoort were upset. They had formed a little group and had become very fond of one another. They particularly missed Ahmed. Even then he was seen as a rallying-point for friendship – a potential leader.

Ahmed went to school in Standerton, as there was no high school in Balfour, and boarded at the local hostel. He fell seriously ill in Standerton and moved back to school in Roodepoort in about 1956. When Ahmed returned a much closer friendship emerged between Ahmed and Jo Jo Saloojee (who turned out in later years to be Ahmed's teaching colleague and comrade). They developed a brotherly relationship.

Returning from Standerton to Roodepoort in 1956, Ahmed boarded at Ebrahim "Bob" Amejee's together with his cousin, Iqbal "Baboo" Dindar, with whom he had grown up in Breyten. Special arrangements were made with Bob to accommodate Ahmed and Baboo as boarders and they were allocated a room that they shared.

Mohammed Bhai Haffejee had first met Ahmed in 1956. Roodepoort was a very close-knit community, with both Muslim and Hindu families living together in harmony. Haffejee recalls: "The elderly members of the community that included Haji Timol, Molvi Patel and Ebrahim Seedat would always be engaging in political activities, discussing in Gujarati the World War of 1939." I remember Haji Timol during later years sitting close to the radio and listening attentively to the news. Occasionally, he would sigh after hearing a news story.

As his business did not prosper in Balfour, during December 1956 Haji Timol and his family followed Ahmed and returned to Roodepoort and were tenants at Flat Number 2 in Choonara's Building, 76 Mare Street. Haji Timol and Hawa stayed in this small, two-bedroom flat, with one shared bathroom and toilet, with Ahmed, Aysha, Mohammed, Haroon and Ismail. Zubeida had married Rashid Ahmed Chotia earlier that year and had moved to Machadodorp in Mpumalanga.

Haji Timol opened a fish and chips café on Gustav Street in Roodepoort. One fateful evening, rushing off to perform his *magrib salaat* (evening prayers) during the holy month of Ramadan, Haji Timol forgot to switch off the chip fryer and the entire café was burned down.

Haji Timol had very poor eyesight and underwent an eye operation at St John's Eye Hospital in Johannesburg. He had advanced cataracts and additional eye disorders. I remember playing around with his heavily magnified glasses, which he used for reading newspapers, when I went there for holidays. Eye operations such as these were very costly and money was always scarce in the Timol household. Haji Timol once again ventured into the bicycle business by opening ABC Cycle Works on Station Street in Roodepoort, but as his eyesight deteriorated further he sold this business.

Life at Flat Number 2 was tough for the Timol family. Hawa Timol sewed for additional income. Aysha (Ahmed's sister and my mother) was forced to leave school in Standard Five in 1956. Paying the rent had become increasingly difficult and Aysha had to contribute in order for the family to survive. GH Bhabha had made special arrangements for dressmaking and pattern-designing courses to be held in the boardroom of the Kholvad Madressa. Aysha obtained a bursary from the madressa and, along with 25 other girls, she successfully completed the dressmaking and pattern-designing course. Aysha recalls how she would incur her mother's irritation when she took time "unpicking" while customers were waiting and money was short. She recalls: "Ahmed would intervene and tell Hawa not to force me to attend the sewing lessons." All along, Ahmed was very close to Aysha, who married Ebrahim Cajee – my father – in 1965. It was such remarks about Ahmed's nature that made an impression on me and spurred me to write his story and helped me to grow in the belief that Ahmed would have been an excellent teacher. He knew that people could be encouraged in their aptitudes but never forced to learn against their will.

Some notable Kholvadians were well ensconced in the then Transvaal by that time. Yusuf Dadoo had arrived in South Africa from India in 1927 and worked in a shop for two years. He then went to London and later qualified as a doctor at the Medical College in Edinburgh. When he returned to South Africa in 1936 he entered the political arena. GH Pahad had also returned from India to South Africa in 1935 and was elected as a committee member of the Kholvad Madressa of the Transvaal. During the years 1939 to 1942 Dr Dadoo served as chairman of the Kholvad Madressa and also played a significant role in having the property at 27 Market Street developed. The boardroom at Kholvad House was used on many occasions by the Congress Movement for its meetings.

Dr Dadoo was the inspiration for having a school built in Kholvad, but he is also a legendary political figure in South Africa. He was a prime mover for the "Three Doctors' Pact" – a "Joint Declaration of Co-operation", agreed to by Dr AB Xuma, president of the ANC, Dr GM Naicker, president of the Natal Indian Congress, and Dr Dadoo, president of the Transvaal Indian Congress, on 9 March 1947. The opening paragraph of the declaration by the three doctors said: "This Joint Meeting between the representatives of the African National Congress and the Natal and Transvaal Indian Congresses, having fully realised the urgency of co-operation between the non-European peoples and other democratic forces for the attainment of basic human rights and full citizenship for all sections of the South African people, has resolved that a Joint Declaration of Co-operation is imperative for the working out of a practical basis of co-operation between the national organisations of the Non-European peoples."

The Three Doctors' Pact cemented the relationship amongst the oppressed people of this country. The signing by the representatives of the ANC, representing the African people of South Africa, the Natal Indian Congress (NIC) and the Transvaal Indian Congress (TIC), and the Joint Declaration had paved the way for greater and closer co-operation between the African and the Indian people which was to be of historic significance.

When Haji Timol had returned to Roodepoort from Breyten in 1949 he had regenerated his friendship with Dr Dadoo and GH Pahad. By then the Indian Congress Movement had succeeded in transforming the Indian Congress into a powerful, progressive, militant national liberation movement in association with the ANC. Dadoo became leader of the Communist Party of South Africa, and later the SACP.

During 1942 GH Pahad and Haji Timol had discussions with several committee members in order to establish the Kholvad Welfare Society. The first meeting was held in Carolina. Haji Timol, Dr Dadoo and GH Pahad were some of the critical figures in laying the foundation for the setting up of the Kholvad Madressa. Haji Timol played a profound role in helping to make the Kholvad community more cohesive and integrated as well as to build up the capacity of this madressa. It was not possible to mobilise the broader population without first organising and mobilising the smaller groups.

In Dr Dadoo's statement made at the last meeting at which he served the Kholvad Madressa one can see the clear outlines of an over-arching South African nationalism, not just that of Indians or sections of Indians. It was a harbinger of the national unity that was to emerge as part of the struggle for democratic statehood a generation later and it echoed the Three Doctors' Pact.

"Insulating ourselves from the national and international development of society would be nothing short of suicidal. We can no longer afford to remain narrow, sectarian and fanatical. We either march forward with the rest of the world or condemn ourselves to stew in our stinking juice. We must cultivate that healthy progressive national outlook, which alone can lead us to our salvation ... In South Africa, it is criminal to identify ourselves as Kholvadians only; we belong to and are part of the great South African Indian community and nationally oppressed Non-European people." (From the Madressa Anjuman Islamia of Kholvad 80th Annniversary Brochure.)

In this Dr Dadoo was reshaping Indian nationalism in a manner that laid the groundwork for our own participation as African nationalists in South Africa. Ahmed was Dr Dadoo's most emblematic inheritor, making the absolute sacrifice for his vision of an African unity across ethnic and racial divides. Even in the Eighties it was significant that my father threatened to send me back to India for my own safety if I persisted with political speeches. His intentions were not in any way racist. He was simply concerned for the safety of his son. But the symbolism remains important: India was a place safe from the temptations and risks of the pursuit of the struggle for liberation.

Ahmed suffered from bronchitis and was one of Dr Dadoo's many patients. This contact was a turning point in his life and ensured the steady growth of his non-racialism towards the African majority. Ahmed's association as a patient and Haji Timol's friendship with Dr Dadoo provided opportunities for Ahmed to engage with Dr Dadoo's political thinking as well as that of his other family and friends. Ahmed's niece, Fatima Chotia, recalls Ahmed's protests against the typical habits and patterns of racial hygiene of the day. "Why must the [black] helper have different dishes [to eat from]?" she recalls him asking his mother.

Haji Timol and Goolam Pahad were close friends and so were their wives, Hawa Timol and Amina Pahad. Naturally, Ahmed had formed a close relationship with the Pahad family, including the sons, Essop, Aziz, Zunaid, Ismail and Nassim. Ahmed spent so much of his time with the Pahad family that his mother would refer to him as Ahmed Pahad.

As indicated earlier, life for Haji Timol and his family was a continuous struggle. The family had been constantly on the move; Breyten to Roodepoort, Roodepoort to Balfour and finally back to Roodepoort. Haji Timol had attempted different business ventures after moving from Breyten and had not always succeeded. Despite his attempts at various business ventures and the family not settling down permanently in a fixed residence, Haji Timol's family remained a close-knit unit. He had succeeded in sending his sons to school.

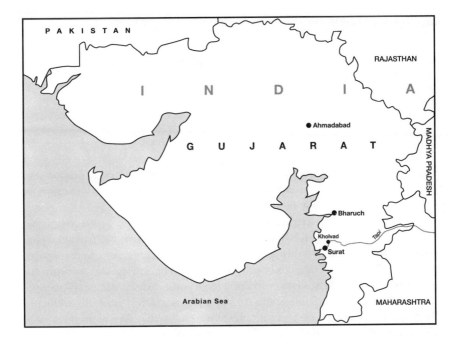

2

EDUCATION

The Indian community has traditionally placed heavy emphasis on education, and put as much of its resources as possible into it. This is arguably a major reason for the community's success in South Africa.

The Cape Town Agreement between the governments of South Africa and India took place from 17 December 1926 to 12 January 1927. The Union government recognised that Indians domiciled in the Union, who were prepared to "conform to western standards", should be enabled to do so with the government undertaking to do everything in its power to lead to the upliftment of the Indian community. Some South African Indians attached great importance to the Cape Town declaration and interpreted it to mean that they, as South African citizens, would be accorded all possible opportunities to qualify for full citizenship rights. But later events clearly showed that successive South African governments failed to pursue a policy of upliftment among South African Indians and particularly after 1948 things went into reverse.

Many years later, Ahmed would write at some length at the Lenin University in Moscow about the struggle he faced to obtain an education in South Africa and how it influenced him:

"After completing my primary school at Roodepoort the problem of attending a secondary school was slightly difficult as there was none in Roodepoort and the only high school for Indian children at that time was in Johannesburg, catering for thousands of children. This was 12 miles away and scores of us travelled daily to school for an hour or so, getting up at dawn to be in time to take the early train to the city. My family were sure in the belief and I in the hope that I would see the completion of my secondary education at the Johannesburg Indian High School and then go to university, as was the case for a short period in the past with some fortunate children who had been to the JIHS (Johannesburg Indian High School) and who were successful to obtain some places made available at that time to the non-white students in South African universities.

"Friedrich Engels had something pertinent to say for people having such precious hopes. He wrote, 'That which is willed happens but rarely. In the majority of instances the various desired ends cross and conflict with one another ... The end of the actions are intended but the results which flow from these actions are not indeed.' And this quotation appropriately sums up my position at the end of my first year at the high school. The educational authorities of the ruling class arbitrarily refused admission of pupils to the school coming from outside the municipal area of Johannesburg. This decision simply meant that hundreds of school children were thrown out into the streets with no prospect of any education. The Indian community was utterly shocked at this callous decision of the authorities.

"Once again as in the past struggles, Congress under its able leadership took the initiative by calling upon the people to establish an independent secondary school free from government control. The Congress mobilised maximum support for this venture, funds were collected, buildings hired and a highly progressive teaching staff cutting across racial lines was recruited. For the first time in the history of school education in South Africa, teachers of different races were on the same staff at the Central Indian High School (CIHS).

"Because of the nature of the school and its known links with the Congress Movement, it was frequently subjected to police raids. Men of the calibre of Duma Nokwe (Secretary-General of the ANC), Alfred Hutchinson, gifted writer, Michael Harmel, the headmaster, journalist and member of the Central Committee of the Communist Party, and others were at one time or another members of the teaching staff. The response shown to the school and the support that it received was magnificent and in direct consequence of this popularity the repressive authorities started their harassments and victimisation campaigns against teachers and pupils of the school. As a result of this the school was forced to close down in the early 1960s after a few years of existence.

"The birth of the CIHS had a positive reaction from the repressive authorities. Once they realised that the nature and composition of the school was in conflict with their rigid racially sectarian outlook, they were forced into opening two more secondary schools, one in Roodepoort and the other to the east of Johannesburg. These were some of the events that had an influence on shaping my thoughts and future."

Aziz Pahad, deputy foreign minister since 1994, recalls, "When the apartheid regime decided to enforce the Group Areas Act, they compelled Indian schoolgoing children to attend schools in Lenasia. Congress in protest decided to establish the CIHS. There were no real facilities and we had to relocate to different premises on many occasions. Most of the teachers were leaders of the Congress Movement and we were therefore fortunate to have a politically grounded education. Many of the students were active in Congress politics. Because of the nature of the school it was raided by the police continuously. Parents had to contribute financially to their children's education and, as could be expected, the teachers were not paid regularly or timeously."

Mohammed Hanif (MH) Desai recalls Ahmed, aged 15, making a speech in class in 1956 about the nationalisation of the Suez Canal by President Nasser of Egypt. The teacher, Mr Baker, warned Ahmed that his speech was political.

Mohammed Bhai Haffejee, a close friend of Haji Timol, recalls Ahmed frequently visiting their place in Roodepoort when he was attending high school. Mohammed Bhai's two sons, Sulaiman, born in 1955, and Ahmed Sayed (1957) were both deaf. Ahmed had formed a tremendous bond with these kids and he would spend every moment of his spare time with them. Mohammed Bhai could not believe the amount of patience Ahmed had for his children. He vividly remembers Ahmed sitting on the floor and playing with his kids with their toys. Ahmed had mastered the art of sign language and communicated better with Sulaiman and Ahmed Sayed than their own parents. Ahmed communicated with them so well that he practically got them screaming with laughter. From his teenage years, he possessed the art of getting through to children.

Ahmed had obtained his senior certificate with matric exemption in 1959 at the Johannesburg Indian High School. It was here that Ahmed had come into contact with Essop and Aziz Pahad, who later became his closest friends. Essop was two years and Aziz one year older than Ahmed. The relationship of Haji Timol and the brothers' father, GH Pahad, had resulted in an enduring link of friendship between the two families.

GH Bhabha, a fellow Kholvadian, was a close friend of Haji Timol. GH Bhabha's sons, Ahmed, Cassim, Hamid "Buster" and Farouk, were very closely linked to Ahmed. Farouk says: "We practically lived together in one house. My cousin, Mohammed Bhabha, also lived with us. The Timol and Bhabha families were very closely knitted." Ahmed, Cassim and Mohammed now live in Canada.

FIERY BRUSH WITH LAW ON A TRAIN
Ahmed had early brushes with the brutal new order that was gaining ground in South Africa. Ahmed and his close friend Jo Jo Saloojee were once among a group of students travelling by train from Roodepoort to Johannesburg to attend high school when one of the students claimed to have a leaked exam paper. The group looking at this leaked paper began questioning its authenticity. Ahmed and Jo Jo took the view that they were heading for big trouble and that they should burn the paper. A small fire was made and, as the paper was smouldering, a white conductor entered the coach and asked who had made the fire. He immediately locked the doors of the coach and proceeded to the next coach.

The conductor assumed that the fire was politically motivated and that the students were burning banned literature. As the train approached Langlaagte station, a group of Railway, uniformed and Security Branch policemen took the students into custody. Ahmed and Jo Jo managed to escape. However, other students gave their names.

The police came to Ahmed and Jo Jo's homes and questioned both of them. Hawa Timol urged her son to provide them with the names they were looking for so that the police would leave. Ahmed refused to co-operate with them. It was this defiant stand that Ahmed was to employ against the security police and authorities for the rest of his life. Even in Ahmed's final moments, the security police were highly displeased with the level of "co-operation" they thought he was giving.

In the train incident the authorities were looking for a political motive and this was now a Security Branch matter, a serious development. Some of the detained students mentioned that it was a leaked exam paper that they were burning whilst others, under duress, claimed that it was political literature.

The Security Branch wanted to establish who was principally responsible for the fire. Ahmed and Jo Jo refused to co-operate. Suliman "Babla" Saloojee took Ahmed and Jo Jo to a lawyer, NG Patel, who was in Becker Street (now known as Gerard Sekoto Street). Patel convinced the prosecutor that they had not meant any harm. They were kids and were ready to apologise. They apologised and were released without any action being taken against them.

Saloojee was at the time working for NG Patel, and this incident, with its happy ending, might have encouraged his faith in the law. If so, he was in the end cruelly disappointed; in 1964 he himself died in police detention. He remained active in the TIC and ANC after its banning in 1960. He had been detained for over 100 days the day after he had been engaged to Rookaya Saloojee in 1962. He was banned during their engagement and marriage. Often when Babla was spiriting activists out of the country Rookaya did not go home, afraid that the Security Branch would come looking for Babla.

The death of Suliman "Babla" Saloojee had a tremendous impact on the whole Indian community.

Fawzia Denath, who first met Ahmed at the Johannesburg Training Institute for Indian Teachers in 1963, tells the story of Saloojee: "Babla, a 32-year-old clerk in a law firm, was active in the TIC and ANC after its banning. Babla had been under 90-day detention (justice minister John Vorster's specialty in dealing with dissent) for 65 days. The last time his wife Rookaya saw him was 10 days before his death, and he had asked her to pray for him.

"Babla was detained on 6 July 1964 and on 9 September allegedly fell 20 m to his death from a seventh floor office in Security Police Headquarters, The Grays, in central Johannesburg. Saloojee was the fourth detainee to die while in detention. Babla had been detained for 100 days just two days after his engagement to Rookaya. They had been married for two years when he was detained for the last time."

Pupils from the Lenasia and Roodepoort Indian High School went on a full day's fast and held a peaceful demonstration outside the Fordsburg police station in sympathy with Babla's family. Over 200 children, many of them in school uniform, gathered outside the Saloojee home and carried various placards, one reading: "Release 90-day detainees". The pupils stood silently for over 30 minutes outside the Saloojee home, while others wept openly. About 3 000 people of all races from many parts of the Transvaal attended Babla's funeral at the Croesus Cemetery.

Jo Jo and Ahmed discussed at Babla Saloojee's funeral the fact that they were convinced that a real cadre of the movement would never kill himself – as had been suggested by the authorities. Insiders in the struggle are adamant that suicide was never a prescribed option for political detainees. Though all would accept that people who had been detained and tortured could be driven to wishing to end it all and maybe forced to do it – a far cry from voluntary suicide. During their discussion at Saloojee's funeral both Ahmed and his friend Jo Jo agreed that they would never commit suicide. This was of significance in view of Ahmed's ultimate fate.

After Babla Saloojee's death, Jo Jo and Ahmed distributed leaflets issued by the TIYC (Transvaal Indian Youth Congress). They also distributed a beautifully produced commemorative document on Babla and were almost caught during the distribution. As Jo Jo and Ahmed saw the police van approaching they ran into the Roodepoort Muslim Club. They jumped two fences and the police did not see them. Ahmed had escaped – for the moment – to fight another day.

ROODEPOORT MUSLIM CLUB
As there were no public sporting facilities available, and no public library accessible to Indians, the Roodepoort Muslim Club was the only option available to members of the Roodepoort Muslim community. Its facilities included a swimming pool, dartboards and table tennis equipment, and social activities were planned on its premises.

The Roodepoort Muslim Club had decided to expand its membership. They wanted to get the youth off the streets and to prevent them from getting up to mischief. A number of persons were invited to join. At first Jo Jo and Ahmed refused to enlist as this was a sectarian club for Muslims only and members from other religions and races were barred from becoming members. At a follow-up discussion, Jo Jo and Ahmed decided to join (this was Ahmed's decision) but also to politicise it. They slowly set about doing this.

On one occasion a big event was hosted by the Roodepoort Muslim Club. The property was owned by the community and ridiculously low rentals had to be paid by the community. People who endorsed the policies of the government of the day managed the club. At this special event, only the rich were invited. The lower-income group was never invited and this included poorer Muslims. At this event Ahmed demonstrated by way of an outburst directed at the so-called rich leaders of the club. Ahmed explained to the audience that he failed to understand how people were enjoying this lavish party when other people in the community had no food and the rich looked down on them. Ahmed's outburst resulted in a major confrontation and he and Jo Jo were brought before a disciplinary hearing. In the event, they won the day. Their case was unanswerable and in line with enlightened Muslim thinking, Ahmed and Jo Jo were let off the hook.

Ahmed believed that the only way to change a view was to confront it and argue it out at the table, as was in fact South Africa's eventual happy fate in the negotiated revolution of the 1990s.

Ahmed was an active and highly political member of the club. At one of the club's annual general meetings he raised the issue of membership being restricted to Muslims. Jo Jo and Ahmed were asked to leave the meeting. Despite this they both remained members of the club. They felt that this was a good forum to conscientise others. It made other people re-examine their political beliefs and some became political activists.

Moosa Waja, a fellow-student at the Indian Training College, remembers Ahmed's answer to the question of why he was a member. Ahmed mentioned that it was very difficult to fight people from the outside but easier from the inside of a meeting. As he put it, "One can shout abuse from the outside, you can shut the doors and the windows and you won't hear the abuse. In the front door, you can transform their views and fight any view from the table. This tells you where the man comes from, his characteristics and of the deep thinking of the man." Ahmed knew that he could not change people's views overnight but that one had to work on this consistently and openly.

STUDY CIRCLE AND POLITICS

Ahmed was receiving treatment every week from a speech therapist in Johannesburg for stuttering. The bright, neatly turned-out matriculation student with a stammer was slowly getting involved in real, deadly politics that would change and end his life. Ahmed Bhabha (now in Canada) and Samad Ravat were the principal organisers of a small political awareness group, the Roodepoort Youth Study Group. Ahmed Bhabha was responsible for recruiting Ahmed (who was completing his high school), Jo Jo Saloojee and Mohammed Bhabha (also now in Canada) to the study circle.

Living in such times, Ahmed could not help but become involved in organising colleagues at school for strikes and demonstrations, collecting funds for the movement, selling progressive journals and newspapers, and a variety of other activities.

Jo Jo recalls: "I convinced Ahmed that we could not achieve much politically as individuals, and we therefore decided to belong to an organisation. We were at an age when we were both vibrant and active in our minds. We constantly took up issues such as 'justice in our society' and would discuss at length and in great detail the kind of society that South Africa was and should be. I distinctly remember Ahmed's contribution. There was a contradiction in South African society from an Islamic perspective, he argued. This influenced me. Ahmed stated that you could not be a good Muslim and not fight apartheid. We therefore joined the Roodepoort Youth Study Group, which was in some ways linked to the Transvaal Indian Youth Congress (TIYC). In essence the objective of the study circle was not only to discuss the political situation in South Africa but also in different parts of the world. It had a world dimension."

Mohammed Bhabha and Ahmed regularly attended the TIC meetings in Johannesburg, particularly at the Gandhi Hall. The ANC had already been banned in 1960, but the TIC and TIYC were politically active. Chief Albert Luthuli, in a brief moment of freedom between banning orders, was scheduled to be the guest speaker at a meeting at the Gandhi Hall. This was part of a political pilgrimage which took him to other centres, such as Cape Town, where whites wept openly at his meetings as they got to know something of this remarkable man that they were hearing for the first time in five years. Mohammed recalls: "Ahmed and other members of the Roodepoort Youth Study Group formed the guard of honour for Chief Luthuli as he entered the hall in front of a jubilant audience. After his speech Chief Luthuli had a new banning order placed on him. These orders precluded banned persons from meeting more than one person at a time. This eliminated social life, stopped them from earning a living, prevented them from writing anything for publication or attending meetings which neutralised them politically and could hamper their lives in a variety of other ways. It was, quite simply, a state of civil death."

The meetings of the Roodepoort Youth Study Group usually began with a general chapter-by-chapter discussion of one of the illegal books they bought for their library. One book that Mohammed Bhabha remembers was *Time Longer Than Rope* by Edward Roux, a wrenching account by a leading left-wing political figure of the liberation struggle which deeply influenced a whole generation of young thinkers.

Different spokesmen with different points of view would also address these meetings. Although political activity at the time was not banned there were a number of individuals who were "named" or banned under the Suppression of Communism Act and were, therefore, banned from attending any gathering and also from participating in any political or social activities. Even a social meeting of three was deemed to be a "crowd" and therefore closed to a banned or listed person.

As these meetings were not publicised the political study circle would invite those "banned" activists to address them. One such person was Ahmed Kathrada, who was to spend nearly three decades with Nelson Mandela in prison. Occasionally an African speaker from the mines would also attend and address this study group. Renowned South African writer Ezekiel (Es'kia) Mphahlele was also a guest speaker at the club in 1956. Mphahlele's invitation to the club's study group was not advertised as members of the club would not have sanctioned his appearance. Mohammed Bhabha (14) and Ahmed (aged 15) found this a most unusual experience. This was their first experience sitting and talking to a black person who was not a servant or a labourer. Mohammed recalls, "I was enthralled by this black intellectual whose potential would make him the equal of any white South African writer but who, at the time, was irrelevant in South Africa." Mphahlele spoke about having to leave his country of birth to go to Nigeria in search of artistic freedom. He was banned because of his stand against apartheid and emigrated from South Africa in 1957.

Mphahlele had a profound impact on the life of Ahmed. Mohamed Bhabha states: "Today, Es'kia Mphahlele has probably heard of Ahmed Timol, the brave warrior of Umkhonto we Sizwe. He probably knows of Ahmed's death but is unaware that he met him a long time ago. The irony is that Mphahlele is unaware of the effects that his words had on Timol and will never know the true extent to which he contributed to Timol's ideological destiny with the speech he made to the Roodepoort Youth Study Group."

Political material would be read and discussed at the weekly Friday meetings.

Ahmed Bhabha remembers that the book *Naught For Your Comfort* by the Anglican priest of Sophiatown, Father Trevor Huddleston, was discussed. These activities would go on after 10 pm at the Roodepoort Muslim Club when most people had already left. After the discussions had finished the group would sing political songs. These activities were not known to the other members of the club and lasted for about 12 months. This was when Ahmed was on the verge of completing high school. Iqbal "Baboo" Dindar (Ahmed's cousin) was invited by Ahmed to attend.

The activities of Ahmed and his close friends at the Roodepoort Youth Study Group might not have appeared politically significant at the time. Yet these activities were viewed as unusual and radical in those days. Most of the elders of the Roodepoort community were totally uninterested and opposed to these kinds of political discussions. For example, if they had known about the study group's invitation to Mphahlele they would not have sanctioned his appearance. The significance of the youth study group was that it made Ahmed and others politically aware of the situation in South Africa at a most convulsive time. It allowed them to channel their thoughts and ideas constructively in a certain direction. It also assisted them to develop sensitivity towards the injustices and racism committed by the apartheid regime. It was the Roodepoort Youth Study Group that was responsible for putting Ahmed on the road from an instinctive humanism to analytical politics.

Mohammed Bhabha and Ahmed assisted Ahmed Bhabha in the door-to-door sale of a Congress-aligned publication called *New Age* that advanced the sensible demands of the Congress Movement but was viewed by conservative and racist whites as extremely radical for those times. Its notions were revolutionary not only to the white power structure but also to the Indians. The mere mention of the words "freedom" or "equality of the races" in those days resulted in one being branded a communist. Even the mild philanthropy of the liberals was branded communist, which explains the detention and banning of some prominent liberal leaders such as Peter Brown.

Mohammed Bhabha says that in 1964 after the Rivonia trial that led to the imprisonment of the ANC leadership and during a massive spate of detentions throughout the country, "we would go regularly to the Jeppe Street police station in Johannesburg where my cousin, Ahmed Bhabha, was being held in solitary confinement. We had made an agreement with the police officers to allow us to go with them to the rear of the police station, where the detention cells were located, to deliver the food that we had brought.

"While we were not allowed to speak to my cousin, this provided an opportunity for his mother to see her son and to be reassured about his well-being. Timol and I also used this opportunity to communicate messages to my cousin. One of the ways in which we did this was by wrapping the food in newspaper pages that carried appropriate news."

The outward impression of timidity that Timol projected – for instance he had a paranoiac fear of cats – contrasted sharply with the real inner courage that he possessed and which exhibited itself from time to time when the need arose. It allowed him to act bravely in the face of real and absolute fear. It was the courage that made him leave the safety and close associations of exile in London (years later) because he felt that there was work that he needed to do in South Africa. He knew the risks involved. He was in South Africa during the Rivonia swoop and subsequent trial when the whole underground apparatus of the ANC was exposed and destroyed by the Special Branch. Thousands were placed in solitary confinement where they were tortured and some were killed.

Babla Saloojee's death eerily foreshadowed Timol's own destiny, even down to the pictures of a bruised and battered body showing signs of physical torture. But none of this deterred him from returning to South Africa to carry on the resistance against injustice and tyranny.

TEACHERS TRAINING COLLEGE
By 1959, after Ahmed completed his secondary studies, his father had to undergo another eye operation, the third in three years. This naturally affected the family's material situation, and raising income to maintain a large family of eight was no easy task.

Here is Ahmed's own description: "For the Timol family this period was marked with anxieties, tensions and stresses, a basic characteristic of practically all family life in capitalist societies, especially those families which are vulnerable to the uncertainties of economic political factors."

Ahmed's sister Aysha was forced to leave school, and with their mother Hawa did all the household chores – washing, ironing, polishing the wooden floors in the flat and the floors outside their flat. They also did the cooking.

So at the beginning of 1960, despite his matric exemption, Ahmed began to work as an office clerk at a bookkeeper's office in Johannesburg to augment the family income so that his younger brothers could carry on with their education. Zubeida had married in Machadodorp and Ismail, Mohammed and Haroon were attending school in Roodepoort. Haji Timol, meanwhile, had opened a small trading business.

Ahmed had the personal experience of a remarkable, generous man, GMA (Goolaam Mohamed Ahmed) "Goramota" Khota of Kholvad House in Market Street, Johannesburg. He played a key role in getting Ahmed and many others into bookkeeping. He was one of the very few "non-white" bookkeepers in the Fifties and Sixties. Indian businessmen asked Goramota to teach their children the discipline. Goramota agreed and students from all over the country (including the rural areas), Ahmed Timol among them, came to him for free bookkeeping lessons. There were few training institutions available for Indians, and as a result Goramota was unofficially running his own bookkeeping school. This "school" was unique as Goramota paid the students for working for him. There were no financial gains for Goramota.

Knowledge, as Francis Bacon said, is power. This was Goramota's contribution towards the upliftment of Indian youth, by empowering others with his knowledge. Many of the hundreds of students who went through Goramota's hands are successful today and owe this remarkable man a debt of gratitude.

Goramota remembers Ahmed as a disciplined worker and very soft-spoken. The families were close. Haji Timol was always having lunch at Goramota's place.

In 1964 Jo Jo and Ahmed were walking in downtown Johannesburg when they read a newspaper headline, "Mandela & Co Sentenced". Jo Jo recalls, "We became very angry and emotional and started shouting political slogans. The police then chased us and Ahmed insisted on us standing our ground. Ahmed had his fists clenched and was ready to fight. I had to convince Ahmed that we were not going to win and that it was better for us to run. Ahmed's open defiance was delayed for another day."

Ahmed obtained a scholarship from the Kholvad Madressa to do a teaching course at the Johannesburg Training Institute for Indian Teachers, the only institution of higher education for Indians in the province of Transvaal. He studied there from 1961 to 1963, when political movements were illegal and all forms of mass struggle banned.

Later, when he was living in London, Ahmed was sent to Moscow for training and as part of his course he was required to write an autobiography. The passages reproduced in this book are from that autobiography. Here, for example, is how he described his college years:

"My activities were confined to student problems and in the period 1962-1963 I was elected vice-chairman of the Students' Representative Council and in that year we got the college union affiliated to the National Union of South African Students despite the annoyance and threat of victimisation by college authorities. At college most students saw the bankrupt nature of the courses that were offered; idealistic philosophy and bourgeois ideology permeated our courses, and this idealistic mish-mash contradicted in the most visible and naked terms the realities of the majority of people's material existence in South Africa and most parts of the world which were under the domination of either colonial or imperialist powers, or by their own reactionary national rulers."

Essop Pahad, having already met Ahmed at school, grew closer to him when Ahmed went to the teachers training college. "Political ideas had already formed in Ahmed's head and now began to take concrete form. Political discourse and discussions were now held in a more meaningful way. Ahmed and I exchanged views and Ahmed became acutely aware of racism not only in Roodepoort, but also on a larger scale nationally," he recalls.

Ahmed's cousin from Breyten, Farouk Dindar, commenced his medical training at the University of the Witwatersrand in 1961. He was staying at the Wadee home on Nugget Street. The Wadee patriarch had been a close associate of Chief Albert Luthuli. The Wadee residence was also a venue for the underground for their monthly meetings – several leading anti-apartheid figures were politicised there. Farouk was becoming politicised by simply being there. It was the Wadees who gave Nelson Mandela refuge in 1962 and he shared the bedroom for one week with Farouk.

Ahmed would periodically meet Farouk and would discuss politics with him, as he no longer perceived Farouk as a politically conservative cousin. Farouk has vivid memories of Ahmed discussing the bantustans with him. Ahmed was appalled at what was happening to the Africans under the migrant labour system and would often say with passion, "The bantustans are a reservoir of cheap labour." It was obvious that his sympathy and solidarity for the oppressed Africans ran very deep. "Ahmed spoke with intensity about the poverty of the Africans. Ahmed never spoke about the poverty of Indians and always spoke about the African struggle," adds Farouk. His views were in line with those Indians who refused to be compartmentalised by apartheid and sought common cause with Africans and other groups in the face of growing repression. He would have seen the dangers ahead but was clearly not to be put off course. Farouk began to share Ahmed's views on the migrant labour system and other issues and he viewed Ahmed's politics as those of an enlightened member of the TIC.

Moosa Waja, correspondence secretary, 1963-64, and director of student welfare, 1964, at the Johannesburg Training Institute for Indian Teachers, vividly remembers Ahmed's last speech at the Institute. The students had already taken their seats in the hall when the rector, vice-rector and other senior lecturers entered. Ahmed's speech "knocked them off their feet". It focused on the condition and brainwashing of the students and amounted to a powerful exhortation to them to learn to "think" and to "read" the media. Moosa recalls that if he had been a "white" person that day, he would have sunk into the floor or moved out of the hall discreetly without anyone noticing. Ahmed was a very clear, powerful and forceful speaker. The audience were too scared to move their legs lest a squeak or noise would disturb things. For days people spoke about Ahmed's speech. It was obvious that this man Timol was special. Someone who had understood the essential evil of the society in which he lived and was prepared to do something about it.

After the speech Ahmed was called to the office of John Smith, the rector, who was white. He said he concurred with what Ahmed had said, but reminded him that the teachers training college was still a government institution. Ahmed was told that he was in a very serious situation and that in his own manner it was he who was brainwashing students. The incident illustrated the ruling dogmas of the day. Smith was supposedly liberal-minded yet he was a captive of his own environment.

In Fordsburg, the Congress Movement grew from strength to strength. Moosa lived in High Street where everything happened. There were numerous visits and raids by the Security Branch. Residents would jump roofs and move to other yards to avoid the Security Branch policemen. Neighbours all spoke in one voice and were firm. They would deny everything the Security Branch members asked. The more the Security Branch visited, the more it strengthened the beliefs of the community. The Security Branch members would hit and punch the people and think nothing of it. The law was on their side.

While Moosa Waja and others were involved in politics it must be noted that this was at the lowest level. They would question their own actions and have doubts about what they were doing. Parents at that time encouraged youngsters not to be involved in political activities since they knew the risks involved. Moosa was saved from arrest only because the security police had wrongly spelled his surname and so couldn't find him. He left the country for Canada in October 1968.

Those were horrendously repressive times and education was no exception. Apart from the segregated institutions Afrikaner nationalist lecturers would draft letters to newspapers and the more malleable students would be forced to put their names to them. The police would use threat and financial reward and the bestowal of privilege to secure support. Filling out application forms for college, a job or security clearance one could expect to be asked if you were a communist and what you thought about the system. Students would be forced to sing the national anthem, *Die Stem*, and they were picked out if they did not. Some of the principals and headmasters supported the apartheid system, either out of conviction or professional prudence, for it was in their own career and financial interests to do so.

Such considerations formed the background to Ahmed's period at the teachers training college. Ahmed was marked out as a bold student, despite his slight build and stammer. He was not shy to correct political statements that he thought were dubious or racist. He was apt to use precise, candid language even if this was to his own detriment in the atmosphere of intimidation and corruption that marked the administration of education in those days.

Moosa Waja asserts that Ahmed could be placed in the category of steadfast anti-apartheid radicals such as his close friends the brothers Aziz and Essop Pahad, who both achieved high office after democracy came to South Africa in 1994. People speculate whether Timol would have followed suit or perhaps concentrated on his first love – education. He fitted into the mould of young struggle leaders of the day such as Thabo Mbeki with whom he was later to study in Moscow. "Ahmed could walk through anything," says Moosa. "Whilst others were studying, Ahmed would walk in, chat a little and be off.

"Ahmed was one of those students who would listen to a lecturer and immediately grasp what was being said. If five bullet points were given Ahmed would add two and diplomatically tell the lecturer he was talking nonsense and that this or that is how it really was. This was Ahmed." He was vocal in his political beliefs and refused to accept the paternalistic and racist treatment handed out to the students.

There are a number of people who have vivid and cherished recollections of Ahmed. Jo Jo Saloojee mentions that Ahmed influenced many students when he enrolled at the teachers training college. He encouraged them to stand up for their rights in an organised manner and to be treated as human beings. He also played a very important role in the political organisation of the student body, not only in the college but also in a much wider sense.

Hassen Jooma, a friend who was also later detained, had entered the Johannesburg Training Institute for Indian Teachers in 1961 and his recollections of Ahmed are vivid. They were the first group of students to have done the junior high school course. During their second year of study, they were told they had to do a lower or higher diploma of three years' duration. The authorities made it compulsory for all males to complete the three-year diploma but females could still do the two-year diploma.

Hassen and Ahmed shared a desk in the classroom and frequently communicated in Gujarati. They felt that the SRC was not strong enough and not making sufficient headway with principal Smith. The staff was white and the lecturers were of pensionable age. At the end of 1961, the SRC was steadily becoming more progressive. At the beginning of 1962, Smith introduced specialisation subjects such as mathematics, Afrikaans and history. A minimum of five students was needed for each of these disciplines. Ahmed vehemently refused to do Afrikaans which he referred to as the language of the oppressor.

On one occasion lecturer JJ Browdie called Ahmed a "bloody communist" and chased him around a table. Ahmed was also seen proclaiming: "We are on the threshold of a national disaster," as he stood on his desk between lectures. In 1961 a lecturer, JT Verster, asked the class when the *Communist Manifesto* was launched. Hassen could not answer but Ahmed responded by saying in 1848. Ahmed and lecturer Verster used to debate the question of social ills. Verster would state, prophetically, that young Afrikaners would one day have a change of heart and he claimed that they were conscience-stricken about their racist role. Ahmed would disagree with this subtle optimism and would challenge him.

The SRC at the college was becoming vibrant and started having contact with SRCs at the Johannesburg College of Education and at Wits. There was a conference at Botha's Hill, near Durban, where Ahmed spoke. It was a significant moment in Ahmed's political education. He was noted as one of the more outspoken speakers and was vehement in his criticism of the apartheid regime. Ahmed showed that he was deadly serious about the politics of the country.

Mrs Badenhorst was one of the white lecturers at the college and was nearing her retirement when Ahmed was there. Hassen mentions that she had a good heart. If you did not obtain an A symbol in her class there was something wrong with you. Mrs Badenhorst had a soft spot for Hassen and would refer to him as the Bachelor of Hearts. Hassen would ask that students in her class be excused for SRC meetings and she would always oblige without any questions. Hassen once told Mrs Badenhorst that he did not mind apartheid as long as trading rights were granted to Indians. Ahmed was very angry about this statement and responded by saying that there must be freedom for all the citizens of the country. His political beliefs were strong and coherent.

But the odd political difference did not affect their friendship. As students they frequented the Avalon café and the bioscope in Fordsburg, and also the theatre. Because of apartheid, "white" theatres were barred from allowing "non-whites" to attend regular showings. A limited number of tickets were given to the Johannesburg Training Institute for Indian Teachers SRC members at 25c, but only for the dress rehearsals. Intellectually like-minded students such as Hassen and Ahmed invariably went to these dress rehearsals, but they knew it was an individual's choice. Ahmed frowned on the cynicism whereby "white" theatres managed to get audiences for full dress rehearsals by packing them with "non-whites".

One night, Hassen attended a concert in Roodepoort and on the programme was an Indian version of a one-act play entitled *Nanima's Will*. The play was adapted with an Islamic background. Ahmed was the co-ordinator of this play which showed his creative, artistic side. Hassen wondered whether the arts, rather than politics, might secure Ahmed's future attention, but he was wrong.

Hassen remembers Ahmed as witty and an excellent orator. He had a good command of the English language. His usual comment on Hassen's choice of girlfriend was, "Hey man, you only find the ones built for comfort!" This was because Hassen chose well-built females to escort to the cinema and to the theatre.

When Hassen completed his teacher's diploma he began teaching in Lenasia at the Nirvana High School in 1965. Fawzia Denath – a fellow student at the teachers training college who later married Hassen Jooma – taught in Brits at the time. Ahmed successfully completed his teacher's diploma in 1963 and took up a teaching post at the Roodepoort Indian School. It was at this school that he would teach the youth who, in 1971, would be arrested with him in a roadblock, Salim Essop. (Salim was dangled over a 10-storey stairwell, horrifically tortured, hospitalised – and lived. Ahmed died.)

AHMED THE TEACHER

Despite his stutter, Ahmed became a teacher who was able to inspire and motivate his students with his words. He was loved and respected by pupils and colleagues alike. Cassim Bhabha remembers that Ahmed always had deep sympathy for the poor, even before he became politicised. The convictions that led to his death were clearly rooted in concern for his fellow human beings.

Haji Timol was always struggling financially and Ahmed felt this acutely. Jo Jo recalls, "Ahmed said to his father, 'No matter what it takes, one day I will see you come right.'" Both Jo Jo and Ahmed gave half their salary to their mothers.

Haroon Timol, Ahmed's younger brother, described him as one of the most popular teachers in the view of the students. He was always first to greet them and he treated them equally, irrespective of their family backgrounds. He did not believe in failing his students. He constantly reminded his students that their parents were the breadwinners of their families.

His cousin Farouk Dindar considered Ahmed a gifted teacher. Ahmed would first analyse his pupil and then give material to the pupil that would be appropriate. Later on he analysed Farouk's political growth and recognised that he had limited time to read as he was specialising in medicine. He very carefully chose the material for Farouk to read when he was in London studying. All the material he chose for Farouk was appropriate for his needs, the hallmark of a gifted teacher. During Ahmed's stay in London he presented Farouk with Marxist literature.

Jo Jo soon joined Ahmed at the Roodepoort Indian School. He and Ahmed loved to dress well and the students noted this. Jo Jo recalls, "We were regarded as the two best-dressed teachers in the school. We selected our clothes carefully and always together."

Jo Jo stayed in a flat opposite Ahmed's. "Ahmed was an early riser and would wait for me every morning before walking to the Roodepoort School. We would stand and talk every night for hours outside our flats."

Another student, Ebrahim Bhorat, now a prominent businessman in the Western Cape, recalls, "In 1964 my political awareness could be described as virtually non-existent. I came from a privileged background and lived in a community who seemed to exist in a political vacuum oblivious to the iniquities in South African society, especially those affecting the African community.

"In 1965 I was a Standard Eight (Grade 10 today) learner and Ahmed Timol was my teacher in history. The prescribed textbook for South African history was one by Van Jaarsveld. Mr Timol took it upon himself to deviate from the text of Van Jaarsveld and introduced what he considered to be the true perspective on South African history. He became my mentor and confidant.

"A firm believer in education, he assisted pupils like me, who were experiencing problems with the principal who wanted us to leave school in Standard Eight, by fighting for our right to continue schooling after Standard Eight. With his help I was able to pursue my scholastic career.

"My political knowledge was so limited that I did not even know what the acronym ANC stood for. Ahmed Timol introduced me to the struggle. His convictions and value systems began to appeal to me and I became politically active. My political activism resulted in my arrest and detention under the Suppression of Communism Act. I was imprisoned and held under its hideous provisions in detention without trial. During my detention I was physically assaulted and kept in solitary confinement.

"I owe my present political awareness to my initiation through Ahmed Timol."

The Roodepoort Indian School obeyed the government of the day. The Muslim hierarchy of Roodepoort had substantial influence in the affairs of the school. Jo Jo and Ahmed found great difficulty in being accepted as teachers at the school as they were regarded as being too political.

There were enough obvious pointers to the school's acceptance of the apartheid status quo. The mayor and mayoress of Roodepoort and the inspector of education were regular invited guests to all school functions. On 13 December 1965 the Roodepoort Indian School hosted a retirement reception for the inspector of education, Mr Swart, and his wife.

The school had celebrated the founding of the Republic of South Africa in 1961. After the hoisting of the national flag and speeches, pupils were provided with refreshments. The school even sent a message of condolence to the family of Dr Hendrik Frensch Verwoerd, the key architect of apartheid, when he was assassinated in Parliament in 1966. A memorial service was held for him and the school closed at 9 am.

In this slavishly pro-government atmosphere, Jo Jo and Ahmed decided to build a close rapport with the students. Besides their normal teaching functions they began teaching the students that they must be treated as equal human beings and that they must stand up for their rights. This was done in a slow, careful and cautious manner. It took some time, but before long Roodepoort Indian School became a politically active school.

Jo Jo recalls: "Ahmed and I had decided to divide the teaching staff at Roodepoort Indian School into three categories, i.e. the lost cause (reactionaries), the possibilities (in between) and the potentials (possibly to be brought on board). This group included Yusuf "Chubb" Garda, KC Naik, who were both later arrested, and Agie Valliala, who later moved to Canada. The students were fine, but the teachers needed organising."

On one occasion the Roodepoort Indian School was celebrating Republic Day at a festival with many other schools at the Union Stadium in Newlands, west of Johannesburg. At a staff meeting held a day before the celebrations, principal Lorghat set out the logistical requirements to the teachers and at the end of his briefing he enquired from the teachers whether everyone agreed with the arrangements. All the teachers approved with the exception of Ahmed and Jo Jo who registered their opposition to the celebrations as a matter of principle. Lorghat's response was, "If you don't like it, pack your bags and go back to India." The school incident book recorded the following for 10 May 1966:

"Staff Meeting: Mr A Timol indicated at a staff meeting held today that he would not be able to attend the Republic Festival to be held at the Union Stadium on 11/5/66, because of strong personal convictions." Two witnesses, IV Pillay and vice-principal B Devchand, signed the above statement in the school incident book.

Timol's stand bore fruit. As many as 60 per cent of the students boycotted the celebrations at the Union Stadium. There were also slogans painted on the school walls. On 26 May 1966 Ahmed's younger brother, Mohammed, was arrested with seven other school pupils for painting political slogans in protest against Republic Day celebrations. On 13 July 1966 Mohammed was found guilty and had to pay a fine of R20. He received a suspended sentence for a period of three years on condition that he did not commit a similar crime that resulted in damage to state property.

Jo Jo and Ahmed were summoned to Lorghat's office and asked to explain, it being assumed that they were responsible for this boycott. Ahmed responded by saying that he and Jo Jo must have been two very powerful individuals to organise an entire school on their own and, if they were indeed responsible, this was a direct insult to the school's capacity to organise itself. It implied that the students could not think for themselves.

Lorghat issued a direct order for Ahmed and Jo Jo to join their fellow teachers in the Republic Day celebrations. Jo Jo refused and Lorghat threatened to report him for insubordination. Ahmed's response was: "You are welcome to do so because Allah gives us our living and not you."

Jo Jo and Ahmed frequently distributed political leaflets at the Roodepoort Indian School. The school incident book noted on 4 May 1965: "The Security Branch called at the school to investigate the presence of a circular (re Marxism). They were satisfied that there was no demonstration and circulation of pamphlets as such at the school. However, the Principal warned pupils to desist from such activities; otherwise strong disciplinary action will be taken against them. A staff meeting was called to discuss and to combat such activities."

Jo Jo narrates: "The leaflets were secretly produced. The content of the leaflets dealt with various political issues. These leaflets were in addition to the pamphlets that had been produced by Essop Pahad and the others on earlier occasions. I was in charge of the equipment at the school and so Ahmed and I used the school's duplicator machine to produce pamphlets. Later we became friends with an enlightened Imam in Roodepoort who helped us to produce leaflets on his machine."

Jo Jo and Ahmed found one Afrikaans teacher who they were sure was informing the principal about the illegal distribution of leaflets in the school. This teacher disassociated himself from politics and was not progressive. The principal informed the Security Branch who came to the school and questioned the teachers and students about the illegal leaflets that were being distributed there. Jo Jo recalls: "Ahmed and I worked out a plan of action. We both pleaded innocent to the principal and informed him that we might know the suspect responsible for this, provided that the Security Branch didn't disclose their source. We named the same teacher who was responsible for spying as the distributor of these illegal leaflets. The teacher was interrogated by the SB for over two hours. He never reported the distribution of leaflets to the principal again."

Jo Jo and Ahmed had the overwhelming support of the majority of students at the Roodepoort Indian School, as became apparent after another fruitless visit by the Security Branch to the school. Jo Jo had stored his political literature in his cupboard in his classroom. They had initially visited Jo Jo's home and had not found any political literature. Jo Jo was summoned to the principal's office. As he returned to his classroom, accompanied by Security Branch members, convinced that he was now going to get caught, he was surprised to find that his political literature had been removed from his cupboard. Jo Jo's students had done it, and saved him.

The Security Branch used to make regular visits to the politicised school. They raided it one day in full force and took a number of students into custody for questioning and interrogation. They were determined to find the ringleaders responsible for the heightened political activity not only in the Roodepoort Indian School but also in neighbouring schools. Jo Jo and Ahmed were convinced that the students would break down under torture. According to Jo Jo, the student victims of torture included Ebrahim Bhorat, Zunaid Moola and Shireen Areff. He and Ahmed began making preparations to be detained or to leave the country. Despite the brutal torture by the Security Branch, however, not a single student divulged either Jo Jo or Ahmed's name.

During the time they taught at the Roodepoort Indian School, up to December 1964, every Friday Jo Jo and Ahmed, after attending prayers and having lunch, would go by train from the Roodepoort station to Aziz and Essop Pahad's family in Johannesburg. Jo Jo, Aziz, Essop and Ahmed would then go to the movies. Jo Jo and Ahmed would at times spend the weekend at the Pahads' place. There was one weekend when the Pahads had an additional, and as things turned out most memorable, visitor – Gerard Ludi. He had studied with Aziz and Essop at Wits University and had returned from overseas. He kept Ahmed and Jo Jo awake the entire evening with his lectures on Marxism and Leninism.

The following day Ahmed mentioned to Jo Jo, with remarkable prescience, that he had a "bad" feeling about Gerard. Despite the fact that Ludi appeared to be the Pahads' friend, Ahmed did not trust him. Some time later newspapers splashed the story about South African special agent Q107 who had for years been an agent for the security forces while working for the liberal *Rand Daily Mail* as a reporter. This agent was none other than the all-night Marxist lecturer and confidant, Ludi.

The Pahads were red rags to a bull in those days of repression, as this will illustrate. The Roodepoort Indian School was urgently looking for a commerce teacher. Aziz Pahad had completed his studies at Wits and was not working. Aziz knew nothing about commerce but was convinced by Ahmed and Jo Jo that he should accept an appointment. Principal Lorghat had not heard of him and on Ahmed and Jo Jo's advice appointed Aziz to the post. But after he had been at the school for a few hours the Security Branch arrived and requested Lorghat to remove him. Lorghat obliged and Ahmed and Jo Jo had a good laugh about Aziz's rapid departure.

Aziz had been banned under the Suppression of Communism Act in 1964 and it was illegal for him to be on any educational premises. "I believe that this must have been the shortest teaching career of any individual," he said, years later. "I still wonder who informed the Special Branch."

Jo Jo and Ahmed spent a great deal of time with Amina Desai's family when they were both teaching and prior to Ahmed going overseas. Despite the fact that they did not always agree politically they remained the best of friends both with the parents and their daughters. The Desai home was close to the mosque and on many occasions Jo Jo and Ahmed would happen to meet members of the mosque congregation who wondered why the two young men spent so much time with the Desai family. In time, they would know.

Jo Jo and Ahmed found the environment at the Desai home very different compared to their own homes. At the Desai home they were free to discuss politics, culture, books or whatever they liked. This became their second home – a link that would prove to be significant as things turned out. Jo Jo was therefore not surprised when he heard the report that Ahmed had been working at Amina Desai's home using all the resources available without her consent. This was nothing new as Ahmed and Jo Jo had previously done work with Amina's son, Hilmi, who was hiding reams of paper used for manufacturing leaflets in the Desai garage, though Hilmi's parents were not aware of his activities.

The leaflets that were printed in the garage were distributed in the Indian community. They were a reminder to the community that it was their duty to fight apartheid and to oppose measures such as the Group Areas Act. Jo Jo and Ahmed wrote the contents of the leaflets. They dressed in black clothing and distributed these leaflets covertly in the dark of the night. On many occasions they were nearly caught. The community suspected Jo Jo and Ahmed's involvement but had no proof.

3

SPORTING CAMPAIGNS

In the 1950s, as the Congress Alliance became more articulate and the ANC became more radicalised, football and sport in general entered the mainstream of the anti-apartheid struggle. It was a particularly soft spot in the underbelly of the apartheid oppressors who loved their sport, worshipped sports figures and regularly prayed for victory against competitors. This attachment to sport was mercilessly exploited by the liberation movement and led, in time, to all sorts of policy gymnastics by the racists, including the opportunistic notion that sport could be integrated at international but not national or local level. These developments reached directly into Ahmed's life. According to the school incident book for November 1966 Basil D'Oliveira, the England test cricketer, visited the Roodepoort Indian School to give a demonstration and coach the pupils.

Chief Albert Luthuli, President-General of the ANC, was not the only member of the Congress Alliance who was actively involved in rugby or other sport. Dr Yusuf Dadoo was also absorbed in cricket and was patron of the Witwatersrand Indian Cricket Union. In 1959 the TIC launched a campaign against the proposed visit of Frank Worrell's West Indies team on the grounds that it would encourage the government's apartheid policy.

For most people the fact that the Verwoerd government had given its blessing to such a tour was enough for them to see it as hostile to the interests of black people throughout the country. A small section of higher officials of the Indian Cricket Union could not comprehend the significance of this popular revulsion against any form of apartheid, and they spoke about "keeping politics out of sport", which was the white nationalist cry. To show their resentment, and flying in the face of popular opinion, they deposed Dr Dadoo from the panel of patrons of the Indian Cricket Union (ICU) and in his place appointed Worrell, the captain of the ill-fated team. The *New Age* newspaper dated 13 October 1960 reported that

Dr Dadoo was reinstated late in 1960 as a patron of this leading body of non-European sportsmen. By the Seventies and Eighties, the sports boycotts had become indispensable tools of anti-apartheid resistance. Sanctions-busters like West Indian cricketer Alvin Kallicharan were literally spat upon in the streets of their own home countries upon their return there.

During the Fifties considerable progress was made in cricket, soccer, boxing and weightlifting to break down divisions between members of the African, Indian and coloured communities. For example in cricket racial divisions in the South African Cricket Board of Control (SACBOC) were abolished in 1958, after which affiliation was based on area alone. An integrated team from these race groups had already played the touring Kenyan Asians in 1956 and in 1958 South Africa toured East Africa. The outlines were being created for the non-racial sport of a new and democratic South Africa – one that had to wait more than a generation.

Ahmed Timol was among those who fought against apartheid in sport and for non-racial sport in the Fifties and Sixties. This generation of dissent made it possible that, within the space of eight weeks in 1970, South Africa was excluded from the Davis Cup, expelled by the Olympic Movement and rebuffed by the MCC. By November 1971 – the year of Timol's death – the United Nations was calling for a boycott of South African sport. When South Africa was increasingly shut out of world sport the local racists came up with silly notions such as the (whites-only) South African Games, which meant playing against no one but themselves.

Ahmed's main involvement in sporting activism was through the Dynamos Soccer Club, formed at the initiative of Aziz Pahad from a humble beginning in Becker Street, Ferreirastown. The players were mainly from Ferreirastown, Fordsburg, Vrededorp and from Kliptown. For all involved in Dynamos, soccer was their first love. They played it in the streets until early evening. Aziz Pahad was the goalkeeper of the team and Essop Pahad a defender and also the chairman of the club. Dynamos emerged as one of the best teams not only amongst the Indians but also amongst the Africans – although even here apartheid intervened. African teams like Orlando Pirates and Indian teams like Dynamos were not allowed to play against the whites. Dynamos played endless "friendlies" against other teams from other leagues. With each player's parents paying kombi fares and assisting with the fares of those unable to pay for themselves, the Dynamos team would travel to play in Middelburg, Ermelo and Mafikeng. When they played against Krugersdorp they would go by train and occasionally fights would break out against whites that they encountered on their journey.

Essop Pahad recalls, "We went to Durban accompanied by Ismail Pahad, 'Archie Boy' Bhayat (Sampie Essack's brother) and Cas Saloojee and had meetings with Luchman who was a soccer administrator in Durban. It was here that the first discussions about professional soccer took place in South Africa. When we returned to Johannesburg we contacted Orlando Pirates and Moroka Swallows football clubs and discussed the issue of professional soccer. Both the clubs agreed to participate."

Dynamos could not play at the Orlando Stadium because the ground was in an African township and it was only for so-called "Bantus". The Orlando Stadium and the Natalspruit ground in Doornfontein were the only grounds that were properly fenced off. The Dynamos leadership approached cricket administrators Chummy Mayet and Checker Jassat to use the Natalspruit ground. They agreed on condition that a semi-professional league be formed and that the Dynamos leadership should form another team, drawing on a broader and truly regional talent pool, so as to make a true inter-regional league of it. Thus was born Transvaal United.

Essop recalls, "This was a very difficult moment for us as we were good enough to play for Dynamos but not for Transvaal United. However, in the interests of starting professional soccer we agreed, despite knowing that some of us would not be selected to play for Transvaal United."

In Durban they had Avalon Athletics and Berea. A team from Cape Town also participated. This is how professional soccer started in South Africa. Among the administrators nobody was paid for their services although, says Essop Pahad, "the players were paid a few pounds"

Dynamos were well known in the Northern Cape as they had played in Vryburg and Mafiking and had beaten the best teams there. Essop jokingly recalls, "We had beaten the local coloured team in Vryburg. The local coloureds kept on saying that we Indians could only play cricket and not play soccer. People still talk about our beating the coloured soccer team of Vryburg."

As I can attest, the Dynamos were still going strong two decades later. I played soccer for Standerton Dynamos in the Eighties while I was still attending high school. We would play against other towns such as Ermelo, Nelspruit, Barberton, Middelburg, Piet Retief and Kinross on a home and away basis. We would make arrangements with taxi operators from the African or coloured areas who would transport us when we played away from Standerton. Our parents would pay our kombi fares. Rivalry at these games was intense and fights would regularly break out amongst supporters and players.

I also played cricket for Standerton from my high school days. We also played against other towns, as we did in soccer. Again, tensions would run high during these games and would occasionally result in fights breaking out. The opposition from the other towns included family members. While the game, whether soccer or cricket, was played all family loyalties were put aside and the game came first.

But after the game, in most cases, differences were put aside and the opposition team was always invited by the hosts for snacks after a soccer game or for lunch during a cricket game.

Essop Pahad spoke at the Multi-Purpose Community Centre in Alexandra Township on 25 February 2004 and reminded the residents of Alex of the time when Dynamos beat Alex Gunners by three goals to two in Alexandra. The champion among African soccer teams in 1961/2 was Homekillers from Kliptown. Essop recalls: "We played Homekillers in Kliptown. The ground was full of African supporters. Before the game young African boys would come up to us and taunt us by saying that we Indians were so thin – how could we play soccer? Many Africans placed their wages, betting that Dynamos was going to lose. We beat them by three goals to two. I was playing at right-back."

In Becker Street, Ferreirastown, there was another well known soccer team, Young Tigers, led by Ebrahim Adams. Dynamos and Young Tigers took the initiative to form a summer league.

The games were played at the Chinese Grounds in Ferreirastown. This league started without any money. Officials were elected and they would meet weekly to draw up the fixtures. Essop Pahad recalls, "The Summer League became the most popular Sunday League amongst the Indians and coloureds. The best footballers would play in this league. There was Siva from Germiston, who was a great football player, Walter Ntombi from Blackpool, our own Bonke Ndamase from Dynamos – probably the best left-back that South Africa has ever produced. Competition was fierce amongst Dynamos and Young Tigers, who both came from Becker Street. We did this because of our total commitment to soccer and we did this without any financial assistance. We had a league running as well as a knockout tournament. The mineworkers would take off on Sundays to watch Dynamos play."

The arbitrary racial divisions between soccer leagues made for some entertaining anecdotes. Essop Pahad recalls, "Aboobakr Saloojee and I played for a team in the Coloured League. We took on coloured names but everybody knew who we were. Dynamos were the first to break the colour barrier. We were not playing in a league but we played friendlies in Meadowlands, Soweto, and beat (African team) Young Zebras by four goals to one. We were once again taunted by young Africans before the game who commented that we coolies can't play soccer. After beating them, they would say you coolies can play soccer." This was how Dynamos became a household name.

Motherwell was by far the best team in the Coloured League. They played at the Vrededorp grounds. The top South African player, Hashim Rusdien, played for Motherwell. Essop recalls, "We beat them on their own grounds. All the Indians from Vrededorp could not stop congratulating us as they mentioned that this was the first time that they could show their faces as far as soccer was concerned. They would regularly be teased after losing to us on a regular basis.

"We used to train in the evenings at the Natalspruit grounds with no floodlights," he continues. "There were no dressing rooms to change in. Players would change on the ground or in someone's car. After attending university we would take a bus or walk to soccer training. After training, we would come back to Ferreirastown in the dark. We would go for runs three or four times a week for 10-20 km around Johannesburg. The training was done in the most difficult conditions and no facilities were available. Timol was involved and this brought Ahmed closer to Aziz and myself and later to my brothers Ismail, Zunaid and Nassim." Dynamos had a clubhouse in Fordsburg where these relationships grew.

Dynamos was opening to coloureds and Africans. This was a political statement they had made saying that they did not recognise any racial barriers to people playing sports together. They went out of their way to play in the townships and this widened their scopes of contact. Some like Essop Pahad were overtly political. Essop recalls, "When the former head of FIFA, Stanley Rous, visited South Africa I arranged a demonstration outside Jan Smuts Airport (now

Johannesburg International). My photo appeared in the *New Age* newspaper with a banner saying: 'Stanley Rous go home'. He was not welcome in South Africa because we had decided to boycott white sports. Prior to the demand to boycott white sports we would go and watch soccer, rugby and cricket at white grounds and stadiums where the principles of segregation and racial discrimination were strictly applied.

"When we would go and watch Newcastle United playing at the Rand Stadium we would always support the opposition. Whenever we went to the stadiums, we were penned in one section. If one black person had supported the local South African team, he was in trouble. The same applied to the Wanderers Stadium. We would sit on the wooden benches and face the direct afternoon sun.

"When the British Lions came to South Africa in 1955, a young red-haired 18-year-old Irishman, Tony O'Reilly (who now owns the Independent Group of Newspapers), was playing on the wing. In the final minute of the game South Africa scored a try and if they converted it they would have won the test match. The fullback who took the conversion was Jack van der Schyff. His kick went just wide and South Africa lost the match. We had to put tomato cases on our heads to protect ourselves against the bottles that were hurled towards us. Our joke was that Van der Schyff was coloured and that he deliberately missed the kick. We had to wait inside the stadium after the final whistle was blown as the whites were waiting for us outside."

Dynamos had a coloured goalkeeper by the name of Schwartz, who came from the East Rand. He was a policeman and reported Essop and Aziz to the Security Branch for breaking their banning orders.

A Dynamos brochure from the Sixties about Junior Dynamos notes: "This team, led and directed by Zunaid Pahad, youngest brother of Ismail Pahad, together with the genial M Bayat, has added lustre and glory to the name of Dynamos. These backstreet youth had more love for soccer than even their daily bread. They gave not a damn where they played as long as they were able to partake in a match, among themselves or against formidable foes. I remember most vividly a hot Sunday afternoon when these youngsters were trespassing on the lawns of the Magistrate's Court, and this only to play soccer. While the match was in progress a passer-by, seeing that they were young, decided to steal the ball. But, alas, to his detriment because these youngsters were arrested for assault.

"Another incident that I recall is that of one of their potential stars, namely F Dadabhai, ruining his soccer career. They were playing on the street when suddenly he tripped and fell through a plate glass window, severing his wrist. He is unable as yet to make use of the hand. Nonetheless this has not deterred either those arrested or those injured from continuing on the glorious path already blazed by their ancestors on and off the soccer field. Neither has their love for soccer waned in any way. The backstreet soccer still continues, not from lack of competitive soccer but it stems from deep down. Their love for the most celebrated sport in the world still reigns supreme."

Jo Jo and Ahmed were very poor soccer players but they were seen as good organisers. Accompanied by Ismail and Nassim Pahad and Hamid "Buster"

Bhabha, they were the principal organisers of the first Dynamos Festival. Ismail Pahad, later known as the "Fordsburg Fox", had taken full control of Dynamos. This was also the largest amateur soccer tournament ever held in South Africa, in any community. Jo Jo and Ahmed, as organisers of the tournament, used the opportunity to extend their political contacts.

The first soccer tournament held in Roodepoort comprised four teams. Jo Jo and Ahmed had attended various soccer meetings and proposed to increase the number of teams to eight, and to have the tournament over two days. Jo Jo and Ahmed had a dispute with the Roodepoort Football Club.

They boycotted this tournament but planned another. They could not kick a soccer ball to save their lives, but wanted to be soccer organisers and they knew that they had administrative talent. They proceeded to Dynamos supremo Ismail Pahad and made arrangements to use two to three grounds, invite 16 soccer clubs from all over the country and hold the first national amateur soccer tournament.

Ismail Pahad supported this proposal but was not aware of the political angle that Ahmed and Jo Jo had in mind. Influential sportsmen like Chummy Mayet and Rashid Garda were brought on board. No one had ever seen a soccer tournament of this magnitude. Ahmed's responsibility was to look at potential recruits and he did an excellent job of this. People, supporters, players and administrators from all over the country were present. This provided Jo Jo and Ahmed with a perfect cover to conduct political work.

The Security Branch had not one grain of suspicion about their activities. Jo Jo and Ahmed also had the support of all religious denominations, all ethnic groups and people of all political persuasions. Everyone attended because of their love of the sport. Only after Ahmed's death did the Security Branch probe Dynamos Football Club. Jo Jo and Ahmed felt that if they could organise a large-scale soccer festival they could set up a political underground network on a national scale. The word Dynamos began to get new meanings and, of course, it could be traced to the famous Moscow club.

Essop Pahad, who to this day is an avid reader of soccer match reports in the newspaper sports pages, recalls, "The Dynamos Football Club allowed new friendships to be formed and flourish. Ahmed joined Dynamos in 1965 just as professional soccer was beginning to take shape within the country. Dynamos took the lead in developing professional soccer and they were instrumental in the emergence of Transvaal United. Dynamos could not play at Orlando Stadium because of apartheid."

Hamid "Timer" Valley recalls that Ahmed was known as "Tims" (short for Timol) to him and his friends. "Ahmed accepted everybody as his friend," he said. Timer played soccer for Dynamos and Ahmed was the secretary of Dynamos Football Club, and they formed a close relationship. The day Roodepoort had its first turf ground was the greatest day in the lives of Timer and all other sports-crazy citizens. There were no sporting facilities available for Indians, and talent had to be developed on the streets. Timer notes, "Dynamos Football Club was the inspiration of Aziz and Essop Pahad. Dynamos made participants aware of racism as the ethos of the club was multi-racialism. This was not just a football club, but it also made them aware of the political situation within the country. It taught them as youngsters to see fellow Africans as brothers and sisters. People were afraid to come out in the open and express their feelings and Ahmed was not afraid to do this."

He continues: "If anyone showed any form of opposition, or any inclination of antagonism, towards the government Ahmed would automatically become friendlier towards them and provide them with communist-inspired literature." Timer explained to Ahmed that when he was living in Becker Street, Ferreirastown, downtown Johannesburg, and was walking down the street in town one day, elderly African people were on their way home towards Westgate Station when he witnessed a pass raid conducted by young white policemen. The police just grabbed the elderly Africans and loaded them onto the "Kwela Kwela" police vans, as they did not have the necessary "pass" papers. The manner in which the police terrorised these elderly citizens depressed Timer, who was a young boy at the time.

Life was tough for Timer and the family in Becker Street. Every Friday after school Timer would accompany the other hawkers on Eloff Street Extension selling fruit and peanuts. The police raided the hawkers and Timer was also thrown into the big police van, a vehicle dubbed "nylons" by township blacks because of the wire mesh on the windows. Timer was in Standard Six at the time. He remembers sharing the sweets with all the other arrested hawkers in the police van. They were taken to Marshall Square – then police headquarters – and were placed in the waiting cells. Timer witnessed a policeman beating up an African in the police station. The large officer hit the African on his back with his palm and arrogantly boasted to his young colleague how to avoid leaving a mark behind. Timer was fortunate that his uncle bailed him out, but this incident scarred him for life. He pondered over what really happened in those police cells. This only increased his growing hatred of the government. He was not politically active but was becoming a possible recruit for Ahmed.

CRICKET

Ahmed, a true cricketer, was small in stature and a specialist middle-order batsman. A cricketing friend, who was also in detention and requests anonymity, says, "He was a very competent cricketer and an excellent driver of the ball. Ahmed was not a flamboyant batsman but was a fighter on the cricket field, in the true sense of the word. Ahmed was a dependable batsman. He once scored a memorable innings of 49 not out for Wits against Fietas (one of the strongest unions at the time) and won the game for his team. He was carried off the pitch after this innings."

Ahmed's cricketing sensibility summed up his revolutionary temperament as well. My research has revealed a man who was always careful of others and not at all interested in colourful heroics in excess of his brief. Ahmed Timol was a reliable batsman, never tempted by showmanship, possessing an austere elegance and a fierce concentration that is evident in photographs of him at the stumps. His style was unobtrusive and yet somehow always suggested captaincy – he was never a maverick. It was these cricketing qualities, this precision, that marked Ahmed Timol out as an educationist.

People repeatedly tell me of his spontaneous love for children, his considerate ability to take his revolutionary peers along at an appropriate speed, without overwhelming them in ideology or in missions. These were Ahmed's cricketing qualities.

Akbar Moola recalls Ahmed's innings. "We were batting together and I told Ahmed that we had to win the game. Ahmed was not a flamboyant batsman, but a very dependable one. Ahmed was full of life and we were very good friends. The death of Steve Biko had a huge impact on us, but the death of Ahmed was personal. Ahmed was a fighter."

Ahmed's cousin, Iqbal "Baboo" Dindar, recalls getting inspiration on the cricket field from Ahmed. Ahmed was playing for Roodepoort at the time and Iqbal for Zulfikas, a local cricket team. Iqbal could not get into the Roodepoort team at the time as he was a student, was not from Roodepoort, and was probably leaving Roodepoort in a year or two after his studies. Batting for Zulfikas against Roodepoort, Ahmed was fielding at square-leg and encouraged Iqbal to concentrate and bat well. This is exactly what Iqbal did, and he scored a memorable innings of 68.

Rafique Khota (bookkeeper Goramota's brother), himself a very good cricketer, describes Ahmed as a dependable batsman who showed a lot of courage and commitment on the cricket field. "Ahmed was not the flamboyant type. He was quiet and unassuming and a dedicated cricketer who carried these beliefs into his political life. Ahmed never gave his wicket away cheaply. Ahmed batted in the middle order, number four or five, and was a very attractive batsman – short in stature and an excellent driver of the cricket ball. He had a good defence and was an attractive strokeplayer on matting wickets. He scored lots of runs for Roodepoort.

"If Ahmed had played longer, he could have achieved much more. We will never know."

Rafique recalls that the local rivalry in cricket circles was equivalent to test matches, similar to the Ashes series between England and Australia. There was tremendous crowd support and the grounds were always full. People would talk for weeks about the games. There were no sporting facilities available to non-whites in those days. Playing cricket at Natalspruit and Fietas (Vrededorp) on matting wickets, glass and stones sticking out on the sand outfield, resulted in strong resentment towards the privileged white communities which enjoyed far superior facilities, often at taxpayers' cost.

This led to black communities strongly supporting visiting cricketing countries when they toured South Africa, notes Rafique. "Sitting on wooden benches at the Wanderers, caged in fences like animals with the afternoon sun directly in your eyes, the non-white cricketing community fervently urged the visiting nations to beat South Africa. For a period, many went to the stadium merely to watch the game of cricket because of their love for the sport. As they became politically conscientised, the non-white community began to stay away from the stadiums and made a clear statement that they wanted change."

Rafique says that Ahmed was, as a cricketer, a victim of the racist apartheid regime with deprivations suffered from the cricketing and sporting perspective – inferior or no sporting facilities, the difficult environment at home, the inferior educational system, crowded classrooms resulting in the ratio of 40 to 50 students per classroom, while the white students could be as low as 10 per classroom.

The Group Areas Act restricted living conditions, trading licences were curbed and application had to be made for movements from one area to the other. Overnighting in the Free State province was banned outright for Indians.

Essop Pahad confirms that Ahmed was a brilliant cricketer. "He had sufficient talent to perhaps go all the way. We will never know." Racism in sport restricted Ahmed. The cricket leagues were divided according to race and matches were played on an inter-provincial basis, and a national tournament for the Indians, coloureds, Malays and Bantus (the official term for Africans then) was the national tournament, says Pahad. This tournament was the highlight of the cricketing season for the non-whites.

Ahmed and Jo Jo loved cricket. Jo Jo believes that Ahmed should have been a Springbok. He was a superb batsman and represented the Transvaal Indian cricket team and also the South African non-white team. But in those days it was necessary for a cricketer of the calibre of Basil D'Oliveira to go to Britain to play for the MCC, if he aspired to world-class cricket. As it happened, Ahmed went to Britain and elsewhere, but to train as a liberation fighter.

Mohammed Bhai Haffejee, a close friend of Haji Timol, notes, "They would play on the street in Roodepoort with a softball, a paraffin tin in place of stumps, and they would play between four and five games on a Saturday and Sunday. Ahmed was an excellent fielder and batsman. Added to this, Ahmed had a terrific sense of humour, despite his stuttering. Cricket was Ahmed's life and he would play this sport in every spare moment available to him. Cricket was even played during the winter months when others were playing soccer."

Mohammed Bhai had captained a team in the Wits League, and Ahmed played for the team although he was still in high school. They were playing a promotion game and the team was in trouble. Batting second and desperately chasing the opposition's target, Ahmed assured Mohammed Bhai that they would get the runs and win the game.

"Ahmed was always dependable, not only in cricket, but in life generally," he said. "He had a very strong self-belief. Ahmed would always make you feel comfortable and assure you that things will work out".

ARTICLE BY AHMED IN DYNAMOS SOCCER FESTIVAL BROCHURE, 1965
It was in this see-saw atmosphere of growing domestic repression but also international success that Ahmed Timol wrote an article in the Dynamos Soccer Festival souvenir brochure in 1965. He demonstrated a clear mind and sheer determination in the non-racial cause, and he presciently saw the strong link between sport and future liberation. It is worth preserving for a wider audience in this book:

It has become an indisputable fact that in recent years non-white sportsmen, through their respective associations, have successfully strengthened their case for recognition and affiliation to international sporting bodies. This happy state of affairs has materialised primarily due to the undaunted and inspiring efforts of the sportsmen themselves under the watchful eye and guidance of the sporting associations.

It must however be emphatically stated that the task of the non-white sportsman in raising himself to international status has not been an enviable one. His path to achieve recognition through his associations has not been one strewn with flowers – his has been an uphill struggle, hindered and hampered at every turn. His "path" has revealed major obstacles. Above all, his associations have been compelled to tread on dangerous terrain, a terrain that has revealed sharp stones and other obstructionist elements, thus making progress difficult. But in spite of these imposed hardships and with abundance of patience, strength and together with his associations, he has successfully negotiated the "path" destined for international recognition. The words of Nehru that, "Success only comes to those who act bravely and boldly and never to the timid" – must be firmly rooted in the minds of our sportsmen and administrators during their days of trials and tribulations.

We are immensely proud of the achievements of our non-white sportsmen who have stamped their names in international sporting circles. We are proud of them because they have been instrumental in spotlighting the attention of the dilemma facing our sportsmen in their fight to compete as true representatives of all South Africa within the arena of international sporting events. Our hearts go out to a man like Precious McKenzie, the weightlifting hero, who has virtually sacrificed his career, a career which should have yielded him rich rewards and international fame, because he stuck to his principles that he would represent all of South Africa in international events and not only a section of the population. In the golfing world we have our own Papwa who has successfully crashed the barrier to participate in national golfing events within the country and his success overseas particularly in the Dutch Open. In the boxing arena who can challenge the reputation gained by "Schoolboy" Nhlapo, Levi Madi, Joe Ngidi and the one-time Empire lightweight champion Jake Tuli? On the athletic track the half-milers Humphrey Kosi and Benoni Malaka are today the top athletes in our country. On the tennis court David Samaai, Jasmat Dhiraj and a host of others have proven themselves over and over again. On the other hand we find cricketers D'Oliveira, Abrahams and soccerites Johannesen and Steve Mokone have left our country to become sporting exiles and who are presently gaining tremendous prestige and reputation for their sporting prowess.

These are a few of the present sportsmen but what about those who have lapsed into retirement and those who have died, obscured and forgotten by the passage of time? And what about those yet to come, those future sportsmen who are still young and eager, who must be nursed and trained and must yet face up to the rigours of competitive sport? We solemnly ask, must their sporting life be jeopardised because of humiliating affiliations and lack of facilities and thus become victims of political machinations? Must these sportsmen of the future be deprived of sports just because they do not belong to the "right" associations? Must their associations be arbitrarily kicked from the use of their grounds, which were properly administered and controlled for over 30 to 40 years because they refuse, on matters of principle, to subject themselves to subservient affiliations?

We ask these questions because national sports in our country have reached a crucial stage. A situation has arisen where we find our country either suspended or expelled from the sporting fraternity of the world. Suspended from the Olympics and FIFA and threats of expulsion hanging over tennis, swimming, weightlifting, amateur boxing, cricket as well as all other national sports.

It is an inborn human urge that a time comes when one asserts one's human rights. Similarly in the sporting world the day has dawned when our sportsmen are asserting their rights for recognition. They are excelling in sports, their records and deeds justifies them to compete in international events. We therefore call upon the white sporting administrators that the ball is at your feet, it is up to you to square up to the realities of the dilemma facing South African sports. It is up to you to decide whether to sacrifice national sports at the altar of traditional policies or whether to pursue bold, progressive policies. Policies which are within the mainstream of enlightened thinking in the world today. One thing for sure is that if enlightened policies are infused into sports a long lease of life for sports is well assured.

On the other hand the application of traditional policies will undoubtedly contribute to the immediate death of any hope to compete with other countries or to participate in international events – the door will be firmly closed in our face. Traditions are good as long as they do not hamper progress, but once progress is hampered and in this case the progress and very existence of our sport is threatened traditional policies should be quickly done away with.

4

POLITICAL SITUATION

Ahmed was an internationalist. He wrote in his autobiography, "Our struggles at home were inevitably linked with the struggles in Africa and in the wider world. In Africa, the victories of the national liberation revolutions; the aggression of Suez and Bizerta by the Imperialist powers; the Algerian War of Independence and other acts of heroic struggles to rebut Imperialism clearly showed who the real enemies of the people were." His internationalism was tinged by the Cold War propaganda of the era: "On the other hand the undertaking to construct the Aswan Dam in Egypt by the Soviet Union, also its persistent condemnation of reactionary policies in the international councils of the world and above all, with the launching of the first sputnik demonstrated strikingly the fantastic scientific and technological achievements of the Soviet Union under the growth of the productive forces of Socialism."

A DECADE OF STRUGGLE

It was Dr Yusuf Dadoo who was the critical factor in the political development of Ahmed Timol. As Essop Pahad has noted in his unpublished biography, "Dr Dadoo was exceptionally busy on a wide variety of political issues and his popularity and stature and influence were such that any call by him for mass political action was certain to receive the serious consideration of the national liberation and working class movements.

"From the late Thirties Dr Dadoo remained the single most influential political figure within the Indian community. The Defiance Campaign, in which over 8 000 disciplined volunteers courted imprisonment, had been a mighty demonstration of the strength of the African people and of the united front of all revolutionary forces. It signalled an irrevocable break with the old, fruitless, cap-in-hand restrictions of the struggle confined only to deputations, petitions and pleas to the authorities for justice; it marked the decisive shift to unremitting mass struggles including the greater use of the strike weapon. In his presidential address to the

ANC (Transvaal) Conference in 1953, Nelson Mandela introduced the 'M' Plan (named after himself). This plan intended to build a mass membership that was organised into cells at grassroots level and, through a hierarchy of leaders at intermediate levels, would be responsive to direction without the necessity for public meetings. This also allowed for a tighter, more disciplined organisation, closer to the grassroots of the people – an organisation designed for mass action in a hostile and increasingly repressive atmosphere."

Essop Pahad notes in *A People's Leader, A Political Biography of Dr Yusuf M Dadoo*: "The experience of Sharpeville, the illegalisation within days of the African National Congress and Pan Africanist Congress (the Communist Party had been banned since 1950), the massive use of armed force and intimidation to suppress all popular struggles, made it inevitable that the movement should reconsider its reliance on non-violent forms of struggle alone. The revolutionary forces had to find alternative forms of struggle against fascist terror. From this reconsideration of their role was to come Umkhonto we Sizwe (Spear of the Nation), the military wing of the ANC, formed on the joint initiative of the ANC and the South African Communist Party. At the first sign of Umkhonto activity the regime counter-attacked with draconian legislation for detention without trial and legalising the torture and murder of detainees: it subsequently increased its military expenditure, and instituted a system of unrestrained police terror. South Africa had become a police state."

In the book *A Long Night's Damage: Working for the Apartheid State*, Eugene de Kock tells Jeremy Gordin that: "Born less than a year after the National Party took power in 1948, I was brought up to believe that police action was justified if its goal was to protect the system. The Sharpeville shootings of 1960, for example, made an enormous impression on me. I may have been 11 years old but I understood that the state mechanism had been used in the defence of a political system."

The tough-talking justice minister John Vorster had come to power after the assassination of prime minister Dr Hendrik Verwoerd in 1966. This repressive atmosphere set the tone for what was to happen to Ahmed in detention. Vorster's security chief Hendrik van den Bergh made it clear, in remarks to a commission of inquiry (remarks that the government tried to conceal at the time), that his men would stop at nothing if the security of the state demanded this. There can be no doubt about a pattern of deliberate state assassination of comrades in the struggle, something which is highly relevant to the Timol case.

THE TURN TO ARMS

It was in conditions of political emergency that the foundations were laid for the activities that led to Ahmed's death. After the declaration of a State of Emergency in March 1960 following the Sharpeville massacre, thousands were arrested including most of the leading members of the national liberation and working class movements. But Dadoo, Moses Kotane, Harmel and others evaded the racist net. The Communist Party of South Africa, banned in 1950, had been recast as the South African Communist Party (SACP); its existence was kept secret from all apart from its own members. Now it was decided to make the existence of the

Party public. Leaflets were clandestinely distributed throughout the country at an agreed date and time. While underground, Dr Dadoo vigorously argued the case for a radical departure in the tactics and strategy of the national liberation and working class movement – a turn to armed struggle.

Ahmed wrote in his autobiography, "The planning for the new stage of struggle commenced immediately and in 1961 the beginning of an armed struggle was on the agenda of the South African Revolution. As a direct response to the emergence of Umkhonto we Sizwe, the military wing of the ANC that was given the task for sabotage acts directed against the economic pillars of apartheid and the offices and places of discrimination, the ruling authorities introduced the 90-day law. Hundreds of activists were detained in solitary confinement and subjected to barbarous treatment.

"The security of the underground movement was penetrated at several points and numerous trials followed, the famous one being the Rivonia Trial where our leaders comrades [Nelson] Mandela, [Govan] Mbeki, [Ahmed] Kathrada were sentenced to life imprisonment."

Pahad describes how new repressive laws were rushed through the white Parliament, and the first arrests and detentions, incommunicado, were made under these laws. "90-days", "180-days", "sabotage suspect", "detention without trial", "solitary confinement", " torture" – a whole new vocabulary was becoming current in legal-political talk, and with it new images of what was really happening in the country. From prisons and detention centres all over the country horrific accounts of police brutality and consistent tortures began to emerge through information smuggled by the victims to friends or relatives outside.

The involvement of Indians in this new phase of struggle was dramatically underlined in April 1963, when five men, Laloo Chiba, Sirish Nanabhai, Indres Naidoo, Reggie Vandeyar and Abdulhay Jassat were arrested and charged with sabotage. Chiba was subsequently released and Jassat, together with another detainee, Moosa Moola, escaped from prison (with detainees Arthur Goldreich and Harold Wolpe) and left the country, but the other three were convicted of attempting to blow up electricity pylons. They were sentenced to 10 years' imprisonment. Chiba was to be arrested again in 1964 and sentenced to 20 years.

A significant degree of unity was maintained in the Indian community, despite differences on the new strategy – a unity stretching to communist and non-communist, workers, shopkeepers, teachers, nurses, doctors and students. Within the underground itself, this was demonstrated as a unity in which people of African, coloured, Indian and white descent had been successfully integrated, and they were functioning at every level of Umkhonto we Sizwe – not as representing national groups or organisations, but as revolutionaries, functioning under a single unified leadership. The outlines of a future non-racial society were becoming more apparent.

The arrest of a part of the leadership at Rivonia dealt a great blow to the liberation movement. It did not, however, destroy it. A year later, shortly after the Rivonia accused had been sentenced, a fresh wave of sabotage rocked the country and sporadic acts of sabotage continued until 1965. In August 1967, armed combatants of the ANC joined members of the Zimbabwe African People's Union (ZAPU) on combined operations inside Zimbabwe against a combined force of the Pretoria and Salisbury regimes. Things were getting very serious.

Dr Dadoo had been asked by the South African Indian Congress (SAIC) and the SACP to leave South Africa to strengthen the external mission of the movement. Dadoo was not happy with the decision and argued vigorously that his place was in the underground. He was overruled and, disciplined communist and revolutionist that Dadoo was, he carried out the collective decision and left the country in 1960. But he was in South Africa long enough to make a deep impression on student Timol.

After the banning of the ANC, during 1960-1963 volunteers from the Transvaal Indian Youth Congress (TIYC) began producing and distributing ANC pamphlets and posters. South Africa was in a state of ferment. The struggle against the Group Areas Act was the main form of struggle by the Indian Congress. The country was under a State of Emergency and the ANC was banned. The underground network was now being built. Ahmed continued having contact with Essop and Aziz Pahad, Ahmed Bhabha and others. Political ideas started maturing in his head.

Aziz and Essop were banned for five years in January 1964. Although sharing a bedroom they had to get special permission from the then minister of justice to speak to each other. They both went into exile in December 1964.

Sampie Essack recalls, "Before Aziz and Essop Pahad departed the country, they mentioned to me that we must keep in contact. When I arrived to teach in Roodepoort, I was requested to send the addresses of parents through the various grapevines. I was in charge of the admission register at school. Herbie Francis (who went to Canada) was in charge of the register previously, and the responsibility was then handed over to me. I would regularly write down the names and addresses of the parents on a page and post it to them in London. Aziz and Essop would then send newsletters of the ANC's activities to the people in South Africa. When I was transferred to MH Joosub High School in 1974, I did the same thing. Later, at Nirvana High School, also in charge of the admission register, I once again did the same thing. This was how the ANC in London kept the local communities informed about the ANC's political activities."

The Roodepoort Indian High School incident book on Wednesday, 9 August 1972 contains the following entry: "Warrant Officer Van Tonder of the Security Police called at school. He took statements from Mr I Loonat and myself, regarding the pamphlet 'Bangladesh' by YM Dadoo which had been posted to and arrived at school for Mr I Loonat and Mr AS Solomons, a former member of staff, now on the staff of Nirvana High School."

These were the formative years of solidifying Ahmed's political thinking. Ahmed was a loyal and dedicated member of the Congress Movement.

Essop Pahad recalls, "Ahmed was a very good Congressite from the beginning and totally supported the policies and principles of the Congress Movement. The membership of the ANC was limited only to Africans until the Morogoro Conference in 1969. Many political discussions took place but Ahmed was not yet drawn into the underground networks."

One of Ahmed's students, Naeema Khota (now Jassat), was in Standard Seven in 1966 and remembers Ahmed as a good, caring and very helpful teacher. While softly spoken and reserved, he never hesitated to speak his mind and his activism was not limited to the expression of opinions. He collected food parcels for political detainees and encouraged his students to volunteer to bake foodstuffs.

In teaching history lessons, Ahmed constantly reminded his students of the hardships of the apartheid system. The lessons on Napoleon and the Allied effort in World War II against Nazism were used by Ahmed as a backdrop to the struggles of the South African people.

Ahmed's meagre teaching salary went to his family. He spent very little money on himself. Even when teaching in England, Ahmed sent money home to his family in South Africa. His father was semi-blind and unable to work full-time.

Outside their school activities, Jo Jo Saloojee and Ahmed were involved with the movement at large. Jo Jo was regularly visited by the Security Branch and taken to the Security Police Headquarters at The Gray's for questioning and interrogation. Jo Jo and Ahmed had lengthy discussions and were aware that the time was near when they would not be in a position to continue their political work effectively. They had decided that the time had come for them to leave the country. Jo Jo departed for Zambia where he established contact with the ANC.

Before long Ahmed too was to go abroad and sadly when he and Jo Jo went their respective ways they lost contact with each other. They knew in their hearts that, though physically far apart, emotionally they were together and would continue the struggle wherever they were.

Meanwhile, life went on as usual for young Ahmed – politically focused, angry at apartheid, concerned for social equality. But he had domestic imperatives to deal with too. He was considerably concerned about his mother's health. When she went into a severe depression in about 1966, Ahmed and his cousin Dr Farouk Dindar took her to private hospital psychiatrists. She received a few sessions of electroconvulsive therapy, little knowing what horrific tensions lay ahead for her.

Ahmed was Farouk's best man at his wedding in December 1966. The photographer took the wedding party to a white family's private garden to take photographs. While they were there Ahmed whispered into Farouk's ear: "Look at the extravagance." This caused Farouk some anguish, and his facial expression during the photographs showed that.

Farouk and his wife Jameela left for Zambia soon after the wedding – Farouk did his medical internship in Kitwe. He was hungry to read leftist literature but none was readily available in Zambia.

Ahmed's younger brother Ismail had matriculated in 1964. Ismail obtained a bursary from the Kholvad Madressa and went to India to do a BA at Aligarh University in 1965. It was at Aligarh where his father Haji Timol and Dr Dadoo had studied in the 1920s.

Life during these years had become extremely difficult and unbearable for Ahmed. His closest friends Essop and Aziz Pahad were in exile, his good friend Jo

Jo Saloojee was in Zambia. Ahmed told his cousin Farouk that he needed to get out of South Africa but that he would return.

5

PRECOCIOUS PILGRIM

On 25 December 1966, at the age of 25, Ahmed told his parents that he was going to perform *Hajj* and spend a few weeks in London visiting before returning home. At that time it was very unusual for a young man like Ahmed to go on the pilgrimage to Mecca. During those days it was common practice for people to wait until their late fifties or sixties before performing the pilgrimage.

Ahmed quit his teaching post for this overseas trip. Aysha and "Baboo" Nanabhay (a teacher at the Roodepoort Indian High School) were also on the pilgrimage with Ahmed, and Aysha recalls how helpful he was, "always assisting us in the carrying of our luggage".

Moosa Waja makes the point that *Hajj* was a method of getting a passport to leave the country. Those who were "non-white" were not able to get out easily and *Hajj* presented an opportunity for Muslims.

Ahmed was firm in his religious beliefs and never abandoned Islam, Moosa points out. "Communism never influenced his belief in the Almighty. He was certainly not a hypocrite. He believed in equality and fairness. He was rigorously honest in his approach. He was not afraid of the consequences of his political beliefs."

Ahmed went to mosque regularly, completed madressa, recited the Quran and his father, Haji Timol, was one of the few known *hajis* at the time. This served to strengthen Ahmed's political beliefs; fully accepting the Communist Party did not mean that he had left his religion. Ahmed had always retained respect and affection for his own family and the community. He knew that he had to work within that community. Essop Pahad's view is that there was no dichotomy or contradiction as Ahmed continued going to mosque when he returned to South Africa.

Ahmed showed that you can be a good Muslim and a sincere communist without sacrificing cultures. This was the opposite of what the ruling white establishment in South Africa thought.

Ahmed's allegiance to Islam was never insular. This is reflected in his practice of recruiting and working with people who were not Muslim, like KC Naik and

Indres Moodley. It was part of his religious upbringing to work beyond the confines of his religious community.

During the Hajj in Saudi Arabia in December 1966 Ahmed met up with Dr Yusuf Dadoo. This further contributed to his politicisation. It was no doubt Ahmed's own decision to go to London, given the situation in South Africa and his own politicisation. Essop Pahad adds, "Ahmed had decided to come for political talks and discussions. Dr Dadoo probably confirmed his determination to go to London." Ahmed also met Molvi Cachalia in Mecca. After pilgrimage, Molvi went to India with Alfred Nzo where they established the ANC offices. This was the first mission of its kind in Asia.

It was normal during those years to go for Hajj and then to tour Europe. Ahmed went to Cairo where he visited Sadique Jina who was studying medicine. There were many other South African students who were studying in Cairo at the time. It was normal for visitors from South Africa to visit fellow South Africans in Cairo without making any prior arrangements. No political discussions took place between Ahmed and Sadique, and Sadique had no idea that Ahmed was planning to go to London. It was Sadique who, when qualified as a doctor, treated Ahmed's parents in their old age. He had become their personal doctor and was always present when his services were required. Sadique did not take any money from the family and remarked that this was his modest way of contributing to Ahmed's sacrifices.

In April 1967 Ahmed turned up unannounced with his suitcases at North End House, West Kensington, where the exiles and other South African students had foregathered. Comradeship was automatic and courtesies unnecessary. The apartment consisted of a living room, four bedrooms, and the usual kitchen, two bathrooms and two toilets. Ahmed and the Pahads were roommates.

In 1967, Ahmed took up teaching in London at the Immigration School at Slough. "Teaching was also a means of income for Ahmed. This made Ahmed financially well off compared to the other residents of North End House. Ahmed was a generous person and always contributed for social activities. People could always rely on Ahmed for assistance," says Essop. Ahmed sent much of his salary home to his family.

Ahmed was teaching children from the Indian sub-continent (India, Pakistan and Bangladesh), which made him aware of the racism that existed in the United Kingdom. There was a continuation of old political discussions and comradeship. This expanded Ahmed's horizon and political thinking. Essop had completed his MA in African politics at Sussex University, and political discussions continued between Essop and Ahmed around the Vietnam War and the India-Pakistan conflict. Aziz was at the same time completing his Diploma in International Relations at University College, London.

Meg Shorrock, who later married Essop Pahad, recalls, "Timol was always concerned and helpful about people. He was out most of the time in England as he taught at the Immigrant Reception Centre and was also studying part-time. He was also a member of the National Union of Teachers and took an active interest in its activities. In his last year in the UK he worked among the immigrant community in Slough.

"Ahmed was a teacher who was respected throughout the community for his dedication to his work and for the tremendous effort and sacrifices he made for his students and friends in every aspect of their lives. Those that had the opportunity of meeting Ahmed for the first time or of renewing old acquaintances were impressed by his dedication and his abhorrence of injustice, whether it was in the UK or in South Africa.

"Wherever Ahmed taught, he would work closely with particular pupils who needed coaching. He would do extra work with them, and go to the trouble of finding them additional material to read. He believed in treating his pupils as individuals and responded to their individual needs." Meg says Ahmed must have been a most impressive teacher.

While teaching, Ahmed was doing his A level course. One of the subjects that he was doing was sociology. In London at that time you would first complete your O levels – equivalent to a South African Standard Nine. In order for one to do a tertiary course or degree you had to do A levels. This was a prerequisite for you to be accepted into university or polytechnic. Ahmed was not studying to enter university but rather to broaden his mind. He studied on a part-time basis and attended classes in the evenings. Essop recalls: "Ahmed enjoyed doing sociology. After class we would have talks on 'bourgeois society/sociology' and Ahmed often raised the issue of not being brainwashed by the bourgeoisie. This was rather ironic, as I had completed my studies at a bourgeois institution.

"Ahmed displayed great passion for sociology and showed more interest in the theory than in the practical aspects. He found the A levels in sociology stimulating. He was also exposed to the science of Marxism and Leninism. He was serious in his reading and this enabled him to think in terms of social structures. Coming from South Africa and aware of the struggle, Ahmed now had an opportunity to think in a theoretical way. As a young South African revolutionary Ahmed was automatically attracted to Marxism and Leninism. There was a bookshop in the West End of London called Collett's. They sold material and literature relating to left-wing organisations across the world. Ahmed would frequent this bookshop and buy leftwing material. This gave him a better and deeper understanding of world politics. Our discussions focused on South Africa's problems within the world context. Fierce discussions would take place about what was written in the left-wing literature. This process continued the expansion of Ahmed's political and ideological development."

MEETING RUTH LONGONI

Coming to London to rekindle his relationship with his old comrades Essop and Aziz Pahad, and unable to tolerate the living conditions under apartheid in South Africa, Ahmed was set to meet the true love of his life, Ruth Longoni.

Ruth was 22 and working for *Labour Monthly*, a journal edited by Palme Dutt Ranjit who was a founder member of the Communist Party of Great Britain and one of the founders of the magazine. It was aimed very much at trade unionists and what was regarded as the wider labour movement. Ruth's job as editorial assistant was to organise sales of the magazine, type up articles and attend editorial meetings.

Ruth remembers, "I met Ahmed around Easter in 1967 at an Aldermaston march, organised by the Campaign for Nuclear Disarmament. It was the day before the march reached London, and Ahmed was busy talking to people on the march about their reasons for being there. Ahmed was very interested in people and very enthusiastic about this sort of demonstration. About a week after that I got a phone call from Ahmed asking whether we could meet up."

Ahmed came out to visit Ruth at Arkley, in Hertfordshire – little more than a hamlet outside High Barnet – which was where Ruth was living at the time. Ruth immediately realised that they shared a great deal in common, despite coming from different backgrounds. Emotionally they were on the same wavelength. Ruth was a member of the Communist Party of Great Britain.

He shared his experiences of living in South Africa with Ruth and spoke about the daily humiliations that Indian South Africans faced in all kinds of ways. The fact that there were restaurants he couldn't go to. That, if he was out with friends, the car would pull up and they would have to get drinks from a kiosk, and other similar problems.

Ruth adds, "I think Ahmed also was aware of the particular experience of Indian South Africans. He knew about the whole history of indentured labour of the Indian community. He also knew that humiliating and horrible as the experiences of Indians in South Africa were, it was infinitely worse, he felt, to be a black South African. He had tremendous feelings of compassion and anger at the treatment of black South Africans.

"He was a man of tremendous compassion and he empathised a great deal with the oppressed people and wanted to change their situation. He couldn't tolerate that level of suffering and injustice."

Ruth also recalls that "Ahmed also spoke about his deep affection that he had for his mother. He spoke of her as a kind, simple and loving woman."

The Vietnam War was raging at this time and that was very influential in Ahmed's thinking in its internationalist and anti-imperialist emphases – and in Ruth's thinking as well. Ruth adds, "It influenced a whole generation. So I suppose by that time I had moved from my earlier pacifism to a support for the armed struggle in Vietnam and I think both Ahmed and I believed that in years to come a similar sort of struggle would be taking place in South Africa. And one of the things that Ahmed talked about was that he had to go back because we were seeing the most terrible images almost daily on television about what was happening in Vietnam. And he couldn't envisage staying in England, however happily, marrying me, having children, and seeing those kind of images coming back to him from South Africa. That I could understand very well."

Ruth and Ahmed were very close and committed to each other. Ruth adds, "There were times when we couldn't do things together which I would have liked us to do. One of these occasions was the World Youth Festival in 1968, in Bulgaria, in Sofia. That was a sort of communist youth movement organised on an international basis where delegations from almost all over the world met and discussed and celebrated together. Ahmed explained to me that he couldn't go. There would be difficulties with his passport, with his visa.

"The Pahad brothers went. Various other people that we knew went and Ahmed was very keen that I should go, because he was very generous in that respect. If he couldn't share an experience with me he still wanted me to have that experience. So my friend Lesley and I went and Ahmed and I decided that we would have a holiday together in Devon that summer."

Ahmed Suliman Kaka (known as Ronnie) and Dr Yussuf Saloojee (not to be confused with Yusuf "Jo Jo" Saloojee) point out that Ahmed and Ruth were totally into classical music. They would often go to the theatre and his flatmates would tease him about this.

Ahmed was teaching in Slough, and this was a long journey from North End House where they lived. Like many British commuters, he would leave early in the morning and arrive late in the evening. Ronnie, Yussuf and the others were students and would hardly see Ahmed, as Ahmed and Ruth would often go away for weekends.

Yussuf remembers attending a "soul concert" with Aziz, Essop, Meg, Ahmed, Ruth and Yasmin at the Hammersmith Odeon. The artists included Otis Redding and Sam and Dave. Ahmed was receptive and open to many cultural influences. They remember Ahmed as "nature's gentleman". He was soft spoken, caring and a considerate friend. Nothing could expose the brutality of the apartheid regime more than the contrast between his kindly life and his violent death at the hands of the Security Branch.

Ahmed was very studious, always reading in his room, and Ronnie and Yussuf never inquired about his motives for coming to London after performing Hajj. They did suspect that Ahmed was there for training – but he said nothing about it to them. Part of the self-discipline of the revolutionary was to never disclose significant things to anyone – particularly if the plan was to go back to repressive South Africa. Everything was on a need-to-know principle.

London gave these South Africans unfettered access to all types of literature. Ahmed constantly brought back books from Collett's bookshop. Ronnie has a very strong mental image of Ahmed's cousin, Dr Farouk Dindar, sitting in the room in London reading Marxist-Leninist literature, a most unfamiliar sight. It was obvious that Ahmed had some influence over Dr Dindar and the doctor confirmed this.

Farouk adds, "I would regularly visit the Pahad flat where I would meet Ahmed. The Vietnam War was in full swing and most of the discussions we had were around the horrors of that war. Ahmed gave me a book by (dovish US senator and unsuccessful Democratic presidential candidate) George McGovern to read. Ahmed introduced me to the *World Marxist Review*. This was a monthly publication of articles written by communist parties across the world describing political activities in their respective countries. Essop Pahad was later appointed to the editorial committee of the *World Marxist Review* based in Prague.

Farouk continues, "When I got a job in Sedgefield in Durham County as a senior house officer I was busy doing medical reading. But in my spare time I had a hunger to read political material. The British were very tolerant of different political ideas and there was no censorship. The readily available leftist literature was overwhelming. It was here where Ahmed was of tremendous help to me.

Whenever we met Ahmed would advise me on what to read and what not to read. I respected Ahmed's very sound judgement. Ahmed had recognised that I was busy specialising in medicine and so very carefully chose material that would not overwhelm me. This was a hallmark of a good teacher."

North End House was like a transit zone but Ahmed was completely different from the normal flow. Here was Ahmed, in the London of the swinging Sixties, quietly dedicating himself to the struggle. A picture of neatness, almost a figure apart, he would move around the chaotic flat with all sorts of people coming and going. His hair was always perfectly combed and he would be dressed meticulously, even wearing a dressing gown as he went to and from the bathroom – towel, toothbrush and comb in hand. The slight stammer added to the image that, to this day, is carried in the memories of those who knew him then. For although he had brought his stammer under control, he would stutter when excited.

Ahmed's younger brother Mohammed had completed his schooling in 1967, and Ahmed invited him to come to England to further his studies. Mohammed was given a scholarship by the Roodepoort Muslim Society to study textile engineering at Leicester Polytechnical College in England in September 1968. At this time there were a number of South African students studying in Leicester. Mohammed stayed with Ahmed at the Pahads' flat in West Kensington for two weeks.

Meg, a frequent visitor to the flat in West Kensington, recalls that its numerous occupants included Essop, Aziz, Timol, Ahmed Pochee, Ronnie Kaka, Dr Yussuf Saloojee, Vijay Rama (now deceased), and, for a while, Yasmin Pahad (now Dadabhay). She remembers Timol as a kind person, very considerate, thoughtful and helpful to everybody. "He was always like that," she comments. He might occasionally tease somebody, but she never remembers Timol being cross or upset.

In the four big bedrooms, many people slept. There was a single bedroom and Timol moved into that one, as he had a lot of studying to do at the time. But when Yasmin Pahad, Essop and Aziz's niece was 11 or 12 Ahmed gave up his room to her without anybody asking as she was a young girl amongst all the men and needed her privacy.

Yasmin tells her poignant side of the Timol story: "I had a very unusual upbringing in that I was brought up in a house full of men, one of whom was Ahmed. My grandmother was there for periods but moved from South Africa to London and then to India. I was the only little girl and consequently spoiled rotten by the men. They all entertained me, taking me to the movies, theatres, the park, etc.

"My most vivid memory of him is when he caught me smoking. I stole a couple of cigarettes from somebody's packet and went to the bathroom to experiment. Being a bit näive, I didn't even bother to open the windows. As I came out, there was Ahmed standing waiting for me! He gave me such a talking to, he didn't shout or get angry, and I have no idea what he said to me, but up to today I have never smoked again! Throughout my teens, with all the peer pressure, I just never touched another cigarette.

"When I used to get home in the afternoons after school at times he was there with Essop. The three of us would sit and watch a television soapie called *Crossroads*. I remember his girlfriend called Ruth. They once went away and when they got back they brought me presents, a handbag and a huge bar of Toblerone chocolate. I once helped him address envelopes for mailing ANC/CP literature to South Africa. When my passport was taken away by the security police, one of the things they had was one of these envelopes with my writing on it. To think I was only 11 or 12 at the time."

Yasmin's arrival made Meg realise what a nice person Ahmed was. Everybody else in the flat behaved normally to Yasmin, but Ahmed really cared. Meg recalls that Essop was like a father to Yasmin, and Ahmed more like an uncle to her. When Meg heard the distressing news of Ahmed's subsequent arrest and torture in South Africa she kept on thinking about how he never did anything to hurt anybody, how gentle he was, how he seemed to live always for other people. He was totally non-egocentric. Ahmed put himself last in the important things in life. As he saw it, the important thing was always to do what one could be proud of, to have complete integrity and to be kind and gentle.

Residents of North End House were very security-conscious. If anyone went abroad, explicit details were never mentioned. It was mentioned once that Ahmed had gone to Sweden or Finland (or somewhere north, where it was cold). Meg and the others had no idea that Ahmed had really gone to the Soviet Union for his political training. Some suspected this but it was never discussed.

Ahmed faced wrenching personal dilemmas. He told his girlfriend Ruth that he truly loved her but he could not marry her as he did not have a future. This was similar to what Essop told Meg at the time. If you were in the Struggle you did not have a personal future. There were many comrades in the Struggle who could not marry, as they could not take family responsibilities upon themselves. They were married to the Struggle. A mitigating factor was that many of the young activists had relationships with people of similar left-wing views in the UK and elsewhere abroad, and there was therefore a more ready understanding of the point by their partners.

Farouk Dindar recalls that Ahmed and Ruth came to visit him and Jameela and they went to the Lake District for a weekend. At that time Ahmed was deeply in love with Ruth. Ahmed had long hair during this time and he had begun to dress more casually. Ahmed came to speak to Farouk about some major events that had occurred in his life. Farouk had the impression that Ahmed wanted at least one close cousin to know what was happening to him. Ahmed told Farouk that Dr Dadoo had invited him to join the Communist Party and that he was honoured. He was going to the Soviet Union for training and would be returning to South Africa. Ahmed told Farouk that he was very saddened to leave Ruth but his duty to South Africa would override his love for her. Ahmed had a duty to the liberation struggle in South Africa.

Ruth recalls, "There were however many happy times together. We went to Brighton in January 1969 and had a lovely holiday staying in somebody's flat. It must have been the flat belonging to a friend; maybe there were connections with Sussex University and friends of the Pahads. So, again, we had a delightful time staying in Brighton and going for walks on the South Downs, getting on buses, going out somewhere, going on these lovely walks. At that stage I was aware that Ahmed was hinting to me that there might be a long separation in our relationship.

Ruth and Ahmed spent their last night together at her parents' house in Barnet. Ruth vividly remembers Ahmed leaving in the early hours of the morning, with her thinking that she would never see him again.

LENIN SCHOOL

Membership of the Communist Party at that time was totally secret and was not disclosed, except to members of a particular unit. It was only known that Essop belonged to the Party when he left for Prague in 1975. Party members had secret branch meetings only known to branch members. The ANC was a larger organisation and its membership was known. The underground structures of the ANC and Party were separate. People would gather at social occasions and could assume from Essop and Aziz's discussions that they were Party members.

Ahmed held separate discussions with Dr Dadoo, whom many called Doc or more respectfully Mota (meaning elder brother). Ahmed had clearly displayed that he was interested in carrying out serious work for the movement. At this time the anti-Vietnam War demonstrations were taking place in London. What was to be done in terms of the Struggle?

It was agreed that it was important to build underground structures and intensify the armed revolutionary struggle. Ahmed's two-year stay in England had brought him to the conclusion that he had to go back to South Africa to be an active participant in the underground to intensify the Struggle. Doc and the Communist Party leadership decided that Ahmed had to go to the Party School, the Institute of Social Studies, also called the International Lenin School, in the Soviet Union.

In his book *A View from Moscow* Vladimir Shubin writes about the Lenin School: "Better known by its underground name, the International Lenin School. The decision to resurrect this School (it had existed in Moscow in the Thirties and had been attended by Moses Kotane) was taken on December 1961 to meet an increasing number of requests from foreign communist parties and later from liberation movements."

OR Tambo, President of the ANC, described 5 April 1963 as an historic day in the history of the South African people when direct contact between the Communist Party of the Soviet Union and the ANC leadership was established. As a result of this significant and historic agreement, many cadres in the movement were given opportunities to receive political and military training in the Soviet Union for many years to come.

Essop recalls, "Ahmed had been selected to go to the Party School with Thabo Mbeki and was excited at being selected. It was a personal victory for him to be selected. There was no doubt that when Ahmed returned from his training, he would be returning to South Africa. Ahmed knew of the political consequences that would flow upon his return to South Africa. The movement required cadres to build the underground.

"A decision had been taken in the early Sixties to send members to the Party School. Members were to obtain political and ideological training and would thus come back better equipped in terms of theoretical and practical understanding of Marxism and Leninism. For the others returning from the Party School, unlike Timol, it was not clear if they were to be sent home to South Africa or tasked to do other work.

"In the case of Ahmed it was very clear that he was specifically trained to go back to South Africa. There could have been other members from MK that were sent back to South Africa to set up the underground cells. The Party School was to equip Ahmed with the theoretical background that was required when developing underground units, not just the distribution of pamphlets and leaflets, but also to give political leadership to other structures that were formed. Ahmed was expected to produce and write his own political material. He was to equip himself politically, and specifically target the Indian community. This is why Ahmed was sent to the Party School, and this is exactly what he accomplished."

Prior to Ahmed's going to the Party School, Essop and Ahmed held many discussions as to what it would mean undergoing political training and what life was going to be like in Moscow. "Ahmed, like others, totally supported the position taken by the Soviet Union on imperialist countries. They understood the role and place of the Soviet Union and the other Socialist countries in terms of the struggle."

Recollecting Ahmed's stay in London, Essop says, "This period marks the most formative period of Ahmed's political upbringing. He was developing politically and displayed a greater consciousness of the struggle and of other people's struggles. The relationship between the working class and national struggle was a hot topic of discussion among activists.

"During this political development phase of his life, Ahmed never stopped being himself. He maintained his personality, character and all the wonderful personal things about him. He displayed a great sense of humour and was one who never got angry. Ahmed remained the same easy-going person, someone who was always easy to warm to." This had been reflected when he used to pay for Essop's bioscope tickets in South Africa.

"It was easy for other people to know Ahmed. Early on after meeting Ahmed you could detect a very honest, sincere person, always trustworthy, honest in his dealings (inherited from his father). You could entrust Ahmed with money without keeping books. You knew that your money was safe with Ahmed and it would be returned to you without your asking for it. Ahmed's determination to start working when he returned to South Africa in late 1969 fits with his character. If Ahmed was asked to do something, you could rely on him."

Essop points out that when the decision was taken for Ahmed to go underground and mobilise the Indian communities, he became a full participant of the Communist Party and MK. This moulded Ahmed into taking a conscious decision to participate in the underground structures of not only the ANC but also actively recruit for the Party. The ANC and Party had separate underground structures. Some activists did work only for the ANC, some only for the Party and others for both. The notion of recruitment for the Party, in addition to recruiting for the ANC, meant having some sort of ideological certainty in order to join the Party.

Joining the SACP meant taking real additional risks. The Security Branch regarded the Communists as enemy number one and hated them. Their racial thinking was that the Africans would be fine as long as they got rid of the Indian and white communists. The presupposition behind this was that Africans could not think for themselves and were duped by communists. This utter rubbish and mindset of the security establishment in South Africa explained why people like Ahmed Timol were so grotesquely treated, even killed. The experiences in detention of people like Salim Essop, who was arrested together with Ahmed in 1971, bear testimony to this.

When Ahmed went for his political training in the former Soviet Union in 1969 he wrote in his autobiography about his time in London as follows:

"My experience in England was invaluable because of the following reasons: Firstly, the myth of the Welfare State and classless society was exposed. Secondly, the opportunity of observing how bourgeois parliamentary democracy operates, in the present crisis stage of Monopoly Capitalism in Britain, in the interest of vast monopolies and against interests of both normal and menial workers who are being deliberately deprived of their 'limited' parliamentary rights; thirdly the peddling of abstract political concepts masked in hypocrisy and deceit like freedom of speech, justice, democracy, equality and so forth.

"I joined the Communist Party of South Africa after I had discovered – by reading a few Marxist works and journals in England – that I was always a communist at heart. I also fully realise that sincerity alone is not enough; one must either understand the social forces which move society onwards, or become the blind tools of forces which one cannot understand and therefore cannot control or bend to our will."

STAY AT THE LENIN SCHOOL

Accompanied by Thabo Mbeki, Ahmed went to the Party School in the Soviet Union on 17 February 1969. They completed their studies on 15 October, eight months later. Ahmed had barely two years to live.

Ahmed worked very hard and had lots of material to read. He attended various courses, including political economy and philosophy, social psychology of a people, how to work with people, history of the CPSU (Communist Party of the Soviet Union), how to set up dead letter boxes, setting up of underground structures, how to recruit members, radio communication. The training instructors used their own experiences during World War II to empower the students. Returning from his political training, Ahmed told Essop that he had found the Party School an enriching experience.

Essop states, "Ahmed did well in his courses. Ahmed was not a brilliant theoretician, but a deep thinker. Given his own personality, Ahmed's thoughts were always within the framework of a sympathetic approach to those who were struggling for freedom, not only in South Africa, but also all over the world. The Party School helped to mould Ahmed (as it did for many others) and gave him a better understanding of the Communist Party, better grounding of Marxism and Leninism.

"The months that Ahmed spent in the Soviet Union allowed him to make a real leap forward. Ahmed came to grips with the theory of Marxism and Leninism. This period reinforced Ahmed's commitment to the Communist Party and the ANC. It also crystallised and solidified Ahmed's political upbringing."

At the end of the course, an oral examination was done. Recruits also had to go to another area of the Soviet Union to undergo "practice". This meant meeting the local Party structures, interacting with trade unions, going to factories and learning practical things. There were one to two weeks of holiday allocated to the recruits.

"Ahmed got along very well with the staff. He was always a warm, gentle, human person. This was displayed in his personality. Ahmed got along with the other students that were also at the Party School. Students from across the world attended, e.g. Brazil, Paraguay, Iraq, Syria, Jordan, Germany, Denmark, Finland and Norway," recalls Essop.

When Ahmed returned to London, he and Essop had lengthy discussions about his stay in the Soviet Union. Essop recalls, "Ahmed had returned with a photograph that was taken with him standing at the beach. I agreed that Ahmed could return to South Africa with the photograph. If he was questioned about it, he could simply state that it was taken at any beach, as he was touring Europe."

The photograph of Ahmed standing in front of the Hermitage, a museum in Leningrad, now St Petersburg, in Russia, was another matter, however. This could not be passed off as the British Museum – it might have betrayed his training, it was not to return with him. Likewise his conspicuously Soviet-made camera, which Essop swapped for his own less tell-tale watch.

Essop continues, "Part of Ahmed's training meant going to Leningrad, the cradle of the October Revolution. Recruits were taken to 'Smolny' and you would be shown where the first cannons were fired."

Essop underwent the same course at the Party School in 1973. A lecturer in philosophy, Arkady Gregorian, and Essop became very close friends. Essop would visit his house and meet his wife and daughter. The lecturer would visit Essop's room and would always stare at Ahmed's photo on the wall which Essop had taken with him to Moscow. One day Essop told him that this was his closest friend, Ahmed Timol. That he had been sent back to South Africa to set up an underground cell for the Party and that he had been murdered. The lecturer's eyes filled with tears and he confirmed to Essop that he had been Ahmed's philosophy teacher. Mbeki later confirmed this.

Gregorian told Essop that Ahmed was very diligent in his studies and that he was a very nice, warm person and always hard-working. Ahmed understood philosophy but was not theoretical, though he would engage in theoretical discussions. The lecturer was reticent to say more about Ahmed, as they were not to discuss their students.

Essop also spoke to the interpreters about Ahmed. The interpreters were at the Party School for a number of years and one interpreter was allocated per group. Essop adds, "There were no untoward incidents that Ahmed was involved in. Ahmed always maintained high levels of discipline and showed great enthusiasm while studying. He always did whatever he was asked to do and never complained. Ahmed had received a monthly stipend and the Party School regularly took recruits to attend the Bolshoi Ballet. This gave Ahmed an opportunity to know Moscow better." Ahmed also spent time talking with Thabo Mbeki. The future president was aware that Ahmed would return to South Africa and knew that his mission would be to help build the underground structures of the Party and of the ANC.

RETURNING TO LONDON FROM THE SOVIET UNION

Ahmed had visited Ruth at the *Labour Monthly* offices after returning from the Soviet Union. Ruth says, "I think he was very divided. I didn't think he doubted he was doing the right thing about whether he should go back but he'd got these other feelings and connections to me and how could he reconcile the two? He'd got two irreconcilable commitments, it seemed to me – one to us being close and having an ongoing relationship and on the other hand a path which precluded that. He couldn't do both. He couldn't combine the two.

"When I think back to our relationship, I think there were certain ambiguities in it. I knew that Ahmed was passionately concerned and was involved in the anti-apartheid movement. I didn't quite know the extent of his involvement in the ANC, certainly in the very early days."

Ahmed was a sensitive and kind human being, but never emotional, and would not talk about his relationships on a personal level. Finally, he was forced to give up his relationship with Ruth Longoni to come home for the sake of the Struggle. Such was the degree of sacrifice that Ahmed was prepared to endure. Others would have responded differently. But Ruth understood.

Meg recalls, "Ahmed only told Ruth that he was going to South Africa to work in the underground. None of the other friends ever knew this. There were never any discussions about structures and operational issues, but there were general discussions. All the South Africans who attended Aziz's and Essop's double wedding in 1971 were questioned when they returned to South Africa. It was, ironically, the year of the death of their boyhood friend Ahmed."

Ahmed continued receiving additional training for a period of four weeks in 1970 at Jack Hodgson's flat. Jack was one of the communists most feared by the apartheid government. He was a military expert and teacher in the use of explosives and sabotage and he was, coincidentally, himself from Roodepoort. Ahmed and Jack worked very closely together and had many political discussions. Jack was not a technician but a political figure who got his training during World War II. Ahmed had to convince Jack of his readiness to be sent back to South Africa to set up an underground network. Jack had to submit reports to the Communist Party leadership on Ahmed's readiness, once he was satisfied that Ahmed was genuine and possessed the necessary discipline.

After returning from the Soviet Union, Ahmed was full of stories of the Great Patriotic War. Essop remarks, "Ahmed could not help this as he was watching films on a weekly basis on the many Soviet people who were killed. When he went to Leningrad Ahmed could not but understand what the Soviet people went through under Hitler's occupation. Very few people endured what the people of Leningrad went through. People had nothing to eat and families would survive eating one slice of bread a day. They also had to survive the difficult Soviet winter season." Essop adds that when people came back from the Soviet Union, they were full of admiration for the country.

"The communist was always first to be ready to lay down his or her life for the greater cause. The South African Police version of communists committing suicide is absolute rubbish. If one was recruited into the Party and assigned to perform underground activities, you understood, accepted and were ready to sacrifice your life for the Struggle," says Essop Pahad. But not foolishly. Great emphasis was placed, in the conversations between Essop and Ahmed, on the likelihood that Ahmed would come under surveillance and the necessity for him to lay low for a considerable period upon his return to South Africa.

Essop and Ahmed spoke about Ahmed Kathrada and Nelson Mandela, who were on Robben Island, and the sacrifices that they had made. Ahmed would also discuss things in detail with Aziz Pahad. Essop and Ahmed spoke about the meaning of going to do underground work. Ahmed had to be very careful and the possibility of his arrest was very high, especially given his London residence with the Pahads. They discussed the question, if Ahmed was arrested, of what sort of responses he was to give under torture. Ahmed was to give as little information as possible. He was to protect people in the underground inside South Africa and not those in exile. This was reflected in Ahmed's statement that he made during interrogation. The death of Babla Saloojee was also discussed and there was no doubt in Ahmed's or any other of his comrades' minds that suicide was just not an option.

Discussions around Ahmed's family set-up were also held. Essop recalls, "Haji Timol was unable to work, as he was semi-blind, and Ahmed was the breadwinner of the family. Ahmed had taken a conscious decision to stay with the family and to support them when he returned to South Africa. Ahmed could have easily rented a room in Roodepoort. I clearly told Ahmed that he was not to use the flat where he stayed with his parents for underground work activities.

"While in London, Ahmed spoke a lot about Amina Desai, someone whose life was to be radically changed by what happened to him. The Desai family knew Ahmed very well. I had informed Ahmed not to conduct his underground activities from his parents' place and not to leave any incriminating evidence – he was to use Amina's place if forced to. This was less an instruction than a discussion."

Ahmed could have moved out from his parents' flat and rented an apartment. This would however attract unnecessary attention in the community. But it was not always possible to wait for optimum conditions to present themselves. These were difficult discussions, conducted in London. Ahmed was told to lie low in the beginning when he returned to South Africa and not to be in a hurry to recruit for the underground structures. It was not unusual, says Ronnie Kasrils, for comrades to lie low for two or even three years, as was the case with successful cadres like Raymond Suttner and David Rabkin. There were also long discussions about Ahmed maintaining contact with Nassim, Ismail and Zunaid Pahad, as Ahmed had been close to them prior to going abroad. It would appear strange if contact were now lost with them as Ahmed had stayed with Essop and Aziz in London.

Personal events at home underlined the political factors that were drawing him back there. He wrote home to Amina Desai on 5 February 1969 after her husband had died:

My Dear Aunty Amina

I was deeply grieved to hear of Papa's death from a letter I received from home a few days ago. The feeling of profound tragedy and of personal loss to me characterised the news of his passing away. Had he lived his life in a free country he would have inevitably displayed his true potential in public life and played a positive role in its well-being. Unfortunately having had to live in South Africa his activities were naturally curtailed, but in spite of this he stood out as a firm believer in his convictions and principles and refused to be drawn into supporting both prevailing political and religious dogma – both in essence being reactionary in nature.

Dear Aunty Amina, I am also confident in my hope and belief that you would once again draw on your own resources and obtain sufficient strength and courage to overcome the sadness and anxieties which prevail at home. The image and presence of Papa will linger on for a considerable length of time within the house. All of us will miss him dearly, especially you who lived all your life with him and Leila and Hilmi who were so close to him. His departure leaves a void in the house, but I am sure that you have sufficient capacity and energy to restore the well-being of the house and preserve the equilibrium which is so necessary for the goodness of the family. I can imagine the problems and difficulties that you are faced with, but as time moves on things will look much better and you will be helped by your intelligent and sensible daughters. I hear from Faried Sallie that you intend recalling Hilmi from Sweden, permit me to express my disapproval if the intention is to call him back permanently, however if you are thinking of calling him back temporarily by all means do so. His permanent return cannot solve any problems, especially so, if he is studying and moreover receiving a grant from the Swedish government.

More than anyone else, dear Aunty Amina, I am concerned about you, your health and all the strains and stresses that you are subjected to daily. Why don't you seriously consider going for a long holiday either within the country or come along to England with Leila. I shall be most pleased to have you here. You need not worry about accommodation or money for all that can be taken care of. Please consider my suggestion seriously and try to get away, if only for a few months from that country. I look forward to the day you decide to come over. You rightfully deserve a long holiday.

Finally, may I sincerely express the desire and hope that peace and tranquillity will return soon at home.

Salaams
With Love
Ahmed

"The decision taken by Ahmed to return to South Africa shows Ahmed's courage, loyalty and determination to leave his partner behind," adds Essop. This was a difficult decision for Ahmed. Essop and Ahmed agreed that, once he had returned to South Africa, they were not to send messages to each other. There were not to be letters sent by either of them and Essop would not specifically ask about Ahmed after he had returned to South Africa. Family and friends visiting London would indicate to Essop that Ahmed was well and that he was teaching.

Essop and Ahmed discussed the additional risks that Ahmed would face. They also spoke about how Ahmed was to mobilise the Indian community using the existing structures. Ahmed was to work within the religious environment and to identify suitable people to work with. He was to provide political guidance and leadership when issues were discussed without people knowing about his underground activities.

A critical event formed the background to Ahmed's activities. In 1969 a resolution was taken at the historic ANC conference at Morogoro in Tanzania to actively promote the development of a political underground, so as to balance and supplement the armed struggle.

In that year, Ahmed's friend Jo Jo Saloojee moved from Zambia to Canada, via London, and established the first ANC unit in Canada.

Farouk Dindar and Jameela went from England to Canada in that same year. In 1970, Farouk returned to England to write the British examinations MRCP (Member of the Royal College of Physicians). After completing this Farouk could not get back to Zambia so he decided to return to South Africa in January 1971.

The night before Ahmed was to leave for South Africa in February 1970, Essop and Ahmed exchanged gifts as a token of their close friendship and relationship. They exchanged Essop's watch for Ahmed's Soviet-bought camera, as mentioned earlier, and Essop also gave Ahmed a small gift.

6

UNDERGROUND WORK

After his time in London and training in Moscow, Ahmed was ready to return to his country of birth.

Haroon Timol recalls that when Ahmed came back from London in February 1970, nobody at home expected him. He arrived at the airport in Johannesburg and took a taxi to the Johannesburg railway station. He boarded a train from Johannesburg to Roodepoort. His return could not have been more casual. Ahmed did not believe in inconveniencing anybody.

Hawa Timol was in the kitchen cooking *kurma* (cooked lamb that is fried, normally done after the celebration of *Baqri Eid*, when animals are slaughtered) when she heard a knock on the door. She opened the door and saw Ahmed standing at the door. Ahmed explained to his mother: "You are the reason for me coming to South Africa. Nobody could have stopped me from coming home."

Haji Timol, despite failing health, was now a commercial traveller. Ahmed Khota (also known as Quarter) was a general dealer at 27 Market Street, Johannesburg. Quarter recalls, "I lived for eight years at Flat 8 at Kholvad House and 20 years at Orient House. Haji Timol would join us for lunch every afternoon. He would take goods from my store and we had our own terms of agreement regarding payments." With tears in his eyes, Quarter refers to Haji Timol as his father and says he is alive today because of Haji Timol's prayers. Quarter was working in an underground cell in the early 1960s but was unaware of Ahmed's underground activities in 1970. He had served 145 days in solitary confinement in the Rosebank police station in 1964.

Travelling was one of the safest businesses to be in. It was hard work but you were virtually guaranteed business from fellow Indian retailers. Since a great deal of this business is on trust, Haji Timol coped. He sold knives, watches and locks and travelled all over the Transvaal. Shop owners supported him and the family survived. As a child I remember Papa in his green Peugeot station-wagon coming to Standerton. Because he was semi-blind, he had an African driver who took him around.

As soon as Ahmed arrived back in South Africa, he made contact once again with the Dynamos. This is where Moe Essack met Ahmed. Born in 1950 in the Durban suburb of Morningside, Moe was radicalised by the frequent Security Branch raids on the home of his neighbour, Dr Monty Naicker. Most of the trade in the Essack family's hardware store came from Africans. Moe was outspoken about his political beliefs and Ahmed observed this. Moe made an impression as persons from Durban were regarded as parochial. There was rivalry between Durban and Johannesburg people.

Moe had many discussions with Zunaid and Nassim Pahad. His immediate impression of Ahmed was that of a very pleasant and calm person – somebody who was easy to get along with and who was intelligent. The turning point in their relationship was when Ahmed picked Moe up with a woman friend from Newclare. Ahmed was not doing any talking, his friend was. Moe instinctively knew that he was being observed and recalls Ahmed telling her, "Listen to that, listen to that." This was in response to Moe's comments during the discussion.

Moe was drawn into Ahmed's pamphletting activities, initially commenting that the pamphlets were mere "rhetoric". When Ahmed explained that the point was to reach the masses, not intellectuals, Moe posted the pamphlets. He had no training but was considerably street smart. He had an admiration for Al Fatah, the Palestinian nationalist movement, as well as for Che Guevara and Fidel Castro.

Ahmed resumed teaching at the Roodepoort Indian High School on 10 April 1970. He taught history and commerce and was studying for a BA at Unisa. It was Amina Desai who had written out a cheque to Unisa for Ahmed's study material. He had one further examination to complete his first year of study.

Ahmed had to endure the pressures of living in a small, cramped two-bedroom apartment with his family, while still trying to do his clandestine work. It should be noted that Ahmed was a full-time teacher and by definition not an underground operative. He was dedicated to teaching and that is why his students loved him. But it was stressful living more than one life. He had to make preparations for school, endure family pressures and continue his underground activities, all at the same time.

Salim Essop's house, number 12 Small Street, was in close proximity to the Timol family's flat in Roodepoort. Ahmed taught Salim when he was in Standard Eight and Salim was now studying medicine at the University of the Witwatersrand – in fact, sitting on the University bursary committee – and travelling by train to Johannesburg. Roodepoort had a close-knit conservative Indian community, and certain sectors of the community were extremely wealthy. Salim would pass the Timol flat on Mare Street on his way to the railway station in Roodepoort and the two of them would greet each other after Ahmed returned in February 1970. They slowly started talking and very soon a friendship developed between Salim and Ahmed.

Salim trusted Ahmed from the day they met. They were like brothers. Despite the age gap between Ahmed (29) and Salim (21) they were close friends and co-workers. Ahmed began testing Salim's political interest. Salim hated apartheid and could not condone the daily violence that was lashed out against the African people. They respected each other's views and trusted one another. They began to visit each other regularly and spend their weekends together.

Ahmed was spending more time at Amina Desai's place. The football ground at the back of Amina's house provided easy access for Ahmed. The sporting facilities were limited to the privileged. Returning from school, Ahmed would leave his school bag and books at Amina's place and dash off to the sports grounds.

Amina continued her husband's business (The Shoe Agency) after his death in February 1969. Amina recalls, "When Zarina left the country in the late Sixties, she left her yellow Anglia motor vehicle behind. I had a driver and he taught Ahmed to drive. Ahmed would often take his sick mother to the doctor with the car. Ahmed would take me to Johannesburg on Saturdays to post the shoe agency letters. They had to be posted before 11 am. He would drop me at a cousin's place and would collect me at 6 pm. I never questioned Ahmed about his whereabouts as we had a mutual understanding between the two of us. In this manner Ahmed would at times ask to borrow the car for the evening and I would oblige."

Ahmed was acting as Amina's chauffeur and it was not her business to monitor his activities. She also used to cash his salary of R154 a month through her business account. This was convenient for him, as he did not have to wait for the seven days' clearance.

Amina's children were all away at the time. Zarina, the eldest, was a doctor in Ireland. Bahiya, 15 months younger than Ahmed, was studying at Salisbury Island, Durban. Hilmi was studying in Sweden. He had been detained at the age of 15 for writing anti-apartheid slogans on a wall. On his release, his father had sent him to Lawrence College in Rawalpindi in Pakistan, a secondary school which had been set up for the children of men in the British Army who could not afford to send their children to England for education. Adella, who was 16, and the youngest, was sent to London to complete her schooling.

Amina describes Ahmed as an intelligent person. "Ahmed realised that in order for one to progress in life, you had to study. This was the type of relationship we had. Ahmed was like a son in my house. I remember Ahmed writing on the desk marking the names of firms and individuals that had judgements against them from the credit report 'Informer', when we heard a knock at the door. There were a few men from the local welfare who had arrived to collect their cheque for charity. I saw one of them nudging the other and leering. They were ignorant, mean and narrow-minded young men. They were horrible. They saw me, a widow, sitting with this young man who called me Gorima (Auntie) and having evil thoughts in their minds. My conscience was clear."

Salim Gabba had met Ahmed through their association with the Dynamos Football Club. He says Ahmed was "politically far superior" to the others. In 1970 Salim had already played for the Dynamos first team.

Just as his letters home from London had shown his continuing links to the home front in the apartheid struggle, so too Ahmed's letters from Johannesburg to Ruth reflected the real personal costs that his commitment imposed and that they both accepted.

My Dearest Love Ruth
Your letter went straight to my heart. And it is from the heart that one's emotions

and feelings go out to their loved ones. It is also in the heart that one's cherished memories are stored, and your loving image and spirit has flickered continuously in my heart.

Darling, I think of you a lot and miss you very much. I feel that it is by no chance that on the very day that you were thinking of me last week and wrote to me I was also thinking of you and did the same, my letter you must have received by now. It made me tremendously sad to read how unhappy you are. My heart and soul goes out to you in these moments of unhappiness. Always remember darling that I shall be with you, if not physically then in spirit. We shall live for the day we are together again. And that day, I assure you my darling must come. If it is not possible at the present times then definitely in the future. In the meanwhile we should strive to "pull" ourselves together, consider the realities of our present situation, and work hard so that we can achieve our noble ideals and beliefs. Especially in the belief that we shall be together again.

Darling you should in no way feel that there is no one in the world who does not care for you. I care for you and shall always consider you as my only love. I shall be always interested in your thoughts, in your dreams and ambitions, in the work that you are doing, in the people that you meet, places you visit and the books you read. Not forgetting the many films that you will see, the plays and concerts you will go to and in every other thing that you will involve yourself in. In terms of cultural life I feel absolutely cut off around here. No "good" books or journals to read, no thought provoking films to see and no chance to see any theatre shows or be present at a concert recital. Culturally, I am absolutely starved, and it shall be most wonderful if you could partially carry this need of mine.

In your letter you asked me a rather silly question as to whether I was married or not. Of course darling I am not. With whom do you expect me to get married around here? There is no one I would consider above you. I love you and therefore cannot marry anyone else. And I am told in most cases when people marry it is for love and I am sure this applies to me as well.

I have become an enthusiast of Beethoven's music and have a collection of all his works of symphony on cassette tapes played on a portable tape recorder which I bought. I discover that I also take a lively interest whenever I listen to Mozart's music over the radio and since seeing that Mum is a Mozart fan – I would be pleased if you could ask her which of his works should a "budding" enthusiast like me obtain.

I must end this letter now because it's already about one o'clock in the morning and I must be up by at least seven if I were to be at school on time. One more thing, I think it would be best that you do not mention to any of "my" friends that we are in touch with each other again. Not that I mind particularly but apparently in some of my past letters to you I mentioned certain things which you inadvertently may have passed on to them and for which I was questioned about. Give my fondest regards to Mum and Dad. Look after yourself, and always remember, my love for you is deep and eternal.

NB For a teacher I think I make a lot of grammatical errors in my writings, so therefore if I do make some minor or grave errors in my choice of words or in my sentence construction do not hesitate to correct my mistakes by informing me about them. I think it is about time that I learn to write correctly. My speech I feel is quite good despite the occasional mispronunciations.

Ahmed

The humility of the postscript, where the revolutionary reaches out for elementary grammatical assistance from his distant beloved, is a direct glimpse into the humane depths of Ahmed Timol's soul even while he was proceeding to set up links on behalf of the Communist Party in London with whom he was in regular contact. The police claimed to have found relevant correspondence in his possession when he was later detained at a police roadblock. Says Stephanie Kemp in one of the coded letters, "The Central Committee sends its heartfelt congratulations to you on the progress you are making in the difficult missions which you have accepted. Your letter was indeed inspiring in its dedication to our work and the steps you have taken to implement the tasks. We are confident that you will go about them with all necessary care and that you will ensure all necessary security." Kemp sees Joe Slovo's stylistic influence here. "Such was Slovo's tone looking back today, of combining words of encouragement and caution," she says.

Stephanie Kemp joined the SACP in 1962. After spending one-and-a-half years in prison, whe went into exile and was based in London from 1966 to 1990 when she returned to South Africa. During her time in London she worked for the SACP. Today she is a member of the provincial executive committee of the SACP in KwaZulu-Natal.

According to the police files, Ahmed's first report-back to London was on 24 April 1970 in which he noted that he had compiled a mailing list of 8 000 names (predominantly African) and he had identified a need for political literature to assist students who were becoming politicised within a theoretical vacuum; regular messages from anti-apartheid leaders to mobilise the masses as well as "scientific justification of our common humanity", exploding the myth of genetic superiority of the "White Race" for the benefit of a generation that was "growing deprived of such progressive literature". Such material would go out in a monthly student newsletter. "Incidentally," he added, "Salisbury Island students in state of unrest, degrees no longer to be conferred by Unisa but autonomous body 'University of Indians' from next year."

In light of the intense religious activity then current, Ahmed specifically requested material of a religious nature. The Group Areas Act, with its racialised re-zoning and forced removals of people, was causing discontent in the Muslim community, particularly where mosques were affected. "Literature by religious leaders justifying our struggle, as was the case in India, can be most helpful." Joe Slovo, who later joked that Dr Dadoo was possibly the only leader of a Communist Party to have the status of Haji, would have appreciated Ahmed's acuity. "I remember meeting him on his return to Heathrow Airport in London," Slovo said recalling a picture of Dr Dadoo speaking at Wits University in 1991, "head shaven, kettle in hand and white robe."

Ahmed began to identify candidates for recruitment, whether into the formation of a newspaper for Indians or for full recruitment into the movement and its political work.

On 12 May 1970 Ahmed filed a further report highlighting the opportunities created by the economic boom which had sharpened the contradictions that might be exploited by the Party: 68 per cent of Soweto families lived below the poverty line, he said, citing a recent study. The repressive distribution of wealth was allied with consumer price inflation and rising busfares, which further sharpened discontent. Coloured households were spending half and more of their incomes on food alone. "I am convinced our strategy of protracted struggle will be met with growing response from urban proletariat. Spontaneous recent stone-throwings at police in Tvl and Cape symptomatic of charged polt. situation. Events in Lesotho, struggles in Indo-China/M East, fully publicised here contributes in raising our people's consciousness – far-sighted members of ruling class raising alarm. Predict gloomy future for economy, discuss how to avoid future Ind Strikes, gravely disturbed about white labour shortage. Commis. of police admits P/force under great pressure, cannot attend to all social crimes therefore priority given to manning country's borders. Convinced that regular coordinated 'sparks' in our cities will cause real panic and put pressure on our enemies." Ahmed had identified passages from Lenin's *What Is To Be Done?* that might usefully be published in pamphlets. "Greeting to all – to Thabo and Anne especially," he ended, singling out his comrades from the Russian school for special mention. "Please do not mention the names of Thabo and Jenny in the open text" a subsequent letter from London admonished, after this friendly habit continued in further correspondence.

The South African Communist Party in London responded to Ahmed in a letter dated 17 May 1970. The letter suggested he identify additional "clean" addresses through which to receive material "but remember each person you approach for this purpose must not suspect you are an activist of some sort". The same letter gave Ahmed the go-ahead to proceed with the production of an Indian newspaper as soon as he could find reliable comrades for this; and that a message from Dadoo for the first issue was in preparation.

The letter also contained evidence of the close monitoring that the Party maintained over its operatives. "If you wish to write to Ruth Longoni please do not discuss any form of politics. She has been given similar advice. Please give us more details of a matter you mentioned in a letter to her (posted by someone in London) which suggests that you may have been visited by a suspicious character soon after your return home."

Ronnie Kasrils, in his book *Armed and Dangerous*, writes about the secret communication system that was set up, "The originals would have arrived at various 'safe' addresses in London or quiet villages in the home counties. The originals would be an apparently innocuous letter to someone's friend or relative. On the reverse side of the page would be a hidden text written in invisible ink. The form of address indicated what invisible ink had been used, and consequently, what developer was required to bring out the hidden message. 'My dear Aunt Agatha' would indicate one type, 'Dearest Aunt Agatha' another. We used a variety of chemicals, usually dissolved in alcohol or distilled water. The writer would use a clean pen to write out the secret text. Steam from a kettle would be applied to the paper to iron out any indentation marks left by the pen. After the paper had dried, the innocent text would be written or typed in."

In the letter of 17 May 1970 the Party elaborated its signals for use between Ahmed and London as follows:

> *Letters with no secret text will have the date written thus "23-12-69". Letters with secret text on back of innocent text using formula "A" will conclude with "REGARDS TO ALL". Letters with secret text on back of innocent text, using formula "B", will have a postscript on the innocent side of the letter. Letters with a secret message, using formula "C", will have the date written thus: "23/12/69".*
>
> *All letters with secret messages will be numbered in the hidden text i.e. J/S/2/6/12/69 that this is the second letter from J to S, posted on 6 Dec 1969.*
>
> *Formula "A" refers to the dry method Carbon Z which requires the impregnation of Dithizone powder into the paper then the use of a soft pencil, followed by steaming for between one and two minutes. The words would then be rendered visible by the recipient by application of a developer applied with a tampon of cotton wool. Formula "B" uses hydroquinone and Formula "C" uses two drops of blood dissolved in two-and-a-half tablespoons of distilled water.*
>
> *Where these elaborate concoctions are impractical, a book code is used with the master text being Roman Britain by IA Richmond in the Pelican History of England series. A colon indicates a page, a semicolon a line on a page, a comma the letter in the line. Thus 10: 7; 2, 5, 10 would indicate page 10, line seven, letters 2, 5 and 10. All chapter titles and sub-titles counted as lines. Lines counted from top to bottom and letters from left to right.*

The letters as transcribed by the Security Police end with a recipe for gunpowder, which is odd given that Ahmed was not trained or deployed for the actual placement of bucket bombs. This may have been a Security Police embellishment. Pamphlets for distribution arrived in boxes of Darjeeling tea. Stephanie Kemp raises an eyebrow over the exhaustive, almost encyclopaedic quality of the secret methods detailed in the letter: "What struck me was how extensive this was including almost every method used from the Sixties until late Seventies (book codes were used with Chris Hani when he was in Lesotho around 1978.) This seems pretty redundant and I wonder whether other cadres had such extensive technical training in London. We certainly didn't use such a variety of methods with any one cadre. And I am also struck that he knew both ends of each method. These methods were rolled out as the situation changed over the years. I am surprised that this was all laid out from A to Z in our correspondence to him. What was the purpose? Clearly he was successfully using the Dithizone method – why did he need to find his own source of Dithizone. I would have prepared a book of (not visible) carbons for him in London. I don't recall that the need arose for him to use any other method. I seem to recall this need did arise in the case of the Rabkins (this was later) and we then sent instructions of a new method." The extra information could have been an embellishment added by the Security Police.

On 23 July 1970, Ahmed received notice from London of approval for his suggestion of an illegal newspaper "with all the trappings of illegality involved in terms of policy, content, production etc – a paper reflecting problems affecting all facets of Indian life and openly advocating a policy of resistance. It does not follow," London added, "that initially such a newspaper should in so many words espouse the programme of the liberation movement." Rather "it should begin to explain thoroughly the reasons for, and the need to understand, the move towards a policy of violence rather than an immediate call to support MK."

Above all, the newspaper was to emphasise the need for organisation and resistance (even short of violence) around the immediate issues facing the Indian people. "Insofar as it is possible we must put our policy in a 'clever' way so that the enemy will not find it easy to pin a charge based on the contents. We must remember that for many years there has been minimal organised activity of any sort amongst the Indian people and it becomes necessary to bring them into the stream again by well thought-out stages. It is especially necessary to emphasise the common plight of all the black people while not neglecting the special factors applying to the Indian group." The student newsletter was also approved as a way to begin reaching more advanced cadres. "Its title should not commit it to being merely a student journal."

The Roodepoort School incident book reported that Republic Day celebrations were held at the school on the 29 May 1970. A member of the South African Police hoisted the national flag and the school choir sang the national anthem. Unlike Ahmed's objections to Republic Day celebrations in 1966 he did not publicly voice his objections to the celebrations. He was now operating as an underground operative and did not want to attract unnecessary attention.

On 26 June 1970 ("Freedom Day" in the movement's calendar), leaflet bombs and street broadcasts were simultaneously activated in Johannesburg and all the main cities. Ronnie Kasrils writes in *Armed and Dangerous*: "Jack (Hodgson) finally came up with a design which involved using a small explosive charge in the bottom of a bucket that launched a little wooden platform some 30 metres into the air. A pile of leaflets could be placed on the platform and these would waft down to the ground. A timing device was used to ignite the powder. Another exile, Ronnie Press whom we called 'the Professor', developed a compact electronic device which could function as a public address system. Consisting of a cassette player, electronic amplifier and car loudspeaker placed in a small box, it could broadcast a taped speech and freedom songs with a time-delay of several minutes."

In a letter dated 26 July 1970, Ahmed reassured London. "I can safely say that I am not under any SB observation. My mail is not tampered with. When I arrived back I was however visited by a local Indian connected with the SB. The call, I was told, was of a routine nature. Such checks are observed on all persons coming from abroad. However another incident was a bit more intriguing. Some six weeks after my arrival two persons visited Quarter Khota's shop in JHB wanting to see me and asking for my phone no. or address in Rdpt. They claimed that they were told to contact me by my friends in London (which friends they did not mention to Quarter) – and that they were on their way back to London after spending their holidays in Durban. However, they never came to see me and that was the last that I heard of them."

Ahmed then asked London to distribute political literature (such as United Nations information) to a number of promising recipients. He had obtained their addresses indirectly without them suspecting his involvement. Those taken most seriously and identified for potential recruitment into the Party would, however, not receive even marginally political material by mail so that absolutely all risk of compromising them was removed.

One of these potential recruits was KC (Kanti) Naik who had been a science teacher at Roodepoort Indian High School in 1966. Kanti knew Ahmed exceptionally well, as Roodepoort was a tightly-knit community. Kanti comments, "The Roodepoort community liked Ahmed as he was always friendly and his outlook in life was open. Ahmed was not afraid to speak his mind and principal Lorghat was aware of Ahmed's political activities." According to Kanti, "Others were active in politics but nothing compared to Ahmed. Ahmed's fellow colleagues were aware of his political beliefs and would not have been surprised if the Security Branch detained Ahmed." Kanti remembers Ahmed's sensitivity on the question of social equality, and, for instance, his discussing the salary discrepancy suffered by African teachers at the school during staff meetings.

Ahmed explained his recruitment strategy to London in a letter of August 1970, "Much attention is being given towards finding quality persons capable of organising and developing an internal apparatus. In studying possible cadres for M Units, I have been motivated by the criteria that such persons show potential for embracing our communist ideology and not merely stop at liberal or petty-bourgeois democratic politics. At the moment I recommend one person who in my view admirably satisfies this criteria. He is Mohamed Salim Essop, who lives at 10 Smal St., Rdpt and is a 2nd year medical student at Wits."

When Ahmed came back from London, he was initially very secretive and did not try and recruit Kanti overtly. However, Ahmed was still as engaging as ever. "This was evident and he was not hiding this," says Kanti. Ahmed got busy mobilising and recruiting people. He was looking for pilots to fly planes and to take photographs of strategic places. He made a deep impression on people and was instrumental in raising political consciousness. Says Naik, "Ahmed had a natural gift for hyping up people, and was indeed a dynamic person."

During 1970 Indres Moodley had worked for a drug-manufacturing company in Troyeville, Johannesburg. Indres recalls, "Ahmed phoned me at my home in Lenasia and we made arrangements for him to visit me at my place around July 1970. We had general discussions and I immediately realised that we had a lot in common. Ahmed was very sincere and very dedicated. He was very moved to do something about the political situation. He was not just frivolous and not doing things lightly."

"I had grown up in Fietas and witnessed the brutality of the police beating up African people. I went to Congress School and witnessed the protest marches and demonstrations that took place. The Group Areas Act had uprooted communities and we were forced to relocate to Lenasia. My father read a lot, and we were not

Madressa Anjuman-e Islamia in Kholvad, India,
in the late 19th century. Kholvad lies on the
banks of the Tapi River near Surat which formed
a pivotal centre for trade and commerce
between India and other countries.

Courtesy of Kholvad Madressa.

On 12 September 1957, Ahmed Timol, at the age of sixteen, received this picture of himself from Saber Saith. "Wish you all the luck in this season's games" was written on the back.

The logo of the Dynamos soccer club, designed by 'Archie Boy' Bhayat.

Ahmed Timol addressing the farewell party for the graduates at the Training Institute for Indian Teachers in December 1963. Standing on the right is the principal, Mr J.J. Smith.

Timol family album.

Ahmed Timol with Ruth Longoni during a visit to the Lake District in England in 1968.

Courtesy of Dr Farouk Dindar.

Ahmed Timol with his old friend
and political mentor Essop Pahad
in front of North End House, West
Kensington, London.

Courtesy of Essop and Meg Pahad.

Ahmed Timol photographed outside
the Hermitage Museum in Leningrad
(now St Petersburg), Russia, in 1969.

Source: Timol family album.

The funeral procession on Friday 29 October 1971. The coffin was taken by hearse to the cemetery through the main street of Roodepoort. Men, schoolchildren and students followed the hearse on foot.

The body of Ahmed Timol is carried at the
Roodepoort Cemetery for the *Janazah* prayer.

Haji and Hawa Timol at the time of
Ahmed's death, outside court.

Helen Joseph addressing the community outside
the Timol flat in Roodepoort.

The legal team for the Timol family, with family
members at the inquest that started on 24 April
1972. From left to right: Issy Maisels, George
Bizos, Ismail Ayob, Mia Ahmed Loonat,
Mohammed Timol and GH Bhabha.

Source: *The World.*

Friday 29 October 1971. Ahmed's parents mourn
the death of their eldest son and pray for the safety
of their youngest son, Mohammed.

Source: *Rand Daily Mail.*

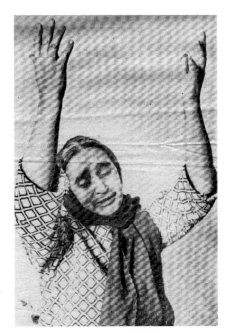

Mrs Hawa Timol mourning
29 year old Ahmed who died
in police custody.

Source: *Post.*

Sergeant Kleyns
who was at the
police roadblock
at the time of
Ahmed's arrest.

Source: *Rand Daily Mail.*

Sergeant Joao Anastasio Rodriques, of Security Police headquarters, Pretoria, who said Mr. Timol "dived" through a window at John Vorster Square.

Captain J. H. Gloy . . .
with Timol minutes before
he fell.

Captain Gloy and Lieutenant-Colonel WP
van Wyk, the two interrogators responsible
for Ahmed Timol prior to his death.
Inset: Gloy as he looks today

Lieutenant-Colonel W. P. van Wyk . . . the senior interrogator.

Source: MuseuMAfrica, Johannesburg. *Rand Daily Mail* 24/4/1972 3-630.

Above is the police photograph of room 1026 where Ahmed Timol was held and where the police alleged that he jumped out of the window. The window is clearly visible in the picture as is the desk and the arrangement of chairs that are referred to by the police in their statement as follows:

"At 3.48pm Captain Gloy and Captain Van Niekerk left the room and Rodrigues and Timol remained behind. Rodrigues sat on the chair marked A and Timol sat opposite him – B. Timol asked to go to the toilet and stood up with Rodrigues at the same time. Rodrigues moved to his left and bumped into the chair marked C. Timol rushed to the window, opened it and dived out. Rodrigues could not stop Timol."

politicised but felt the oppression of the state. I was not indoctrinated but it was natural to feel the oppression of the state. We had no alternative at the time. There was an information blackout. We had no news of what was going on in and out of South Africa. There was a total clampdown by the government after the Rivonia trial. Security police were even visible at parties. One was always suspicious, even about your friends. You were always discreet and very wary not to step out of line. The climate that we lived in was highly charged and difficult for the youth of today to understand."

"During my studies at Salisbury Island as a student I felt the campus was run like a police state. We set up awareness meetings in the form of social clubs where political discussions would take place. This was a difficult time to organise."

Ahmed had made his intention clear to Indres on setting up cells. Indres says, "I made it clear to Ahmed that I was not a violent person but that I was willing to assist in doing underground work. We had discussions on the cell structures and on how security was to be maintained. I was to head one cell and was not to have any links to any of the other cells. Ahmed made no mention to me about members of other cells."

Indres remembers Ahmed, "There was this deep intensity about Ahmed in the way he felt the pain of oppression. It was his intensity that you could share and commit to with Ahmed. It made me want to work with Ahmed and take the struggle to a different level. Ahmed offered this hope that we could achieve this freedom."

Indres left Lenasia and in the new year relocated to Durban. He had married. At the beginning of 1971 he started working as a lecturer at Salisbury Island in the pharmacy department. Indres says, "Ahmed was delighted that I was moving to Durban as I could set up a cell here. The varsity would serve as perfect cover."

Faruq Varachia (also known as Jap, and now in Canada) grew up in Roodepoort and was finishing his last years as a high school student when Ahmed was teaching at the Roodepoort Indian High School. This is what Faruq recalls, "During August 1970, Ahmed came and asked me if I could accompany him to Lourenço Marques or LM (now Maputo) to go and watch a soccer match between Portugal and Brazil. The main reason for our trip was to watch the famous Portuguese footballer, Eusebio. Ahmed and I flew down to LM.

"During this trip to LM I realised how well informed Ahmed was on world sports and also noticed his commitment to caring for others. One specific incident comes to mind. As Ahmed and I were queuing to purchase our match tickets, Ahmed asked to be excused. About 10 minutes later, Ahmed returned and asked to purchase an additional three tickets for the game. I did not question Ahmed's request and obliged by purchasing the tickets. After receiving the three tickets, Ahmed walked over to a young Mozambique family of three, a father and his two sons. He handed the tickets to them. I later found out from Ahmed that the family of three had travelled from a remote part of LM to attend this match. Arriving at the stadium, they could not afford to pay for the tickets. That evening Ahmed gave me a quick history on the Portuguese oppression of the people of Mozambique.

Faruq and Ahmed had met up in LM with "Pops" Govind (now in Canada),

Dr Ahmed Desai (Jakoo) and Yakoob Varachia and other friends who had arrived from Durban. Faruq and Jakoo have confirmed that they were being followed by the South African Police in LM. When returning to South Africa from LM Faruq was detained and questioned about their trip and about Ahmed's activities in LM. They wanted to know if Ahmed had made contact with other people in LM. This was an indication that Ahmed had come to the attention of the Security Branch.

Khadija Chotia (known as Dija) met Ahmed at the Wits Student Ball at the Planet Hotel in December 1966. When Ahmed returned from London in February 1970 Dija was working at Cajee's Jewellery Shop in Roodepoort. Ahmed's father would visit the shop regularly, as he was now a travelling salesman. Ahmed would take a train from Roodepoort and collect Dija from Newclare and they would go to Johannesburg. They would go to Joubert Park and play chess on the big outdoor chessboard. Although the chessboard was for whites only, this never bothered Ahmed, says Dija, "It was as if he was inviting a confrontation."

On 28 October 1970 Ahmed was told that a "present" would be arriving the following month containing leaflets and Ahmed was told to post them. In his letter of 10 November 1970 Ahmed apologised for "inefficiency and lack of discipline in not maintaining regular contact. There is also no reason or justification to blame this inadequacy on the petty family problems besetting me at the moment." He undertook to improve his "style and tempo of work" despite the constraints of living in a close communal neighbourhood. He announced a "temporary stalemate" over the newsletter, partly because of a need to organise regular contributors and further because of the need to acquire suitable printing equipment.

He identified places where letter bombs might be placed. (The fact that he identified the sites does not imply that he placed the letter bombs – separate units may well have done that.) These sites were busy commuter hubs where masses of blacks and Indians tended to congregate – station entrances, bus stops, lunchtime meeting places, routes habitually taken to work, pass offices. "We warm to your frank self-criticism and we hope your personal problems are being solved," replied London. A complete summary of the overall position was now requested. How many persons were now in the main group? What outside contacts had been established? What problems remained?

Ahmed had asked Dija to type out names and addresses on envelopes. Dija's immediate reaction was, "When I saw the names on the list, I knew Ahmed was involved." Dija then enquired from Ahmed about the names and Ahmed responded that it was a mail-order business. Dija did not probe any further but was convinced that Ahmed was politically involved. Dija adds, "With Ahmed there was no in between."

Ahmed and Salim Essop then posted the envelopes, beginning in August 1970. When Ahmed was detained, he wrote in his statement, "The first occasion when I distributed pamphlets was some time in August 1970. The posting on this occasion was done by me and Salim Essop from the Jeppe Street Post Office after 8pm. About 400 to 500 were posted by us simultaneously. Soon after the distribution comments of the distribution were being heard and also advertised by the daily papers. I think ANC (CP) headquarters in London sent me a letter of congratulations through Jack

Hodgson.

"The addresses on the first occasion were typed out by Khadija Chotia and typed onto the envelopes using my typewriter. I gave her R3 for her work. She was given the envelopes and was not told for what purposes they were for. The list of the names was sent in the packet containing the pamphlets. The pamphlets were on this occasion sent inside a box containing Darjeeling tea to PO Box 446, Roodepoort in my name. Around 1 000 pamphlets were sent in the box. After having received the printed envelopes I then personally put them into the envelopes, bought the stamps and posted about 400 to 500 together with the assistance of Salim Essop. (Salim Essop only assisted in posting.)"

Captain Carel Joseph Dirker in his statement made during the inquest stated that he was assigned to investigate the distribution of pamphlets that took place all over South Africa commencing on 13 August 1970. Dirker added: "There were a total of 18 instances when these bucket bomb explosions took place in Johannesburg, Cape Town, Port Elizabeth and Durban. Simultaneously as the bombs went off, a recording from a tape recorder started playing". The pamphlets that were on this occasion distributed were "THE ANC SAYS TO VORSTER AND HIS GANG: YOUR DAYS ARE COMING TO AN END".

On 14 August 1970 the *Rand Daily Mail* reported that two explosions had taken place in Johannesburg that scattered hundreds of "subversive" pamphlets at the Faraday Station and outside the offices of the *Rand Daily Mail*. It also reported that there was distribution of illegal pamphlets in three other centres. There were two home-made explosive devices that blew up at different centres in Durban, showering anti-government leaflets, reported the *Rand Daily Mail*. In Cape Town it was reported that an explosion spread subversive pamphlets. It was one of three attempts to spread the leaflets. The two others had failed. A tape recorder found near the blast was quickly stopped, reported the *Mail*. A dustbin of pamphlets was found in Port Elizabeth but no blasts were reported.

It was evident that there were a number of underground cells that were operating simultaneously. For security reasons members heading their main group were not aware of the existence of other cells operating at the time. Operations had been timeously planned and co-ordinated. Ahmed and Salim were only responsible for the posting of the leaflets and not the bucket-bomb explosions that took place in the country.

Salim Essop, whom Ahmed had successfully proposed to London for main group membership, recalls, "I was eager and keen on doing additional work. The golden rule that applied between us was that we were not to know what each other was doing. This was our basic modus operandi. Ahmed maintained communication links to London. For the production and distribution of leaflets, equipment was required. We had to procure photographic equipment and visited Quentin Jacobsen's studio."

Salim had paid for the equipment that was procured, and all his photographic equipment was confiscated when he was detained. Salim's hobby was photography from the age of 10. His sister had bought him a camera. Salim had set up his room as a "darkroom". Salim and Ahmed had also used the Roodepoort school's equipment for the production of the newsletter. They were prepared to make financial and personal sacrifices in order to set up underground structures despite a lack of resources.

Ahmed was informed by London in a letter dated 28 October 1970 that he was to receive, towards the end of November, mail containing a leaflet that was to be posted to the address list received in the "present". This intention was to target the youth.

Ahmed recommended Indres Moodley to be part of the main group. He wrote, "He is a science graduate from Salisbury Island, lives in Lenasia and works at SCS Pharmaceutical Labs, in Johannesburg. His permanent home is in Durban. I have had several discussions with him and am confident that he will prove to be a devoted comrade in furthering our struggle."

Ahmed informed London that suitable places had been identified where future "bombs" could be placed. He also made reference in the letter to the recruitment of a Cornelius from Dobsonville and Stephen who was working at the American Mission Press. Ahmed told London that the *Searchlight* newsletter, that was provided from London, was having the desired effect on the youth. This newsletter was specifically designed for the Indian community.

Ahmed had received a pamphlet in his father's post-box in early 1971. During interrogation Ahmed wrote, "The second occasion when I received pamphlets through my father's post-box: 446, Roodepoort was in the early part of 1971. This time the pamphlets (headed "Sons and Daughters of Africa") were concealed under a box of chocolates and there were about 500. I personally printed some 250 and posted these also from Jeppe Post Office after 8pm." Stephanie Kemp comments that this was a large number of pamphlets to be posted in a single drop. Normally the practice would be to drive around to various post-offices and do the mailings in batches no larger than 50 at a time. According to a statement made by the investigating officer, Captain Dirker, at the inquest, these pamphlets were distributed in the entire country from around November 1970.

Ahmed went to Durban with Bahiya Desai (Amina Desai's daughter) and Omar Vawda at the beginning of January 1971. They drove down in Amina Desai's yellow Anglia. Ahmed had visited his friend Yakoob Varachia, formerly from Roodepoort, on a social basis. Yakoob had studied at the Textile Engineering College in Leicester during the period 1967-1969 and returned to South Africa immediately thereafter. Yakoob had met Ahmed in Leicester and occasionally at the Pahads' flat at North End House. Yakoob had last met Ahmed in LM in 1970 when Portugal played Brazil in the soccer friendly.

During Ahmed's stay in Durban he had visited Indres Moodley at his home and had given him two books with the titles *What is Marxism?* and *Marxism versus Positivistic Philosophy*. Indres adds, "My responsibility was to recruit suitable candidates for the cell. I was checking out prospective candidates by chatting with them informally. Ahmed gave Dr Saths Cooper (later vice-chancellor of the University of Durban-Westville) and me a lift to Johannesburg. Even Saths did not know about my political association with Ahmed. Saths knew that Ahmed was merely a friend."

Ahmed and Salim had succeeded in the distribution of pamphlets and were active for a period of 18 to 20 months. Salim adds, "I firmly believe that we needed another five years to operate. We had operated in the Roodepoort-Johannesburg vicinity. Ahmed did a lot of work in 18 months. He set up processes and procedures for the setting-up of underground structures. We were successful in the production and distribution of leaflets, procurement of photographic and printing equipment, communication had been set up with London and we were laying the foundation for something huge. However, there were difficulties that we faced. We operated in a very hostile environment in the late Sixties and had to be very cautious. This showed Ahmed's discipline."

Salim continues, "Our aim was to promote work for political education, mobilising of people to act against apartheid, realign people in terms of options they had living under apartheid as most people living in South Africa opposed apartheid at the time. Also emerging at the time was the government's strategy of co-option. People were afraid of participating in illegal activities. Ahmed's task was to set up underground structures, to produce and distribute leaflets and newsletters. Ahmed had to promote the ANC as its leadership was in exile and imprisoned on Robben Island. We were attempting to set up a base structure and to make the organisation viable. This was during the time when ANC networks were crushed and there was a power consolidation by the Nationalist Party. Afrikaner capitalism was emerging and the Afrikaner people were very self-confident during this period. It was in this context that we were operating."

Essop Pahad comments on the underground work done by Ahmed, "Accept the fact that Salim and Ahmed were doing underground work. This was not a routine process. They had to explore and worked undetected for over 20 months. Ahmed's characteristics were displayed: not to go beyond the framework outlined to him. Ahmed showed concern for other people's lives. Committing a mistake could lead to serious consequences. Ahmed preferred being cautious rather than taking risks. However, he was forced to take risks to get the work done."

Indres was concerned about Ahmed being too lax regarding security. He recalls, "I told Ahmed that I was worried about the way he was operating. Ahmed was too relaxed. He had written a letter to me and posted it through the normal post. This was not safe. One knew how good the cops were. Friends were regularly detained for other activities and you had to be vigilant. Ahmed agreed."

Ahmed wrote in his statement under duress during interrogation, "By about April I had not heard from him (Indres) and decided to write to his wife implying very clearly in the letter that he should contact me and questioned him as to why he has not done so. I did not receive a reply from Indres to this letter and did not again hear from him."

Ahmed's cousin, Dr Farouk Dindar, had returned to South Africa in March 1971. Farouk recalls, "I was visiting my family in Breyten, when my father informed me that a local policeman by the name of Van Niekerk had informed him that my mail was tampered with. Prior to me returning to South Africa, Essop Pahad had asked me if I wanted to do some work for the ANC when I returned to South Africa. I agreed and had a few training sessions with Ronnie Kasrils. I was shown how to distribute leaflets and methods of secret communication. I understood the principles of how the ANC was distributing its leaflets in South Africa." Farouk was given a medical textbook on ECG that was "treated". When he commenced work as a doctor at Coronation Hospital, the textbook was stolen. Farouk had already made a decision not to carry out the tasks and chores assigned to him by Essop Pahad and Ronnie Kasrils as it was not safe for him to do so. If Farouk's mail was tampered with in Breyten, would they not have done the same with Ahmed?

Farouk often visited Ahmed at Amina Desai's house and says, " I had an inkling that Ahmed was responsible for the leaflet distribution. I expected Ahmed to be in the thick of the underground movement and never discussed what he was doing. We spent many hours talking world politics. It was totally unsafe for me to question Ahmed. I was aware of what was going on. Ahmed continued to be totally devoted in the work he was doing". Hawa Timol would tell Farouk in Gujarati to "tell him to leave the work". Ahmed would look on and not comment. Hawa's comment is a clear indication that she knew that Ahmed was doing political work. She had no idea what the consequences of Ahmed's work would be.

Despite the fact that Ahmed was earning an income, life in the Timol household remained difficult. Farouk recalls, "I never heard Ahmed ever complaining about the difficulties facing his family. Despite these financial difficulties, Hawa continued to be hospitable to family and Ahmed's friends. The flat was always clean, neat and tidy. Life for the Timol family was tough after leaving Breyten." The constant hardship that Ahmed's family continued to face must have made him more determined to continue the struggle. However, greater challenges lay ahead for Hawa Timol.

According to Ahmed's cousin, Yunus Moola, Ahmed kept a very low profile after returning from London in February 1970. Yunus was already aware of Ahmed's political activities from when he was one of his students at the Roodepoort Indian High School. During the holidays of July 1971, Ahmed asked Yunus if he knew Indres Moodley, a BSc lecturer at Salisbury Island in Durban. (Yunus was studying there.) Yunus acknowledged that he knew Indres and Ahmed gave Yunus a letter to deliver to him. During Indres's trial he mentioned that a courier from Ahmed Timol had delivered a letter to him. The police had failed to establish who the courier was. Yunus now knows of the political content of the letter, which Ahmed at the time did not make clear to him.

In London's letter dated 7 March 1971, Ahmed was informed about London's intention to circulate a cyclostyled Party newspaper to coincide with the 50th anniversary of the South African Communist Party on 30 July 1971. London urgently required Ahmed to obtain tape recorders, reference books, tax receipts and travel documents. "If by hook or by crook you should lay your hands on any of these (and we know this is a tall order) please insert them in a 'present' of the sort we send you." Ahmed was assured in the same letter that the reports of the resignations of JB Marks and OR Tambo were a fabrication.

Stephanie Kemp comments: "The correspondence – I seem to remember that we sent out a Party organ quite regularly called *Inkululeko-Freedom* and it was reproduced in South Africa by groups such as Ahmed's which would have meant he would have had to have a roneo machine available. (How cumbersome life was before computers and cellphones!) The tape recorders would have been used for street propaganda with a megaphone blasting at a taxi rank, etc.

"Reference books, tax receipts and travel documents would have been used for forgeries to get to African operatives. If you remember in the Hefer Inquiry, Patrick Maqubela had to collect a parcel at Natal University Library and was then arrested – the parcel contained passes, etc.

"Resignations of JB Marks and OR Tambo, from SACP and/or ANC – definitely this was South African Security disinformation. In the case of these two leaders (for clarity – OR was president of the ANC and definitely not the SACP) there was never the slightest whisper of anything except dedicated loyalty and leadership from them."

In Ahmed's statement made during his interrogation, he wrote: "On the third occasion I received a draft copy of *Inkululeko* and was directed to cyclostyle this using approximation in size. I typed the text on to the stencils (eight stencils used – learning and typing) and duplicated these one afternoon in late July using the school's duplicating machine. The envelopes were given by me to be addressed to Miss Ayesha Bulbulia of Cajee's Commercial College who was completely not aware of what was to be placed inside the envelope. She typed some 300 to 400 envelopes from the address list sent with the packet. This time two different sized brown envelopes were used and I paid her about R3 for her work. The placing of the newspaper inside the envelopes was done by me at home in the night and posted by me from Jeppe Street Post Office at night. The distribution of the paper was to come out by the end of July 1971. This marking the 50th anniversary of the birth of the Communist Party of South Africa and I think some were posted by me from Roodepoort."

Captain Dirker in his statement made during the inquest stated: "I was responsible for investigating the distribution of the newspaper *Inkululeko* from 25 of July 1971 that took place in Cape Town, Port Elizabeth, Bloemfontein, Kimberley and Durban. The newspaper found in Timol's possession was the same as the ones that were distributed."

Amina Cajee from Cajee's Commercial College recalls, "After arriving from London in February 1970, Ahmed was always 'on the move'. I never recall Ahmed staying longer than 10-15 minutes at a particular place. Ahmed would often come to the college, which had been financed by my father in 1966. Referring to me as 'Gori', Ahmed would ask if some typing could be done for him and would refer to it as school work. I would oblige and Ahmed would ask Ayesha Bulbulia, who was teaching at the college, to do the typing for him. Aysha would do a lot of the typing at home and would also type at the college. Aysha was a very loving person. There was no significance attached to this as Aysha was not busy and this was her way of assisting Ahmed accomplish his school work. Ahmed would always visit on a Friday afternoon and would chat with me and the staff and would quickly disappear and reappear. This continued for a long time."

Sampie Essack's contact with Ahmed was re-established when Ahmed came to teach at the Roodepoort Indian High School in 1970. Sampie was in charge of the library, teaching geography to the Standard Fours in the primary school. Sampie recalls, "My relationship with Ahmed went far back. Ahmed had enrolled to do courses at Unisa. His first course was psychology and I had provided books to Ahmed as he had completed his Psych 1. I was in the second year of my degree. I had a personal arrangement with Ahmed, without the principal's consent, that I would give Ahmed keys to the school library every afternoon. With a group of other students, Ahmed studied in the library. The intention was to build a study group. I had no idea of any other activities that took place in the library. Ahmed would return the keys to me after their study sessions. Principal Lorghat was a stickler for rules but nobody interfered with these arrangements. During 1970/1, there was an article in *Time* magazine that focused on Lenin and communism. The library had subscribed to *Time*. Ahmed had analysed and dissected the entire essay. Ahmed showed me the blatant distortion portrayed by *Time* magazine. I had now realised that Ahmed was a brilliant man and very sharp."

Sampie adds, "I was staying in a flat in Vrededorp and the flat had a balcony. Salim Essop and Ahmed would regularly come and visit me and have a cup of tea. We would sit on the balcony and Ahmed would have his camera with him, clicking away taking photographs. Our relationship grew."

When Ahmed was arrested and people were being detained all over the country, Sampie was sitting on the stairs, between the second and third floor of the flats in Vrededorp. Sampie says, "I knew that I was also going to be detained. If Ahmed was detained the police must have got the key to the school library, in which there were a few books on communism and on the freedom fighter Che Guevara. There was a small cubicle at the back of the library, and this was where I had hidden these books. These books were given to me and they were not Ahmed's books. My fear was that the police would find these books, establish that I was in charge of the library, and establish a link between Ahmed and myself."

After Ahmed's death, Sampie would question himself about his close relationship with Ahmed. Ahmed would borrow books from Sampie, they would discuss psychology and many other issues but Ahmed never once raised the question of establishing an underground cell. "In the early years, when we would meet regularly in Fordsburg, we were all asked to form little cells. Three to four persons were assigned per cell. This was Goolaam Mayet's initiative. When Ahmed returned from London in February 1970, till his death, he never raised the issue of the formation of cells. When people were arrested, I would question as to how Ahmed got them involved. It was possible that Ahmed did not want to get his best friends involved," says Sampie.

Bahiya Desai had married Omar Vawda and they were living in Durban. Omar was sent by his company, JP Coats of Isipingo, to the United Kingdom to attend a course. Bahiya accompanied her husband. The fact that Bahiya left the country had probably saved her from being detained. The fear of police intervention was general and may well have contributed to the slowing down of Ahmed's work at this time.

Kanti Naik narrates, "A relative of the family was arriving from Zambia for a holiday. A local policeman by the name of Strydom contacted me wanting me to vouch for my aunt's visit. This was routine procedure. I knew Strydom because he would visit my uncle's café regularly."

"What is happening at the school?" asked Strydom. Kanti realised that Strydom was making a general enquiry and not specifically asking about Ahmed. It was only later that Kanti was convinced that Ahmed was under surveillance.

Kanti had published a textbook on calculations in chemical science. There was significant publicity in the newspapers about Kanti's publication. Gerhardus Petrus van Tonder of the Security Branch, stationed at John Vorster Square police station, was one of the many people interested in Kanti's textbook. Van Tonder had contacted principal Lorghat and requested a copy of the textbook for his son who was doing matric at the time. Van Tonder said that he preferred to meet the author because he did not want to pay for the textbook. Kanti was hesitant, but Lorghat convinced him to give the book to Van Tonder at no cost. Van Tonder and Kanti were set to meet again, this time not discussing the sale of his textbook but dealing with issues relating to national security. They were to meet again at the notorious John Vorster Square. Whether the interest in the textbook was a pretence meant to veil a recruitment effort remains a matter of speculation.

Ahmed's colleagues from teachers training college, Hassen Jooma and Fawzia Denath, married in 1970. Hassen recalls, "I met Ahmed at the flat in Roodepoort a few months before his arrest. Ahmed mentioned to me about forming a cell to further the cause of communism. Ahmed asked me to join, but I laughed it off."

During September 1971 Ahmed went to his cousin MH Desai (Appa Desai's son) and Fatima's house in Azaadville. Owing to the Group Areas Act families were forced to relocate from Krugersdorp to Azaadville on the West Rand. MH recalls, "Ahmed came to the door and asked to spend a few days at our home." MH and Fatima obliged and Ahmed moved into the spare bedroom with his typewriter in a cardboard box and a set of files and papers. Ahmed had parked Amina Desai's car a few streets away (in somebody's garage) and walked to MH's home. MH adds, "Fatima and I never asked Ahmed any questions and we left him for two full nights in our home. We would go to work and return in the evening and leave Ahmed in the house. Ahmed made himself comfortable and would come to the kitchen, have his meals and return to the room." Ahmed informed MH that it was not safe for him to remain in the house and then left. In a month he was dead.

Amina Desai recalls, "Prior to Ahmed's arrest I had received the *Searchlight* in the post. I put a line through it and threw it in the wastepaper basket. When the Security Branch visited me in the early morning of 23 October 1971, they took this pamphlet with them. I was having problems with my telephone and technicians would frequently visit my place. It is possible that they bugged my house." As mentioned previously, after returning from London Ahmed was spending more and more time at Amina's house. "At times Ahmed would be busy with his school marking, it was supper time and Ahmed would stay for supper." Ahmed was like a son to Amina and she was happy to have him around.

Amina once found political literature under one of the beds in the spare room. It was in the form of a parcel and wrapped in newspaper. She told Ahmed that the safest place to keep this material was in the cemetery. Amina suspects that this is exactly what Ahmed later did.

Ahmed's younger brother Mohammed had completed his studies in Leicester in July 1970 but had decided to stay a year longer to get some work experience. The time arrived when Mohammed had to finally leave England. In a letter sent to Ahmed by London dated 5 May 1971 the following appears, "Urgently require information as to why you consider your brother should not return to South Africa. Mota (Dr Dadoo) considers it desirable he should do so in the near future. Reply immediately."

Mohammed explains, "I was arrested in 1966 with other students in Roodepoort for writing anti-government slogans on the school wall and received a suspended sentence. Ahmed did not want to attract the attention of the Security Branch. (The school incident book dated 7/8/1966 recorded: "Ebrahim Bhorat, Sabera Patel, Yakoob Patel and Mohammed Timol have been found guilty by the local Magistrate for writing slogans on the walls of the school. Today the Inspector of Education has warned them that if they break any rules of the school or the Republic in future they would be immediately suspended from school.") The reasonable fear that may have been in Ahmed's mind was that Mohammed, who had a finding as an agitator against him in a court of law, would attract definite SB attention. "When I went to Leicester in 1968, the Security Branch had visited my parents' flat and made enquiries about my whereabouts. It is perhaps for this reason that Ahmed was not keen on the idea of me returning to South Africa," says Mohammed.

Mohammed had discussions with Dr Dadoo and Essop Pahad and decided to leave for South Africa in September 1971. A few days prior to Mohammed's departure from London to South Africa, he had a further discussion with Dr Dadoo. Mohammed recalls, "I must inform Ahmed that they had not received any letter from him or heard from him for some time and that they were very concerned. After I had communicated this message to Ahmed I was to send an encrypted message on a postcard to Dr Dadoo using a safe name and address. The fact that I was carrying this message confirmed that Ahmed was involved in the underground."

Mohammed left for South Africa on 30 September 1971 and arrived at Jan Smuts Airport (now Johannesburg International Airport) in the evening, between 10-11pm. Mohammed was collected at the airport by Ahmed who had driven Mrs Desai's Anglia. Ahmed was subsequently arrested in this car. Mohammed conveyed London's concerns from Dr Dadoo to Ahmed and Ahmed's only reaction was that he would contact Dr Dadoo.

Stephanie Kemp comments: "Yes, I do remember this – the concern would have been two-fold. Have his letters been intercepted and is he in imminent danger? Has he lost heart? There was always awareness of the great danger posed during this period when activity in the country generally was low and therefore units like Ahmed's were conspicuous and also drove the SB crazy because they thought they had crushed everything with Rivonia. I think comrades in London felt a keen sense of their responsibility to protect comrades who were working at home against any activity that put them unnecessarily at risk. But despite the awareness of the danger, of course there was also the clear recognition of the necessity to drive the struggle forward."

The matter was left at that and at no point did Ahmed give Mohammed any indication that he was involved in the underground. But Ahmed warned Mohammed that because he was back in South Africa he must be very cautious as to what he said to people. Mohammed had to refrain from political discussions with anybody, said Ahmed.

The following morning Ahmed went to school and some time later Hawa Timol insisted that Mohammed go for a haircut. At that time it was fashionable to have long hair in the UK – this was not so fashionable, however, in Hawa's house. It was approximately 9 am when Mohammed proceeded to his barber in Roodepoort. When he returned to the flat he was informed by his mother that the Security Police had come to the flat looking for him. Hawa had told them that Mohammed had gone for a haircut and they left a message saying that Mohammed had to report to the Security Police offices in Roodepoort that afternoon. Mohammed was quite shocked but managed to control himself. Hawa told Mohammed that it was the same security policemen that had come to the flat on previous occasions and enquired what Mohammed was doing in Leicester and where he was studying.

Ahmed had returned from school around midday and was informed by Mohammed about the Security Police visit. Mohammed had been back in the country merely 24 hours. What to do? Ahmed told him to report as requested and to establish what they wanted. Mohammed recalls, "I went to the Security Police offices and as I walked in the security policeman, I cannot recall his name, but he was a sergeant who had visited our flat, happened to be in the corridor and he saw me and his first reaction was, 'Oh, I didn't know that you are back from England. But I didn't want you. I was looking for Ahmed – but when did you get back from the UK? I hope that you were not involved in any political activities there.'" Mohammed told the officer that he had got back the previous evening and that he was not involved in any political activities. The policemen responded, "OK. Please inform Ahmed that we need to see him." Mohammed was taken completely aback and his immediate reaction was that the policeman had told Hawa that he wanted Ahmed and that she had mistaken it as Mohammed. Hawa knew this policeman had come previously to the flat enquiring about Mohammed. It must have been a very natural reaction by Hawa to assume that he was looking for Mohammed without thinking that he really wanted Ahmed. Perhaps, on the other hand, this was too much of a coincidence. Mohammed had arrived in the country merely hours before the Security Police were at the Timol doorstep. Mohammed adds, "Put this together with the fact that Dr Dadoo had asked me to give a message to Ahmed that they had not heard from him for some time and that they were worried – meaning the Party was worried."

Mohammed returned to the flat and told Ahmed that the Security Police wanted to see him and not Mohammed. Mohammed says, "If Ahmed was worried or concerned he did not reflect it." The following day Mohammed was informed by Ahmed that he had gone to see the Security Police and it had something to do with his passport and that the matter was now sorted out. The matter was left at that.

Mohammed was encouraged by Ahmed to go to Durban. He had never been there and had a number of friends there who had studied with him in the UK. After discussing it with Ahmed, it was felt that it was best for Mohammed to go to

Durban to look for a job.

On the evening of Sunday 17 October 1971 Mohammed and Ahmed were in the room at the Timol flat. Mohammed recalls, "Ahmed seemed worried and concerned. He took me to task for having a political discussion with someone – I cannot recall with whom. It appeared as if Ahmed had information that I had a political discussion with someone and Ahmed informed me that both of us were under security police surveillance and he suggested that I leave town the following day. I was to go to Jakes Varachia who would provide me with accommodation."

Jakes had studied with Mohammed in the UK and had known Ahmed quite well. He was running a factory in Durban. Mohammed had the address of his cousin Yunus Moola who was studying in Durban at the time as well as Goolaam Rajah. Mohammed was given money by Ahmed and told that it would be best if he left on Monday by train for Durban.

Ahmed went to school that Monday morning, 18 October 1971, and when he returned to the flat he found Mohammed preparing to leave. Mohammed recalls, "This was the last time that I saw Ahmed. Ahmed appeared to be very worried particularly at the fact that, according to his information, both of us were under surveillance. I don't know how he got this information and from whom he got it, but he was very specific that both of us were under surveillance."

Mohammed left for Durban that afternoon. He caught a train from Roodepoort to Johannesburg and a night train from Johannesburg to Durban, arriving on Tuesday morning, 19 October 1971. He stayed in Warwick Avenue with Yunus Moola, Goolaam Rajah and a few other friends.

According to the school incident book Ahmed was absent from school on the following days: 20/10/71, 21/10/71 (Wed, Thurs). The school was closed on 18 and 19 October because of Diwali (Hindu celebrations). Where was Ahmed? Was he moving the material from Amina Desai's house? What was Ahmed thinking?

Dr Farouk Dindar visited Ahmed on Thursday evening, 21 October, and says, "We discussed the coup in Sudan where Numeiry was overthrown. We were both very upset with the developments in Sudan. I had my daughter Nazneen with me when I went to the flat. She was three years old at that time. I made certain that I took my Nazneen with me to visit my aunt (Hawa, Ahmed's mother) so that any spies would view these as social visits. I never met Ahmed alone on a one-to-one basis. This probably saved me from being arrested and tortured like Ahmed's other acquaintances. Ahmed looked well and there were no bruises on his body." This contemporary observation made by Farouk is of pivotal importance in establishing Ahmed's real cause of death and the absence of any pre-detention bruises.

Dija Chotia, still working at Cajee's Jewellery Shop, had not seen Ahmed for over three weeks. "This was unusual as Ahmed would normally just pop in and greet," says Dija. On Friday 22 October at approximately noon, just before Friday prayers, Ahmed entered the store and asked Dija if she wanted a lift to go and see her sister. Dija declined as she planned to do shopping that afternoon. Dija narrates, "I have this image of Ahmed engraved in my mind. He was wearing a pair of brown slacks, yellowish-mustard shirt and a brown sports jacket with a yellow and green flannel on it." Did she know that this was the last time she was ever going to see Ahmed? "Later, I realised that this was Ahmed's way of saying goodbye or he was reminding me to be careful," adds Dija.

Yunus Cajee (living in Piet Retief and son of Amina Cajee) recalls with tears in his eyes, "I was in Standard Eight and Ahmed Timol was our geography teacher. It was the last period of class on Friday 22 October when Ahmed remarked to the class, "I will live for 500 years and I will become more famous than the president of the world."

Yakoob Adam taught with Ahmed at Roodepoort Indian High School. Ahmed used to take him home for lunch after Friday prayers. Ahmed used to say, "Ma has cooked." Yakoob remembers Ahmed saying in the staffroom on the Friday of his arrest that he believed that Babla Saloojee did not commit suicide, but that he had been murdered.

On that same day, at 6.45 pm, Hawa recalls that Ahmed stared at her for a long time before leaving the flat. He looked sad and said that he was concerned about her health. Ahmed told Hawa that he loved her immensely. Haji Yusuf, who returned from mosque just as Ahmed was leaving the house, now saw his son for what would be the last time. Ahmed told his father that he would be back soon but did not say where he was going.

Apart from the forebodings that Hawa later thought were present in her last conversation with Ahmed, the Friday night of Ahmed and Salim's arrest seemed ordinary enough. The Dynamos Football Club would have their regular meetings on Fridays at Kholvad House. For some reason they were training in Mayfair, opposite the Fietas grounds, on Thursday evening. Timer saw Ahmed after soccer training and he was looking for Toby Hatia. Finding Toby, Ahmed told him that he had forgotten the minutes in Roodepoort and that Toby and Timer should collect the minutes for him. They returned to Johannesburg with the minutes and handed over the keys to Ahmed. At some time during the evening Timer opened the boot of Amina Desai's Anglia and unthinkingly took one pamphlet from the boot and put it in his pocket.

"I was shocked and yet not surprised with Ahmed's arrest, as he had been asked by Roodepoort police a few weeks earlier to go to the police station with his passport," says Dr Dindar. "I wondered why Ahmed did not take this as a serious warning and go into hiding. I wondered if Ahmed was slightly reckless in the manner in which he was operating. As an underground operative he might have felt like talking to someone. He must have been lonely. If I could say anything negative about Ahmed, I would say that he was too trusting."

All the signs were that Ahmed was in danger. No one will ever know why Ahmed did not go into hiding. Certainly, he was committed to the struggle and did not want to shirk his responsibilities. Farouk Dindar's mail was being tampered with in Breyten when he returned to South Africa in March 1971. Persons who attended Essop and Aziz's double wedding in London in 1971 were detained when they returned to South Africa, were questioned and were shown pictures of the wedding. This again is a clear indication that the Pahads were under surveillance when they were staying in London. Had Ahmed then also been under surveillance from the time he returned to South Africa in February 1970?

7

ARREST, DETENTION AND DEATH

After leaving his mother and father, Ahmed went to Amina Desai's house and asked for the keys to the Anglia. He had done this on numerous occasions and Amina did not question him about his plans for the evening. As Ahmed reversed the car out of Amina's driveway, Salim waited in the street. "I saw Ahmed come out from Mrs Desai's house without any boxes or anything. Ahmed did not put anything in the boot of the car," says Salim. Salim accompanied Ahmed and they were off for their normal Friday evening rendezvous, socialising with friends.

According to an article that appeared in the *Star* on 8 August 1972 Salim and Ahmed visited Rashida Mangera, a third-year medical student at the University of the Witwatersrand, at her home in Fordsburg. Rashida was ill in bed and it was her 21st birthday.

What happened next? A friend living in Newclare said Ahmed and Salim had visited her that night and the three of them had removed pamphlets from the boot of the car. She insists that there was no political literature at all in the boot.

According to a dressmaker in Newclare, a recent widow with two children to support, Ahmed arrived at her place at 8.30 pm with a parcel from Amina Desai for whom she often sewed. She said police visited her after Ahmed's arrest and wanted to know what he had delivered – proof, she said, that he had been followed.

The police version states that Ahmed and Salim were driving on Fuel Road in Coronationville at approximately 11.10 pm when they saw policemen manning a roadblock with hand signals and torches in their hands indicating that cars must slow down.

This was a common route used by many travelling from Bosmont, through Coronationville and the Western Coloured Township on the way to Langlaagte Road that eventually leads to Fordsburg and Mayfair. They were en route to Fordsburg to have a snack, with no fixed plans. Ahmed and Salim must have expected to pass the roadblock without any concern or panic.

Police statements made during the inquest indicate that at approximately 3.45 pm that Friday afternoon Sergeant Leonard Gilbert Kleyns (No 23123B) and Constable Thinnies (No 152109P), both stationed at Newlands police station, reported for special duty under the instructions of the station commander, Major JM Kloppers. The police had set up a roadblock at approximately 10.40 pm and Ahmed and Salim were stopped approximately 30 minutes later at 11.10. Given that they were under surveillance, was the roadblock designed to reel Ahmed in? But then why would any roadblock have been necessary, when he could simply have been arrested at will?

As the car came to a standstill, a policeman shone his torch on the occupants and on the back seat of the two-door yellow Anglia, registration TU 22315. Salim, who was driving, was asked to step out of the car by Sergeant Kleyns and asked to open the boot of the vehicle. As Salim opened the boot, Sergeant Kleyns shone his torch into the boot and scratched around the contents. There were a number of shoeboxes and papers wrapped in newspaper. Sergeant Kleyns sighed in Afrikaans "*Aahhhhh! – pamflette*", and asked Salim to stand on the side of the road. Ahmed was now asked to step out of the car by Constable Thinnies, and the other policemen at the roadblock, Constable S le Roux (No 152109F) and Warrant Officer AS Verster (No 203465), both came forward.

Ahmed and Salim were now handcuffed and asked to sit in the back of the Anglia. Kleyns and Thinnies occupied the front seats, with Kleyns driving, and they set off to Newlands police station. Ahmed and Salim attempted to communicate with each other and were constantly told by Kleyns, "*Moenie praat nie*" (don't speak). The police version records this as follows: "Sergeant Kleyns observes that the Indians speak to each other in their language." Repeatedly, the official police records refer to Ahmed exactly like that – as "the Indian". Ahmed and Salim now knew that they were in trouble and began to become anxious.

NEWLANDS POLICE STATION

Ahmed and Salim were taken to the charge office at Newlands police station and told to sit on the bench. Kleyns started making a number of telephone calls and Thinnies was keeping a watchful eye on them. Ahmed and Salim continued to communicate and whisper in Gujarati.

"Banned ANC literature, copies of secret communication correspondence, instructions received from the Communist Party in London, material related to the 50th Anniversary of the South African Communist Party, etc.", as the police version would have it. On available evidence it was likely that the Security Branch planted the incriminating evidence. Salim, although assisting Ahmed with his underground operations, was completely unaware that any such material was kept in the boot of the Anglia. Ahmed and Salim had previously discussed the dangers of doing underground work. They were aware that they could be arrested, detained and tortured. This was now becoming a reality.

Salim recalls, "Ahmed held a firm grip on my hand and said, 'Let's hope everything goes all right – not sure what is going to happen – hope we can survive.'

Salim felt Ahmed's warm hand and had a feeling of separation. "It was as if this bond was now ending," says Salim. This was the last time that Salim saw Ahmed close up and in good physical condition.

According to the police version, Warrant Officer Neville Els of the Security Branch stationed in Johannesburg arrived at approximately 12.10 am and inspected the material allegedly found in the boot of the Anglia. Els contacted Captain Carel Joseph Dirker, who arrived at approximately 12.45. Els and Dirker confirmed that the material found was similar to that distributed in the entire country. They realised that they had made a significant breakthrough. Dirker spoke to Ahmed and Salim and obtained their personal particulars.

Salim was taken up a metal staircase to the back section of the Newlands police station escorted by two plainclothes security policemen. As the surviving member of the pair he is a vital window into what Ahmed went through following his arrest. "It was a two-storey building and the office looked similar to any office. There was a desk and the office was not very large." Before any questions were asked, Salim was given a very painful blow in the stomach. "I had never received such a painful blow in my stomach in my life and was now winded." Salim was asked to remove his glasses and place them on the table. The policeman, who was hefty in size, then started giving Salim heavy-handed slaps across his face. Salim says, "I was seeing stars and was really shaken."

This stopped for a moment and then commenced the questions and comments. "Where were you going? Who were you going to see? Come, speak. If you don't speak, do you know what is going to happen to you? You want to live – don't you? This is serious business. Don't mess with us." The questions and comments were posed in English and Afrikaans. The police were under the impression that Ahmed and Salim were on their way to meet someone.

The threats continued. Salim says, "It was as if they were venting their emotions and anger towards me." The kicking and punching continued and Salim was now terribly shaken and in a state of complete shock when he heard the name of Colonel Greyling mentioned. Salim was then taken from the room and told to climb into an ordinary civilian vehicle. Handcuffed and accompanied by a policeman in the back seat, Salim was driven to John Vorster Square by Greyling. Salim realised he was in serious trouble. This was only the beginning of his nightmare. This was only the beginning of physical assault, and the torture had not yet begun. One can reasonably assume that Ahmed's experiences at the same time were similar.

According to statements made at the inquest by the police, Ahmed was transported to John Vorster Square in Dirker's official police car at approximately 2.40 am, accompanied by Kleyns. The material allegedly found in the boot of the Anglia was also taken along. Ahmed arrived at John Vorster Square at approximately 3 am.

JOHN VORSTER SQUARE

After Babla Saloojee's death at The Gray's building in 1964, statements had been made in the media by police that there was to be no repetition of detainees committing suicide and policies would be implemented to effect this. John Vorster Square, built as the new state-of-the-art police headquarters in central Johannesburg, at a cost of millions, was to have special burglar guards preventing detainees from committing suicide.

Barely half a kilometre from the Market Theatre stands Johannesburg's police headquarters, John Vorster Square – 10 stories of forbidding siege architecture. Behind the bullet-proofing, the bomb-proofing, the paranoia of its turnstiles clamping together like metal teeth, it is the ultimate symbol of the bureaucratisation of fear and horror under apartheid. In those days police stations were built for bombardment and repression. The building stands there to this day, at a commanding spot at a bend in Commissioner Street. Heavy grilles, some for protection against the sun, are visible at the windows.

The Security Police offices at John Vorster Square were described as "the last word in security" in a report in the *Rand Daily Mail* on 29 October 1971, shortly before the completion of the building.

"It is believed that the grilles were introduced at the new building to prevent similar incidents to that on September 9, 1964, when a detainee, Mr. Suliman Saloojee, was killed – when he fell from the former security headquarters at The Grays in Johannesburg", reported the paper.

An article appeared in the *Sunday Express* on 15 January 1967, with this headline: "R2m. HQ for Police". The article reported that the building contained a lecture theatre with tiered seats, cinema projector and sound equipment, large fully equipped photographic laboratories and a spacious fingerprint laboratory. It repeated the description that "the offices to be occupied by the Security Branch represent the last word in security". Access to the top two floors of the building was only by two special lifts running from the basement to the ninth and 10th floors. Any passenger stepping out of the lift would be faced by a bullet-proof glass cage that was manned by a policeman who would be checking their identity and verifying their visit before allowing them to pass through an electrically-operated door. Special steel grilles would protect all other entrances to the security offices. The Security Branch offices contained special soundproof rooms with folding steel grilles across the windows. Access to the soundproof rooms was through a thick steel bank-vault door. They were also to have their own darkrooms. Direct-line telephones were connected to the Security Branch headquarters in Pretoria and other centres.

Detention was an horrific experience. The Terrorism Act, which was passed in 1967, allowed the police to detain indefinitely without trial and in solitary confinement anyone suspected of "terrorism" or of having information about terrorism. No court could intervene and no one had the right of access to the detained person except the minister of justice or government officials acting in an official capacity.

The South African government had admitted that the purpose of allowing the Security Police to detain people indefinitely was to enable them to use any means they wanted to extract information from detainees. In 1963 Vorster, who was then minister of justice, said, "It is not a very nice thing to see a human being broken. I have seen it. The man taking these powers must take the responsibility for them."

The Security Police had a team of interrogators, led by the notorious Lieutenant-Colonel Theunis "Rooi Rus" Swanepoel, whose name recurs in statements of torture by detainees and in evidence given at numerous inquests held on those who died at the hands of the police.

At the Rivonia trial in 1964 Swanepoel said, "Ninety-day detention is not for the ordinary criminal. It is a mighty weapon in our hands."

Indefinite detention in solitary confinement is in itself a severe form of torture. One of the commonest methods of "interrogation" used by the South African Police is the "standing torture" during which detainees are prevented from sleeping or sitting down.

There was a proven pattern of systematic Security Branch torture. By 1963 the Security Branch was already applying electric shocks to political detainees and they were physically beaten up. In a chilling experience, which has a bearing on both the Babla Saloojee and Ahmed Timol cases, Abdulhay Jassat, having been arrested on suspicion of sabotage, was hung out of the third-floor window at Park Station police station. This was a traumatic experience. He recalls, "The cell had louvre windows and two chairs were placed on either side of the window. The policemen would climb on top of these chairs, pull you up by your hair and push you, head first; and they would then hold you by your ankles on either side." The policemen would then taunt Abdulhay by asking, "*Gaan jy nou praat?*" (Are you now going to speak?) They would then let go of one leg and Abdulhay would think that he was dead. All he could see was concrete below him. As one policeman would pull the one leg up, the other would release the other leg. Abdulhay says, "If they did not co-ordinate, you were dead. This method of torture is very difficult to visualise. It is very possible that the same method of torture was applied to Babla and this eventually resulted in Babla's death."

They would take off Abdulhay's shoes and socks and would fiddle with his toes. "They would place a hessian bag over your face and you would only see figures. This would make it practically impossible to identify the torturers. Electric shocks were then applied, starting with 10 volts and gradually increasing. You had no concept of time. They would stop the shock treatment, ask a few questions and would continue."

Abdulhay's mouth was dry and he was not in a position to say much. All they wanted was a name, even one name. Abdulhay would think that by giving them a fictitious name he would be released. At the same time it also went through his mind that, by providing them with a name, the police would find out that this was a fictitious name or that the person had nothing to do with this. This would only mean that they would once again put you through the same torture, or even worse for providing them with false information. The only option was to keep quiet and not give them any information.

He modestly points out that he was fortunate in having these thoughts, while others could not cope with the severe means of torture and provided the police with names of activists.

The electric shock treatment would be increased to 220 volts, and Abdulhay had to be carried out of the detention room. Sitting slumped in a chair, Abdulhay recalls a policeman entering the room holding a hessian bag, with a weight in it, and assuming that it was a manual electrical generator (used to generate the electrical current during torture). His body stiff and tired, Abdulhay now had to stand. Leaning against the wall or chair would mean that you were punched and hit on your body – not forgetting that the policemen were huge.

Amazingly, Abdulhay would stand firm only to see a coin dropped by the policemen. He was now told to put his finger on the coin and continuously run around this coin. As soon as he stopped a few punches and kicks would be thrown at him. The torture was administered because the policemen wanted names of the people who gave Abdulhay instructions. Abdulhay was picked up by his ankles and swung like a pendulum, his head hitting against the concrete floor. Yet he never gave in, and stood firm.

Abdulhay is convinced that the South African Police obtained assistance from the Israelis in their methods of torture and surveillance. If the successive Israeli and apartheid governments admit that they collaborated in the making of nuclear bombs, a story well told by the American journalist Seymour Hersh in *The Samson Option*, it is at least plausible that they would also have shared medical techniques, including torture? Explicit evidence of medical collaboration between the Israeli Defence Force and the apartheid military is to be found in the South African Army journal *Paratus*. In November 1975 Tony Leon, who is the leader of South Africa's official political opposition, wrote an article praising the brilliance of the Israeli Defence Force ("How they do it when Israel goes to war") in saving the lives of its own casualties. What remains unanswered is whether, between the horrendous violence of nuclear weapons collaboration and the supposedly benign collaboration in medical treatment of wartime casualties, there was or was not some more sinister collaboration in methods of physical and psychological torture. It would not be surprising if Abdulhay's assumptions were to be proved correct.

Abdulhay believes the South African Police obtained foreign assistance in its methods of torture and surveillance. Prior to the Treason Trial in the fifties, there appears to have been no systematic use of torture on political detainees, though there were individual cases of maltreatment in police cells, such as the Bultfontein case which caused an outcry when it emerged that prisoners were systematically tortured, such as by being dropped on their heads in police custody. After the Treason Trial, in which all the accused were acquitted, the Security Branch realised that they were outsmarted and were forced to update their brutal skills.

In the state-of-the-art John Vorster Square torture facility, at approximately 3.15 am on Saturday 23 October 1971 (the morning after Ahmed's arrest), Dirker and Lieutenant Colonel van Wyk started going through the material allegedly found in the boot of the Anglia. Meanwhile, later that same morning, the Security Police made the first of their many visits to number 76, Mare Street, Roodepoort. Haji Timol and Hawa were busy with the recitation of the Quran when they heard car doors closing and footsteps. This was *sehri* time (during the month of Ramadan, the early-morning eating period when fasting), when three security police arrived and initially knocked at Flat Number 1. They were at the wrong flat and were directed to Flat Number 2, the Timol flat. Warrant Officer Johannes

Jacobus Liebenberg, Captain le Roux and S/Sergeant Joubert knocked on the door and identified themselves as Security Police. Haji Timol opened the door and asked them to enter. In Hawa's statement made to the Truth and Reconciliation Commission she said, "The policemen were very angry and abrupt in their questioning. It was clear to us that something was wrong. After asking a number of questions, that my husband answered, they wanted to know where Ahmed slept. My husband proceeded to Ahmed's room only to find that his bed had not been slept in. This made the policemen angrier and they became very agitated. We were accused of knowing all along that Ahmed was not in the room."

The call for *fajr* (morning) prayer was heard but Haji Timol was not permitted to go to mosque. It was the fasting month and Haji Timol informed them that he had not missed a prayer for many years and he asked that he should be allowed to pray on the balcony of the flat, in view of them. They were initially angry at this request but he persisted and they eventually agreed. Aysha, my mother, recalls, "When Papa would come from travelling, he would immediately perform his prayers that he had missed due to being on the road. He would thereafter have his meals." Haji Timol was closely guarded on the balcony as he performed his prayers at home. Unable to understand his piety they seemed to believe that the prayers were a trick meant to conceal a plan to escape over the railing of the high balcony. They ransacked the house and confiscated Ahmed's typewriter, his passport (Number 68451) and certain documents belonging to him from his room.

Ebrahim Choonara, living at Flat Number 5 in the building at the time, says: "I was returning from *fajr* prayers and, as I walked past Flat Number 2, the Timols' flat, I could smell smoke. This was unusual as it was the month of Ramadan and no one would be smoking. I could sense that something was not right. It was only later in the day that we found out that Ahmed had been arrested."

Haji Timol and his son Haroon were then taken for interrogation at John Vorster Square. They returned home at about 1.15 pm. The presence of the Security Police aroused suspicion amongst the neighbours. Hawa persistently asked to see her son, Ahmed. Before departing, they mentioned that he was detained. The police returned later and searched the entire flat.

At the time of Salim and Ahmed's arrest, the following persons were also detained at John Vorster Square under Section 6 of the Terrorism Act of 1967 (the @ represents what the police called an "alias"): Fatima Essop @ Mayet, Salim's sister from Roodepoort; Kantilal Chaganlal Naik @ Kanti, teacher at Roodepoort; Amina Desai, businesswomen from Roodepoort; Yusuf Garda @ Chubb, Johannesburg shopkeeper; Mohammed Ishmael Momoniat, Johannesburg doctor and social administrator; Yunus Patel, a fourth-year engineering student at Witwatersrand University; Hassen Ahmed Jooma @ Boetie, teacher at Laudium, Pretoria; Dilshad Jhetham @ Dilshadbegum, second-year medical student, Witwatersrand University; Mohammed Hoosen Dinath, a salesman; Gadija Chotia, Johannesburg secretary; Shireen Areef, former student in Johannesburg; Moegamat Noor Matthews, primary school teacher in Bosmont, Johannesburg and Mohammed Amin Essop.

Cornelius Tebogo Lekhogole was detained at the Florida police cells. David

Kennelly Davis, a student of arts at Durban University, and Fatima Wadee, a student at Durban University were held at the Durban North Police Cells.

Indhrasen Moodley, lecturer in pharmacy at Durban University, was detained at the Mayville police station in Durban. Ayesha Bulbulia, a typist from Johannesburg, was detained at the Krugersdorp police cells. Yakoob Varachia was detained at the Rossburgh Police Station in Durban and Ahmed's brother Mohammed at the Berea police station in Durban.

Dr Colin Marquard, a lecturer at Witwatersrand University; Max Katz, a student at Witwatersrand University; Quentin Jacobsen, British citizen; David Smith, British citizen; Martin Cohen, an Australian citizen; and Ian Hill, a fourth year medical student at Witwatersrand University were all detained.

In a statement dated 5 November 1971, Amnesty International reported to all its national sections that on 25 October 1971 between 4 am and 5 am the Security Police had raided the homes of 115 persons in South Africa. The arrest included bishops, priests, lecturers, journalists, students and all members of the executive committee of the National Union of South African Students (Nusas). The Security Police alleged that these raids were the result of leaflets that were found in the car of Ahmed Timol and Salim Essop during a police roadblock.

The newspaper of the Anti-Apartheid Movement, *Anti-Apartheid News*, dated December 1971, reported, "The first detentions took place during a weekend of mass political raids, which are said to have been the biggest since 1964. At least 115 people were raided – 35 in the Western Cape, 20 in the Eastern Cape, 30 in the Transvaal and 30 in Natal.

"They included 62 students, nine clergy, 17 teachers and university lecturers and six journalists. Among the clergy were two Anglican bishops and the head of the United Congregational Church in South Africa. Thirty of those whose houses were searched were connected with Nusas, some were members of Student Representative Councils, six were officials of the black South African Students' Organisation (SASO) and at least five were activists in the University Christian Movement (UCM). Police questioned 11 officials of the recently revived Natal Indian Congress.

"Among the institutions searched were a Lutheran college in Natal, an Indian commercial school in Johannesburg, a hospital in Zululand and the High School in Roodepoort where Ahmed taught. From many places the police took away samples of typefaces and typewriters. One of the things the police were obviously searching for were the sources of the underground literature, much of which was duplicated. An underground newsletter *Revolt* had been circulating for some time in Johannesburg and the South African Communist Party recently sent copies of its duplicated newspaper to the South African press."

The number and variety of people involved in the raids that followed Ahmed and Salim's arrest were out of proportion to the actual work that Ahmed had been doing. This indicates that the authorities at the time were using the occasion to indicate that there was a wide conspiracy underway. This would help the government to intimidate people and also to give white South Africans the impression that government, through its *kragdadigheid*, was keeping them safe.

Ahmed and Salim were in no condition to understand what was emerging in the entire country as a result of their arrest. They were fighting for their own survival. So were their friends and loved ones.

AMINA DESAI

The Security Branch arrived at Amina Desai's house on Saturday 23 October 1971 at approximately 2 am. They went through the entire house with a fine-tooth comb. Ahmed was doing political science as one of his subjects at Unisa and the SBs found his books at Amina's place. Amina's daughter, Bahiya, who was in Durban at the time, was also studying political science.

Amina, in her early fifties, was running her shoe agency business from home and naturally had stationery stored in the cupboards. Her typewriter was confiscated. The search of the house lasted till approximately 8 am that Saturday morning. Amina was then asked to get in the car with the Security Branch officers. As the car, occupied by Amina and her two white male captors, turned at the corner, Amina noticed Mr Bodania, a member of the local community. He did not suspect that she was being detained, but thought that she was leaving with her fellow-passengers for a business conference. So little was the Roodepoort community aware of the high drama unfolding. What's more, Amina was taken to John Vorster Square dressed in a green suit with black trimmings; she had a brooch, bangles, scarf and a watch on.

Amina Desai recalls, "As I was brought to John Vorster Square police station on Saturday morning, 23 October 1971, I remember walking through a tunnel. The police did not mention to me that Ahmed was in their custody and detained. I was taken to the ninth floor and could hear the furniture crashing and moving. Loud screams could also be heard from the office above. They kept on asking about Ahmed. I was forced to stand for 52 hours without any sleep in front of the white policemen. Some of the policemen were Van Rensburg, Visser, Van der Merwe and Brown (English-speaking from Krugersdorp)." Amina was kept in detention for over five months at John Vorster Square before appearing in court.

KANTI NAIK

At approximately 5 am on the same Saturday morning, security policemen visited KC Naik (known as Kanti). His house was ransacked and Kanti was taken to the Roodepoort Indian High School where the school's typewriter and other material were confiscated (Kanti kept the keys for the school). The policemen left only to return later that morning, at approximately 11 am, and arrested Kanti who was working at the local pharmacy. He was taken home, his house ransacked again and then taken to John Vorster Square.

Kanti was brought to John Vorster Square at approximately noon on that Saturday. Naik narrates, "I was kept isolated in an office until late at night and was asked to write a statement. On reading the statement they proclaimed that they were not satisfied with what I had written. I was then assaulted by two burly security policemen on a regular basis.

"Subsequently four security policemen, early on Sunday morning, assaulted me badly using what is known as the helicopter treatment. My wrists were tied tightly with a cloth and were then slipped over my knees. A broomstick was then placed between my knees and the ankles. I was then lifted with the stick and suspended between two chairs with the broomstick. I was left hanging in mid-air for a long time, the policemen rotating me around the broomstick. With both centripetal and centrifugal forces acting on my elbow my muscles in the arms collapsed totally, leaving the arms limp for almost three and a half months. The pain was excruciating and unendurable and I was not able to use the hands for either dressing or eating. This was unfortunately traumatic and I was depressed and cried about the fact that I was not going to be able to use my arms in the future at all! My handwriting being immaculate and also being able to play Indian musical instruments seemed no longer a possibility. I was saddened to know that my arms were totally immobilised and that I was not going to be able to use them at all."

On Saturday night while being interrogated and assaulted Kanti heard Salim Essop screaming in some adjacent room, being tortured by the police. The next morning Kanti was taken to the holding cells and kept in solitary confinement.

Kanti says, "I had supplied Ahmed with hydroquinone, a chemical compound that is an oxidising agent. They had found this in his possession. He said it was supplied by me. They detained me for aiding and abetting Ahmed in furthering the aims of the South African Communist Party. Hydroquinone is a developer and is used in deciphering invisible handwriting. According to the Security Police, letters that came in the form of invisible handwriting to Ahmed were deciphered using this chemical agent. Not being aware of the events from Ahmed or otherwise, I am not sure whether this was done or not."

The Roodepoort Indian High School incident book recorded on 15/11/1971: "Received a Minute from the Department regarding Mr KC Naik. I quote: "Mr Naik has been granted vacation leave without pay with effect from 25.10.71 until further notice in terms of regulation 15(7) and 15(8) of the Conditions of Service in State and State-aided Schools for Indians dated August 26th, 1966. Leave forms not required.""

Kanti was released on Tuesday 7 March 1972.

DILSHAD JHETAM
Dilshad Jhetam had been in Standard Eight in 1964 when Ahmed had taught her history. Dilshad remarks, "Ahmed was very passionate about his job. He was an excellent teacher and was always there for the pupils." Ahmed also taught Dilshad history for part of 1965. Dilshad matriculated in 1966 and went on to further her studies at Wentworth Medical School in 1967.

Dilshad had returned from Salisbury Island in Durban and continued her studies at Wits Medical School in 1971. She was a close friend of Bahiya Desai, who studied at Salisbury Island, and would regularly visit her at her mother's place in Roodepoort. On Saturday afternoon, 23 October 1971, at approximately 5 pm, Dilshad was returning home from the library at the medical school when she was detained by Security Police and taken to John Vorster Square.

Dilshad Jhetam was brought there in the late afternoon. "I was taken to the 10th floor and accused of being a communist. The policemen accused me of assisting Ahmed Timol and Salim Essop in furthering the aims of the South African Communist Party. I laughed and scoffed at their accusations as I could not believe that either Ahmed or Salim could be involved in politics, let alone be responsible for bucket bomb explosions that took place in the country."

Dilshad continues: "They forced me to stand for long periods and forced me to consume bottles of water. When I requested to go to the toilet, they refused. There were eight to 10 white policemen standing in front of me and laughing as I was forced to urinate in my clothes This process continued as they forced me to continue drinking bottles of water. I was told that I was not nappy trained and continuously slapped across my face. At regular intervals, I passed out."

The police had showed Dilshad photographs of her that were taken by Salim. Dilshad adds, "Salim and I were both studying at Wits and Salim was experimenting with his camera. He asked to take some photographs of me and I agreed. I was fully clothed and these photographs were not incriminating at all. The police used these photographs to prove that I was linked to Salim. I heard screams and shouting from the room next door and immediately recognised them to be of Ahmed and Salim."

Dilshad was given dates and times when her white Anglia was allegedly spotted at political meetings in Durban during 1969 and 1970. "I informed them that I had lent my car to Bahiya Desai and my other friends. I had no idea where they had gone to." Dilshad remembers going to hospital for treatment on some of the days mentioned. "I told them to go to the hospital and verify my story," says Dilshad. Dilshad was sent for a cold shower at 4 am and she was tauntingly reminded not to slip on the soap as Imam Haron had (he had allegedly slipped on stairs in Caledon Square police HQ in Cape Town, dying not long after with 24 unexplained bruises on his body and contusions on his back).

An elderly woman warder informed Dilshad of Ahmed's death. Dilshad had to take valium to sedate herself in the evenings.

AMINA CAJEE

During the month of Ramadan, when Ahmed had been arrested, the Security Branch came knocking at Amina Cajee's flat during the early hours of the morning. They were looking for the owner of Cajee's Commercial College. They took Amina to the college. The police, using many vehicles, were waiting outside the college for Amina to open up. They took all the typewriters and recording equipment used for short-hand, cassettes, papers packed in boxes and everything they could get their hands on. Amina was asked if she knew Ahmed and she responded that she did know him. Everybody from Roodepoort, as she was, knew him. By this time Amina had heard that Ahmed, KC Naik, Mrs Desai and others had been arrested. Aysha Bulbulia had also been arrested. Her parents were upset and could not understand why their daughter, just an ordinary worker at the college, had been arrested.

Amina was told to return to John Vorster Square in three days. Students came to class the next morning to find the classes empty with all the equipment taken. No lessons could take place. The huge media publicity given to Ahmed's arrest and subsequent death and the mention of Ahmed's association with Cajee's Commercial College resulted in a loss of income as students and family were afraid of being associated with a college that had links to Ahmed, a communist.

Amina returned to John Vorster Square three days later, as she was requested to do. She proceeded to the 10th floor and went through a number of gates and was once again interrogated about her association with Ahmed. Amina responded by informing them that Ahmed brought his schoolwork for typing and whoever was available at the time would oblige. The typewriters were eventually returned to the college.

The Roodepoort Indian High School incident book recorded on 25.10.71: "During the weekend in the course of raids by the Security Police the typewriters from the typing room, the office typewriter, the duplicator and the adding machine were taken away. Mr AAI Ahmed who has the keys to the typing room informed me that he has been given a receipt for his typewriter that will probably be returned on Wednesday. Mr KC Naik and Mr A Timol have been detained by the Security Police. Their whereabouts are not known."

HASSEN JOOMA

Hassen and Fawzia were living on 4th Street, Marabastad, Pretoria. On the fateful Saturday, Hassen had gone to mosque to perform *Zohar* (midday) prayers when two white men came knocking at his residence looking for him. They identified themselves as coming from a soccer association and wanted Hassen to referee an important soccer match in the township. Fawzia told them that they had the wrong man, as Hassen could not differentiate between a soccer ball and a cricket ball. They insisted that they wanted Hassen, as he was a man of integrity. Fawzia told them she was the one who was sports-orientated and not Hassen. Refusing to accept Fawzia's explanation they asked directions to the mosque on 6th Street.

Hassen noticed two white males approaching him outside the mosque. He was initially excited and full of anticipation at seeing them because a few weeks earlier he had written a letter to the Pretoria City Council requesting a council-built house. He therefore thought that they might have news of this for him. But one of the white males held Hassen by his hand and told him to get in the car. This did not, therefore, appear to be about the council house. The white males then produced their cards, identifying themselves as police.

Hassen remarked, "*My gewete pla my nie* (My conscience is not bothering me)," to the policemen. One policeman replied, "*Dis goed dat jou gewete nie vir jou pla nie, ons gaan vir jou pla*. (It is good that your conscience is not bothering you, as we are going to bother you)." This was definitely not about the council house.

He was driven to his own house for searching. Fawzia immediately realised that something was wrong. The expression on Hassen's face was not encouraging. As the two policemen entered the house they excitedly placed their hands on some of the Islamic pamphlets that were in the house on an old piano and on the desk in the one-bedroom tenement. However, these pamphlets were innocuous. They dealt

121

with the significance of Ramadan. Hassen eagerly supplied them with more of these, doubting, somewhat, that he was on the brink of converting them to Islam.

The police, immune to religious conversion, ransacked the entire house and kept staring at a photograph of the SRC that was hung on the wall. This photo showed Ahmed as an SRC member. The search at an end, Hassen was told to accompany the police. Fawzia unsuccessfully attempted to give him some food for breaking his fast. The policemen said that Hassen needed to be taken to the police station for questioning and would be brought back shortly. Hassen was repeatedly asked if he had an enemy because someone was saying bad things about him. No mention was made of Ahmed as Hassen was driven to the Compol police building in Pretoria.

At this dark and uninviting police station, one of the policemen picked up the telephone and spoke to a certain Lieutenant Smit: "*Ons het hom hier* (We've got him here)." Hassen was asked if he knew his ID number. He responded by saying that they knew everything and should know his ID number as well. The policeman warned him not to be a comedian. Hassen was driven by car to John Vorster Square in Johannesburg. Hassen conversed with them in Afrikaans from the time he was picked up and throughout his incarceration, hoping that this might increase their sympathy towards him and hasten his release. It however seemed to have little effect.

FATIMA WADEE

Fatima Wadee was detained on 24 October 1971 and taken to the Durban North police cells. Fatima recalls, "I was doing my BSc at Salisbury Island in 1971 when I got a call from my parents in Heidelberg informing me that the police were looking for me. I had met Ahmed through Bahiya Desai and only knew him on a social basis. The Security Branch searched my place of boarding and told me that there was something big going on in South Africa and I was part of it. They asked me to pack my clothes and I now became scared." She was detained for 45 days. Released and not charged, she is currently a dentist in Mayfair.

MOHAMMED TIMOL

Ahmed's younger brother, who had had left Roodepoort as instructed by Ahmed, had gone to Durban where he stayed with Yakoob Varachia at his flat in Durban. Yakoob and Mohammed were both detained on Monday 25 October 1971.

Mohammed recalls, "On the morning of 25 October 1971 I was detained at Himalaya Heights, where I had been staying with some students from the Transvaal. I was arrested by Lieutenant Nayager and 10 other officers. At the time of my arrest I was not aware that Ahmed had also been arrested a few days earlier. A small article on his arrest had appeared in the *Sunday Times*, but I had not seen it. My parents did not know where I was staying and hence were unable to warn me. I was taken to the Security Police headquarters in Fisher Street in Durban. The officer in command was Colonel Steenkamp. There I was subjected to interrogation by Lieutenant Nayager, Sergeant Andy Taylor and an officer Botha. The interrogation began around nine in the morning and continued until 11 that night. I was assaulted and made to stand for long periods of time on a brick with two telephone directories raised in the air. The so-called 'golden chair' torture position was also used. During the interrogation I realised that Ahmed had been arrested. The Security Police wanted to know of my activities in the UK as well as my contacts in South Africa.

"At 11 pm that night I was taken to the Berea police station and locked up in a cell. In the cell I had a little time to reflect on the situation. I was very confused. During my stay in the UK as well as during my training, I had read numerous books on resistance movements and operations during World War II. I had also read books on interrogation and torture methods, especially those practised by the South African Security Police. This information helped me to cope during this ordeal.

"On the morning of 26 October 1971 I was taken back to the Fisher Street headquarters, and the interrogation resumed with different officers in charge. It went on until late at night. The same methods were utilised again. I was taken back to the cells afterwards. On 27 October the same procedure was followed once again. However, at approximately 7.00 pm the interrogation took a completely different turn. I was asked whether I wanted anything to eat and the tone of the situation changed completely. The Security Police officers were anxiously hurrying to and fro. The interrogation session was terminated and I was taken back to my cell at the Berea police station.

"On Thursday 28 October, two different security policemen came to fetch me. The previous evening they had given me some paper on which to write a statement. When they came to fetch me they said that I would have to stay in the cell until I had completed my statement. To me it was a breather. It was the first day since my arrest that I was on my own during the day.

"In the evening, at 7 pm, two security policemen came to see me and informed me that they had received a message from Pretoria that Ahmed had died. My first reaction was to ask how he had died. They told me that they did not have any further information. After they had left, the uniformed policeman on duty, who came to give me food, conveyed his condolences. I was confused as to whether this was a tactic to break me or whether Ahmed had really died. The death of Babla Saloojee several years earlier while in detention came to mind.

"That night was extremely difficult from an emotional and psychological point of view. I had to remain strong under all circumstances. I was still not certain that Ahmed had indeed been killed. On 29 October they fetched me and took me to their Fisher Street headquarters. While they drove I saw a newspaper billboard which said, Death plunge, Vorster speaks. I wondered why Vorster would comment on a death plunge. I was suspicious and related this billboard to Ahmed's death. In the lift at the Fisher Street headquarters an Indian security policeman conveyed his condolences to me. These incidents confirmed that something terrible had indeed happened to Ahmed. It was only after my release on March 14, 1972 that I got to know all the facts surrounding Ahmed's detention, death, and funeral.

"From 29 October 1971 there was no further interrogation. I was taken back to Berea police station and kept in solitary confinement until 1 December 1971. I was then transferred by road to John Vorster Square in Johannesburg. During the journey the Security Police repeatedly said I would be released on arrival in Johannesburg and that my parents were waiting for me at John Vorster Square. This was not true. On arrival I was immediately locked up in a cell. From then up until 14 March 1972 I was only questioned twice. However, I was not tortured on these two occasions.

"During this long solitary confinement under Section 6 of the Terrorism Act, I knew that I had to remain strong and maintain my sanity at all costs. I was not allowed any reading material other than a religious book, so I requested an English translation of the Quran. Later I requested a copy of the Bible and the Bhagavad Gita. Every day I became more resolved and determined to pursue the struggle against apartheid. The long period of confinement was extremely difficult, but I survived. I refused to be defeated by my jailers.

"My only real human contact was the uniformed policeman who was responsible for the cells. Despite the Security Police instruction for them not to talk to us they did communicate with us. I developed a relationship with them and in time they gave me cigarettes and newspapers. I also managed to communicate with Amin Saloojee whose cell was next to mine.

"I was released on 14 March 1972. I had not been charged. It is my firm contention that the death of Ahmed at the hands of the Security Police scared them. Hence they did not assault me any further. My return home was very emotional, especially seeing my mother and my family after such a long time. One of the first things my family did was to take me to the cemetery in Roodepoort where Ahmed had been buried. It took days after that initial meeting with family members and friends to gain a comprehensive understanding as to what had happened to Ahmed and the impact it had had on individuals and on the country."

INDRES MOODLEY
During the evening of 24 October 1971 Indres got a telephone call from his uncle in Lenasia. Indres recalls, "My uncle informed me that there were policemen at his house looking for me. I told him that they were probably looking for me because I had not paid a traffic fine. My uncle told me that the interest of the police seemed to concern something far more serious. I immediately burnt all the literature that I had.

"I explained to my wife without explaining the gravity of the situation. She was pregnant and expecting our first child. I had an option to escape out of the country before the police came looking for me. However, I decided to stay and not abandon my wife." Indres then went to sleep.

The Security Police knocked on his flat door in Overport, Durban, during the early hours of the morning. Indres recalls, "They stormed in and ransacked the entire flat. They found two political books that I had forgotten to destroy. They asked me to pack my bags and I laughed at them, indicating to my wife that I would be returning shortly. I was told that I was going for a long time. I was scared but wanted to reassure my wife that things would work out. I wanted to avoid causing her to panic because of the pregnancy." As Indres walked out of the flat he saw that the road had been cordoned off and that there was a heavy police presence. Indres was taken to the Mayville police station in Durban.

DAILY EVENTS AT THE TIMOL RESIDENCE

According to Hawa Timol, the police did not arrive on Sunday 24 October 1971. Such was the suspense and the general feeling of insecurity that the failure of the police to arrive was almost as much of an event as their arrival would have been.

Hawa asked Iqbal "Baboo" Dindar (Ahmed's cousin) to take food for Ahmed, as she was concerned that he had not eaten for two days and was certain that he would not eat the food provided by the police. Without hesitating, Baboo and his wife arranged a food basket and were off to see Ahmed.

Baboo recalls, "It was raining heavily and it was very cold that day. At about 2 pm Jameela and I made our way to John Vorster Square police station. An African policeman at John Vorster Square greeted us and we enquired as to where the Security Branch offices were. He told us that they were on the 10th floor and we proceeded. As the lift came to a halt on the 10th floor and as we opened the lift door we were greeted by a hefty policeman." This is the conversation that took place between Baboo and the policeman:

Policeman: "*Ja, wat soek jy*? (What do you want?)"

Baboo: "*Ons wil net vir Ahmed Timol sien asseblief. Ons het kos vir hom gebring. Hy is seker honger*. (We just want to see Ahmed Timol. We have brought him some food, as he must be hungry.)"

Policeman: "*Nee, jy sal hom nooit sien nie. Dit is hel koud. Daardie donder soek iets om te dra want hy kry baie koud. Gee jou trui hier*. (No, you will never see him. It is very cold. That man is feeling cold and needs something to wear. Give your jersey here.)"

Baboo continued, "I handed over the jersey that I was wearing to the policeman. We had only gone over to deliver food to Ahmed and ended up leaving a jersey for him. The policeman then escorted Jameela and I back to the lift and pressed the button for us to go down. Jameela and I informed Hawa that we had left the food basket for Ahmed. Hawa felt a bit relieved, as she knew that Ahmed was alive, as he had asked for a jersey.

"A few weeks after Ahmed's death, Ahmed's clothes were returned. The jersey that I had given to the policeman was also returned. However, it was returned full of blood."

If Ahmed's experience in detention to this point was all gentleness and polite questioning, as in the police version as later presented to the inquest, then it is difficult to explain where the blood on the jersey came from, not to mention his bruises.

Monday 25 October 1971

According to Hawa Timol, Haji Timol's African driver arrived at the flat and was interrogated by the Security Police. For his own safety, Hawa Timol had instructed the driver to go home as he might be questioned again. The police made numerous visits to the Timol household and closely looked at Ahmed's books on the bookshelves. The police accused the family of removing books from the shelves. Hawa repeatedly pleaded with the police to see her son but had no success in this.

Even after Ahmed's death, requests by Helen Suzman, then the lone Progressive

Party MP, and others to see detainees including Mohammed, Ahmed's brother, continued to be denied.

Tuesday 26 October 1971
During the inquest that followed, this statement was made: "Detective Officer Van Rensburg, Lieutenant Ras and Warrant Officer Liebenberg had visited the Timol residence on Tuesday, 26 October 1971 at 13:30. The following conversation then took place between Ahmed's crying mother Hawa, and Van Rensburg:
Hawa: "I want to see my son."
Van Rensburg: "You can't see him."
Hawa: "Why did you arrest him?"
Van Rensburg: "He was naughty."
Hawa: "My son was never naughty. I have never given him a hiding."
Van Rensburg: "Listen, old lady, a child must get a hiding. If you had at that stage given him a hiding, you would not be crying now."
The reason for the visit was to find a book belonging to Ahmed that had a list of names inside it. On questioning the police about the whereabouts of Ahmed, Hawa remarked to one of them, "Go home and speak to your wife and find out what is it like bringing up a child and not knowing the whereabouts of your child." Hawa continued, "If there was a zip in front of my body, you could unzip me and see how I am aching internally".

Wednesday 27 October 1971
Early that morning, Security Police searched all the dustbins in the flats. They climbed up on the roof of the flats. The landlord of the building was asked to open the storeroom after the *Zohar* (midday prayers). The domestic cleaners from all the flats were interrogated. They were intimidated and forced to state that Ahmed was asking them to distribute papers in the townships.

Then came the shock. After *Magrib* (sunset prayers) while Haji Timol was still in the mosque, Security Police once again visited the family. In a statement made to the TRC investigator, Hawa stated, "One of them pushed me into a seat and then proceeded to tell me that my son Ahmed had tried to escape by jumping from the 10th floor at John Vorster Square police station. I was told to tell my husband that Ahmed's body was at the Government Mortuary in Hillbrow, Johannesburg. I could not believe what was being said and in my confusion I tried to argue with them saying that this was not true." Hawa continued, "I even remember taking them to the flat window, and telling them how difficult it must have been to have jumped from the window at John Vorster Square police station." The policemen shrugged Hawa off by saying that they could not control her son.

Ahmed was dead! What happened to him?

The Roodepoort Indian High School incident book recorded on 28/10/1971: "The morning papers reported that Mr A Timol died yesterday, whilst still in police custody."

This clinical statement contains no hint of grief – no memorial service was held by the school. Ahmed died a troublemaker in their books, just as he had lived in those same "incident" books.

The school incident book recorded on 16/11/1971: "Informed Mr DNJ van Vuuren, in writing, that when I arrived at school on Thursday, 28-10-71, in three different places, 'Our Hero is Dead' had been painted. I had the cleaners remove the paint work."

Not only did the school not mark his murder but the spontaneous grief of the students, expressed through graffiti, was removed and was treated as yet another inconvenient "incident".

INTERROGATION OF HASSEN JOOMA

Hassen Jooma's chilling personal testimony, told for the first time in this book, more clearly than any other experience points most directly to what must have happened to Ahmed Timol in his lonely and brief stay at John Vorster Square. This provides further evidence and confirms Salim Essop's chilling record of torture in detention.

As they entered the lift at John Vorster Square on Saturday afternoon, 23 October 1971, one of the policemen almost lifted Hassen up and angrily said, "*Jou koelie kommunist* (You coolie communist)." Hassen was shocked at this. They told him that they knew everything about him. He was asked to write everything about his life at college, his affiliation to the National Union of South African Students (Nusas) as a student and his position and his supposed religious life since he could remember.

Entering the main building Hassen met Lieutenant Smit who was a small-built man. He was taken to a room where he found tufts of hair and blood on the floor. A bucket and broom were given to him and he was told, "*Maak skoon* (Clean it up)." The policeman then told Hassen that the same fate awaited him. Hassen was still in the dark about the circumstances around Ahmed's arrest. Hassen recalled Ahmed's long hair and realised that it was Ahmed's hair and blood he had seen. Hassen was told that he was not to mention to anybody what he had seen and that he had better tell the police what they wanted to know or he, too, would be dealt with in similar fashion. This was, he realised, what had happened. The police wanted to know to what extent he was involved in communist activities. Lieutenant-Colonel Johan Coetzee mentioned that Ahmed had gone to Mecca to disguise his communist leanings and on his return to South Africa he was to set up a communist-inclined paper called *Al Yusuf*.

Hassen was asked why he was fasting (the true answer was obvious – it was the Muslim holy month of Ramadan). Was it because of the Reverend Bernard Wrankmore, who was fasting at the Muslim shrine of Sheikh Yusuf on Signal Hill in Cape Town in protest against the Vorster government's failure to set up a proper inquiry into the death in detention of Imam Haron?

Elaborate join-the-dots conspiracies played themselves out in the minds of the police interrogators. Hassen was asked if he sympathised with Wrankmore. Hassen responded that, because it was the month of Ramadan, it was compulsory for him to fast as a practising Muslim and his fasting was no more sinister than that. A circle was drawn on the floor of the detention room and Hassen was told to stand inside it. He was warned that he would be severely dealt with if he moved outside the circle.

This was on Saturday afternoon and Hassen still had his watch on. As *Iftaar* (fast-breaking time) arrived he asked the police officer in whose care he was placed, while the other two went out for supper, if he could break his fast with a sweet that he had in his pocket. The policeman consented, reiterating however that he should not move out of the circle. When the officer left him alone Hassen deliberately left the circle as an act of inconsequential but psychologically vital defiance. He walked to the room next door where he was shocked to see what was obviously a torture machine. It looked like a grader used in renovation of roads.

Hassen returned to his designated circle and remained there throughout Saturday evening and for the whole of Sunday and into Monday morning. At approximately 7 am a policeman entered and told Hassen that he was now going to be taken to the police cells. The Security Branch members then took turns in sessions of approximately two hours without interruption to barrage Hassen about his dealings with Ahmed and about his own political views. Hassen had not eaten or slept for over 52 hours. This was the least of his problems as he was more concerned about the safety of his family.

Hassen's wife Fawzia went to the Compol building in Pretoria every day to enquire about Hassen. She would then drive to Johannesburg's John Vorster Square. She had taken food for him on a regular basis but Hassen had never received this. On a day soon after Hassen's arrest, Fawzia had taken his medication and had given it to a police officer by the name of Liebenberg. He took the tablets to Hassen and mentioned that his wife was concerned about him. Hassen at the time was suffering from a constricted bladder in addition to palpitations. He was taking about four tablets a day.

On the Tuesday after Ahmed's Friday arrest, at approximately 3 pm, Hassen was once again brought from his cell and interrogated on the 10th floor of John Vorster Square. One of the interrogators was supposedly a Mr Smith, the other officer was short in stature. As they were interrogating Hassen, he heard a pained and low-sounding gasping or sighing sound ("Aaaaaahhhhhh") from the room next door. Hassen's suspicions were now confirmed that it was Ahmed who was in the next room.

Hassen realised that it would be in Ahmed's interest to trip over himself and fake a faint, which he did. The Security Branch members came charging from the other room and enquired from Hassen what was wrong. One of the interrogators was a hefty policeman by the name of Ferreira. Hassen was trying hard to catch snatches of what was going on in Ahmed's room. There was a lot of activity and people were running around.

Hassen was placed on a blanket and he feigned sleep in the detention room. He was later whisked away to his cell and was not further interrogated that morning. He was still fasting and breaking it with two slices of brown bread and two boiled eggs. One boiled egg and a slice of bread with margarine he ate at the time of *iftaar* (time to break fast) and another boiled egg with two slices of bread at *sehri* (pre-dawn breakfast in Ramadan). Hassen asked for additional water that he used for ablution as required by Islamic practice prior to engaging in each of the five prayers.

Fawzia was teaching at the time and was ostracised by her friends at school. She learned for herself the age-old lesson, that in times of difficulty true friends are hard to find. Hassen's friend and ex-teacher Barry Veloo, as well as Banoo Goolab and Mariben Sita, were the only visitors the Jooma family had during his incarceration. Barry Veloo did not write an exam paper on the Monday as he was supportive of Fawzia and disturbed beyond any possibility of concentration by Hassen's situation.

One morning the two usual interrogators, namely Smit and Liebenberg, took Hassen to the toilet where current copies of the *Rand Daily Mail* were neatly placed, with conspicuous reports of Salim Essop's hospitilisation. Hassen believed that this was an attempt to gauge his reaction to the news and thus verify his familiarity with Salim Essop and the resistance network. Hassen simply pretended that he had not seen the headlines on those copies of the *Rand Daily Mail*.

Hassen was curious to know what had happened to Ahmed. The Security Branch now questioned him on Islam's position concerning suicide. Hassen told them that suicide was unacceptable in Islam and it was a sin. It may have been this response that caused the eventual explanation of Ahmed's death to be attributed (with equal implausibility) to communism rather than to Islam.

This was the first time that suicide was mentioned to Hassen. However, while performing his prayers, Hassen's sixth sense had told him that Ahmed was no longer alive. The police told Hassen that they had obtained Ahmed's diary and that in it he had mentioned his meetings with Hassen. Ahmed was very meticulous and it was highly unlikely that he would have a diary where he would keep notes of his political meetings.

Prior to Hassen's release after three weeks in solitary confinement, Johan Coetzee reminded Hassen that he had not mentioned anything of substance to the police and that he would still be under police surveillance. Coetzee also warned Hassen that in the course of one year if Hassen took any legal steps against the police he would be in serious trouble. He was also warned not to make any statements to the press.

Liebenberg and Smit then drove Hassen to his home in Pretoria. Hassen was kept in the car and warned to refrain from any political activity in the light of the untimely death of his friend, Ahmed. Liebenberg first approached Fawzia and told her that she would not be seeing her husband for a very, very long time. Without any immediate reaction Fawzia accepted his statement. Five minutes later, Hassen came knocking on the door. This showed the gratuitous cruelty of all police, especially the Security Branch members, at the time. They played psychological games.

The community distanced themselves from Hassen, and his family also noticed that he was under police surveillance when he went to mosque in the early hours of the morning or attending memorial services. The couple soon realised that their passports would be confiscated. They therefore decided to perform Hajj in December 1971.

Hassen had mentioned in his statement during detention that he had only known Ahmed as a fellow student and on a social level. He was constantly badgered by the Security Branch to write "anything". Hassen, being a teacher of English, artfully waffled in all his writings much to the exasperation of Johan Coetzee, who complained about the lack of syntax in Hassen's writing.

Senior members of the Security Branch visited Hassen intermittently in his cell. One of them was Colonel Greyling who started his conversation by asking Hassen whether he was the one who had drawn a beautiful woman on the walls of the cell. Hassen said that he believed it was a previous inmate. He later learnt that the artist was Peter Magubane – the famous photographer. On that occasion Hassen told Colonel Greyling that he felt like Prophet Joseph because he was being imprisoned for something he had not done.

Indres Moodley was at the Mayville police station and was asked if he knew Ahmed Timol. Indres recalls, "I was kept in solitary confinement and nothing really happened. I heard the policemen speaking in Afrikaans saying that they didn't have anything on me. I knew that Ahmed was not going to reveal anything, and this put me at ease. They were not aware that I could understand Afrikaans. I was asked to write a statement about myself and my link with Ahmed. I wrote out a statement and they were not happy with the contents of the statement."

This upset the policemen and they now became violent. Indres says, "I was beaten and shaken up. They made me stand with the bricks in my hands raised over my head. I had to stand against the wall with my knees bent. There were the good cops and bad cops and I was eventually led to my cell. The police then suddenly stopped with the physical treatment and I was asked to rewrite my statement."

Approximately a month after his arrest Indres was put into a car with leg-irons and one hand was handcuffed to the lever above the window. Indres recalls: "We drove to another police station and another Indian was placed in the back seat of the car with me. He also had leg-irons, one hand was also handcuffed to the lever above the window and the other handcuffed with me. We were told that we were on our way to John Vorster Square police station. As we stopped at a petrol garage and the policemen disembarked from the car this Indian person told me that he was Ahmed's brother and that Ahmed had died. I immediately dismissed him and told him not to speak to me. I was very suspicious and did not trust him. We arrived at John Vorster Square during the early hours of the morning and I was separated from this Indian who was supposed to be Ahmed's brother." Mohammed Timol confirms the story but states that he and Indres were only in the car from Durban to Maritzburg and not to Johannesburg.

Indres was only interrogated on a few occasions and was kept in solitary confinement. The police continued putting Indres's wife through psychological torture. "They kept on telling her that I was dead. My wife's doctor, Dr de Villiers, wrote a letter to the minister of police informing him that if anything happened to my wife or the baby he would hold the minister responsible. My wife was then allowed to come and visit me in Johannesburg.

"I was visibly shaken, had lost a lot of weight and was unshaven. I had at this stage not heard any news about Ahmed's death besides a 'stranger' telling me in the car when we were brought from Durban that he was dead." Indres kept on asking the police if he was to be charged or released. The police kept on making promises that they were to charge or release Indres on a specific date, only for the time to lapse without any developments taking place.

Sleep deprivation was a common method of torture applied to detainees who were forced to stand for long durations and repeatedly asked to make statements. If the security police were unhappy with the statements made, the papers were thrown in the bins and the detainees were asked to rewrite their statements. A common strategy applied by the police was "to play one detainee against the other". This would implicate a detainee and create great concern and distrust in the mind of the other detainee. What is evident up to this day is that the manipulative policemen that manufactured evidence against detainees succeeded in creating mistrust and animosity amongst them. The suffering and torture in detention still affects the health and well-being of those who were detained, up to this day.

SALIM ESSOP

Arriving at John Vorster Square from Newlands police station early on Saturday morning, Salim was taken to the basement where there was a separate entrance to the Security Branch offices with those two special lifts that ran from the basement to the ninth and 10th floors. Salim was taken to the 10th floor and into a long room that had a vault.

The lines of questioning that had commenced at the Newlands police station continued at John Vorster Square. The questions were asked at different stages. The line was as follows: What kind of work did you and Ahmed do? Who did you work with? What contacts had you made? Did you make contact with overseas? Or was it Ahmed? Names of people in the organisation? Did you set up groups? Are you a communist? Do you believe in communism? Generally, what activities were you involved in? What are your beliefs? These are the questions Salim was asked during different stages of his interrogation.

Salim spent his detention period in the office part of the room on the 10th floor. This room was always guarded. "At most times there were a minimum of two security officers present. At times there were even three to four," he recalls. Salim had the impression that the interrogators were professionally trained to engage in torture in different ways and at different stages. Initially the torture was not that painful, but then the pain became heavier and stronger as they continued till you could not bear the pain any longer. "This is difficult to talk about. They would apply different torture methods at their discretion depending how you would respond," he says.

"The one method was when I was forced to stand in the centre of the vault with my legs slightly apart. There were two security officers standing on either side of me. They wore specific shoes and continually kicked at my thighs. As time went on, the kicking continued. As they got tired their colleagues replaced them and continued with the kicking. My legs were now becoming stiffer and I was forced to stand in this position for hours on end. As my legs became stiffer, the mere touching of my legs would force me to literally scream with pain. There comes a time when you cannot bend your knees as your legs are too stiff. They would then come and push you down. As I would fall down, they would ask me to rise. At this point your body cannot come up again and they then pull you up again like a log. Once I was brought to stand again the same procedure would start all over again." Salim is convinced that these security officers were torture specialists who had conducted these methods of torture many times before. "The idea is to arouse maximum pain to your body. Mentally you are going through something that you are not ready for. Your body and mind start associating with this pain. One way of dealing with it is to scream," he says.

It was while Salim was held in this room that he thinks that he saw Ahmed. Salim says, "I had endured systematic torture for approximately four to five days. At one moment the vault door was open. I was short-sighted and my glasses were removed when I was tortured. I could see relatively clearly through the vault door and the door of the room when I saw a figure being moved along by two security officers. I realised that it was Ahmed. The walk was similar to Ahmed and I noticed that he was not walking normally. He had a black hood over his head and appeared to be in a lot of pain. This happened in a few seconds. Looking at Ahmed's appearance and condition, they must have been taking him to the toilet. I remember the bathroom and toilet towards the end of the floor and I was also taken there. I washed the blood off my face, body and clothes there. At times there was a bucket brought in the vault for me to urinate in.

"As I had a glimpse of Ahmed I was relatively alert in my thinking and wondering how to communicate with Ahmed. I wanted to wave to him to confirm that it was Ahmed. Was he alive? What was happening to him? Were we to be brought together? What was the next stage?"

Salim and many other political detainees suffered electric shocks. Salim was dragged onto a chair and electric shocks were applied to his body. Salim says, "You are not in control of your body movements. They increase and decrease the voltage levels and you are screaming away in excruciating pain at the slightest touch of your body. Your mind and body no longer associate with each other and you feel as if your mind is floating. While the shock treatment is applied to you, heavy-handed slaps are felt on your face. At this point you simply collapse."

This is what happened to Salim, and he continued collapsing on various occasions. He would become unconscious and water would be passed over him. Regaining consciousness, the procedure would continue. Salim recalls, "Lying on the ground and regaining consciousness, I felt that I was wet. I saw these cops standing around me with their penises exposed to me. They had urinated on me and were having a good laugh. I could see that they were enjoying themselves." Salim was emotionally overcome as he related this.

Another common method of torture applied to detainees was when a plastic bag would be put over your head and tied with a rope around your neck. As you breathed and the oxygen became less, you would start to suffocate. "You would be gasping to breathe. You find it difficult breathing and they then pull the bag off your head. At this point you think that you are dead."

Salim was doing underground work but was not prepared for this torture. "Ahmed and I knew the dangers involved in doing underground work. We expected to be tortured, but did not know how to prepare for this. I did not have knowledge of the different types of torture they were using. They would dip your head in a bucket of water. I heard of people dying in detention. I now know that they were killed. I had no concept of time. There was a fluorescent light in the room where I was detained."

Salim was a third-year medical student and, having some medical knowledge, was at this stage working out if he was alive or dead.

"At one stage I was taken to the stairwell on the 10th floor, close to the room where I was held. Two police officers held me first by my body and then by my legs and put me down. They then threatened to drop me if I was not forthcoming with the information they were looking for. At this stage, after going through so much pain and torture, I felt it was better if they dropped me and relieved me of the pain I was going through. You are literally surviving on fleeting consciousness and trying to make sense of your life."

All the time Salim's mind was drifting as he was looking down, his glasses had been removed which obscured his vision. "I was thinking of family, friends, dear ones, praying and making peace that this is now the final moment," said Salim years later in reliving the horror on the spot when we made a special visit to the scene.

Salim recalls, "Human endurance comes to an end. If I had had an opportunity to take my own life, maybe I would have been driven to this. The pain and torture were severe. An opportunity had never arisen for me to take my own life." If Salim had, would this have been dishonourable? Certainly not.

جرجرجر

The person who breaks under interrogation and prefers to die rather than to betray others can be said to show superior courage and dedication to the cause. In the same spirit, Nelson Mandela, facing the possible imposition of the death penalty at the Rivonia trial, said from the dock that he hoped to live for freedom but was prepared to die for it if need be.

The importance of the question of suicide in Ahmed Timol's own death is not the difference between honour and dishonour in his death. The importance is rather one of the moral, legal and political accountability of the apartheid state. The excuse of suicide is an attempt to suggest that the state was not at fault for his death, whereas in fact the state was at fault. It is not Ahmed or any other detainee who is on trial over the suicide question (Ruth First also contemplated suicide during her detention and was years later murdered by the apartheid state). It is the apartheid state that is on trial when we deny the allegation of suicide.

The police version of events as stated during the inquest was as follows: "Salim Essop was in good health with no apparent injuries on his face and body when the South African Police arrested him on the night of 22nd October 1971. At 11 pm on 22 October 1971, Colonel Greyling, commanding officer of the Security Police in

Johannesburg, took over the detainee from the SAP and detained him under Section 6 of the Terrorism Act No. 83 of 1963 for the purpose of interrogation. At that stage Salim was normal and without any visible signs of physical injury. From the time of his arrest on 22 October 1971 and the morning of 26 October 1971, Salim was interrogated by Colonel Greyling and various members of the Security Police, including a Major Fourie, who interrogated Salim on Saturday 23 October 1971.

Salim was removed on a stretcher and taken to the Johannesburg General Hospital on Tuesday 26 October 1971. According to medical staff, he had been severely assaulted, and was suffering from clinical hysteria. Moved later the same day to Pretoria's HF Verwoerd Hospital, he was constantly guarded by police. It was a miracle that Salim survived.

If this is what happened to Salim then what was happening to Ahmed? This is the police version, contrary to all other experiences of political detainees. The details are as follows:

SATURDAY 23 OCTOBER 1971 (POLICE VERSION)

Ahmed was brought to John Vorster Square police station at approximately 3 am. Lieutenant Van Wyk met Captain Dirker and Sergeant Kleyns with Timol in a room. Sergeant Kleyns guarded Timol, while Lieutenant Van Wyk and Captain Dirker went through the material found in Timol's possession. Although Lieutenant Van Wyk did not thoroughly inspect Timol, he did not visibly notice any injuries on his face, hands, etc.

Sergeant Kleyns and Captain Dirker then took Timol to the Security Branch offices of John Vorster Square police station. Sergeant Kleyns guarded Timol until 5.30 am. Lieutenant-Colonel Van Wyk and Captain Dirker then questioned Timol.

At 6 am Captain Johannes Zacharia van Niekerk and Captain JH Gloy interrogated Timol. The names Martin, Henry and Quentin were mentioned and Timol informed them that Quentin was a coloured man and was only a social friend.

At 3 pm Lieutenant-Colonel Petrus van Wyk arrived at John Vorster Square police station. While Sergeant Kleyns looked after "the Indian", Lieutenant-Colonel Van Wyk and Captain Dirker went through all the documents that were found in Timol's possession. According to the information found, it was clear to Lieutenant Colonel Van Wyk that Timol was a communist and that he had contact with the Central Committee of the Communist Party in London.

Detective Sergeant Frederick Robert Bouwer and Sergeant Louw had received instructions from the station commander (at 3 pm) that they were to report to Captain Gloy and Van Niekerk at 6 pm, to perform certain duties.

At 6 pm Sergeant Bouwer and Sergeant Louw reported for duty at Room 1026 and met Captain Gloy and Captain Van Niekerk who informed them they were to return at 7 pm. They returned at 7 pm and met Captain Gloy, Van Niekerk and "the Indian", Timol, and were told that Timol would be spending the night in the room. Bouwer and Louw were shown a blanket and mattress and told that Timol could use this if he wanted to. They were to guard Timol till the following morning.

SUNDAY 24 OCTOBER 1971 (POLICE VERSION)
Captain Gloy and Captain Johannes Zacharia van Niekerk interrogated Timol from 6 am to 8 pm and Bouwer and Louw guarded Timol for the evening from 8 pm.

MONDAY 25 OCTOBER 1971 (POLICE VERSION)
Bouwer and Louw then handed Timol over to Lieutenant-Colonel Van Wyk and Captain Bean at 8.30 am.

From 8.30 am to 7.30 pm Lieutenant-Colonel van Wyk and Captain Bean interrogated Timol. Timol was allowed to sit and stand as he felt. Food, coffee and cool drinks were regularly offered to him. During both occasions, namely 25 and 26 October 1971, Timol was held in Room 1026 under the observation of Sergeant Bouwer and Sergeant Louw. Captain Bean observed that on both occasions Timol appeared fit and healthy. Timol had no visible injuries.

Bouwer and Louw guarded Timol for the evening from 7.30 pm.

TUESDAY 26 OCTOBER 1971 (POLICE VERSION)
Bouwer and Louw handed Timol over to Lieutenant-Colonel Van Wyk and Captain Bean at 8 am. Lieutenant-Colonel Van Wyk and Captain Bean interrogated Timol from 8.30 am to 7.30 pm.

Bouwer and Louw guarded Timol for the evening from 8 pm.

In statements made during the inquest by all the policemen who were responsible for the arrest, detention and interrogation of Ahmed, all stated that Ahmed had no marks or bruises on his body. They also mention that at no stage was Ahmed ever threatened or assaulted.

WEDNESDAY 27 OCTOBER 1971 (POLICE VERSION)
Bouwer and Louw handed Timol over to Lieutenant Colonel Van Wyk and Captain Bean at 8 am.

From 8 am to 3.30 pm Captain Gloy and Van Niekerk interrogated Timol. Timol was free of any visible injuries or wounds. Timol's behavior was friendly and yet not open. Timol was reluctant to disclose information on Quentin, Henry and Martin. He spoke freely about the documents found in his possession and that he was a member of the Communist Party. He admitted having contact with the Central Committee of the Communist Party in London and in this friendly atmosphere disclosed this information in his own handwriting. Timol regularly spoke out about his concern that he would easily obtain at least a 20-year jail sentence.

At 3.30 pm Sergeant J Rodrigues entered room 1026 and brought coffee for Captain Gloy, Captain Van Niekerk and Timol. Timol was still sitting on the one side of the table making notes about his participation with the Communist Party. Rodrigues did not question Timol and met Timol for the first time.

At 3.45 pm a member of the Security Branch entered the office and informed the other policemen that he had identified the other "white" names that were mentioned in the investigation. The name of Quentin Jacobsen was mentioned.

Timol was visibly shocked and looked nervous. Captain Gloy then instructed Rodrigues that he was to stay with Timol while they did additional research on the names of the "whites" that were mentioned.

At 3.48 pm Captain Gloy and Captain Van Niekerk left the room and Rodrigues and Timol remained behind. Rodrigues sat on chair marked A and Timol sat opposite him – B. Timol asked to go to the toilet and stood up with Rodrigues at the same time. Rodrigues moved to his left and bumped into chair marked C (see last page of photo section). Timol rushed to the window, opened it and dived out. Rodrigues could not stop Timol.

At 4 pm Warrant Officer SAO Gabriel Johannes Deysel of the Security Branch based at John Vorster Square police station was on duty and busy walking in the corridor on the 10th floor, when he heard someone screaming that Ahmed Timol, who was questioned by the Security Police, had jumped out of the window, on the side of Commissioner Street. Deysel immediately grabbed two blankets and ran to the lift where he met Colonel Greyling.

Deysel and Greyling found Ahmed lying on his stomach, his right hand under his body and his left hand slightly away from his body. His right leg was slightly bent inwards and his left leg was straight. His legs were slightly apart and his right foot was without a shoe. His mouth was facing the shrubs and the branches from the shrub were on the right side of his chest and shoulders. There were also branches lying under his chest and shoulders.

Upon Deysel and Greyling's arrival, they both checked for a pulse. Deysel said he felt a pulse and Greyling ran to look for a surgeon. At this stage, Deysel did not see any blood. Deysel put the blanket on Timol's left side and attempted to roll him in the blanket. He failed at the first attempt as the body slipped from his hand. He then turned the body around and realised that blood was dripping from his face. Deysel felt that they had to take Timol to a surgeon and with the assistance of his colleagues they took Timol inside the building. He was lying on his back on the blanket.

As they entered the reception area, Deysel checked for a pulse and noticed that Timol was not breathing and that he was dead. Deysel reported to Greyling that Timol was dead and Greyling confirmed this. Timol's body was then taken to the ninth floor, where the District Surgeon examined the body, and then it was taken to the mortuary.

The district surgeon, Vernon Denis Kemp, stated at the inquest: "On 27 October 1971 at approximately 3.55 pm I received a report that I had to report to John Vorster Square police station. Upon my arrival at 4.05 pm I proceeded to the Security Branch offices on the ninth floor where a body of an Indian man was shown to me. After examining the body I confirmed that he was dead. He had just died."

Even the medical practitioner joined in the racialised designation of the Security Branch officers; Ahmed was, for Dr Kemp, "an Indian man."

8

RECKONINGS

"Ahmed had not enough time to polish his skills as a propagandist, in the writing of propaganda material," Essop Pahad sums up admiringly as well as unsentimentally. "The idea was for Ahmed to also do underground writing in South Africa and to write for the *African Communist*. Due to Ahmed's murder, it was not possible to assess, in the short time he was active as an underground operative, how far he had developed his political and propagandistic writing skills. However, his political acumen, insights, courage and commitment were outstanding."

As shock over the death of detainee Ahmed Timol swept the country his father went to John Vorster Square on Thursday 28 October to make arrangements for the funeral. There he met the chief of Johannesburg's Security Police, Colonel Greyling, who offered him sympathy ... and, with gauche insensitivity, a sweet. Even if he had wanted to, Haji Timol could not accept the sweet because of the Ramadan fast.

Ahmed's brother, Mohammed, who was in detention, was not allowed to attend Ahmed's funeral. Prime Minister John Vorster turned down a request that was made on behalf of the Timol family by Marais Steyn, United Party MP for Yeoville. Then Fatima Meer, Natal University sociologist, together with Archbishop Denis Hurley made a second request. Vorster regretted that he could not grant the request.

On Friday 29 October, Haji Timol went to the Hillbrow Mortuary and identified the body of his son, Ahmed, "Body 399/171" at approximately 7.45 am. Senior government pathologist Dr Nicholas Jacobus Scheepers conducted the post-mortem and Dr Jonathan Gluckman represented the Timol family. At approximately 10.45 am the body was driven by Mohammed Khan to Newtown Mosque in Johannesburg for *ghusal*, to be washed and prepared for burial according to Muslim rites.

Salim Gabba adds, "We found out that *ghusal* was to be given at the Newtown Mosque. I remember Yusuf 'Tara' Seedat holding Ahmed's head. They said that Ahmed had died from a fall. It was clear that his neck was broken as his head was just falling back. I saw clearly that Ahmed's fingernails were taken out and his elbows were burnt."

After the Friday prayers were performed at Newtown Mosque, Ahmed's body was placed in a coffin and driven by Mohammed Khan in the Muslim hearse to the Timol flat.

At the Roodepoort Mosque, the owner of AG Ally, who was a close friend of Haji Timol, stood up and requested that the local businessmen close their shops as a tribute to Ahmed.

In the Timol flat women read from the Quran and prayed around Ahmed's coffin. Family and friends insisted that Hawa not see Ahmed's body. They could not stop her. It was her son.

The surrounding balconies on Mare Street were full of people. The funeral was attended by several thousand Muslims from all parts of the Transvaal. Many schoolchildren, including Ahmed's pupils from the Roodepoort Indian High School, were present. Several white university students also mingled with the crowd. Residents of Roodepoort say it was one of the biggest funerals ever seen on the West Rand. Images of the procession survive in the newspapers of the time. The entire community was convulsed by Ahmed's fate.

Ahmed's face was shown to the public before leaving for the cemetery near Main Reef Road.

Faruq Varachia says, "Ahmed's death hit me like a lightning bolt. I never felt anything like that before. I was overcome with some real anger. Since I could do little against the cruel regime at that moment we felt that somehow we had to show our anger, our sorrow and our loss to the rest of the world. While making Ahmed's funeral arrangements I clearly remember how a few of us gathered around and spontaneously decided that we are going to carry Ahmed's body from his home, through the main streets of Roodepoort right through the 'white' part of town. This is the only way we could show the world what their system had done to Ahmed. It was also decided at that moment to open Ahmed's janaazah (coffin) and show to the world how they had tortured and disfigured him."

Stern-faced or crying, the community had filed past the bier for a last glimpse of Ahmed Timol, clad in his white funeral *kaffan* (burial shroud) with his face exposed. The coffin was taken by hearse to the cemetery, about three kilometres away. Men, schoolchildren and students followed the hearse on foot. Traffic police escorted the procession and many shops along the route stopped trading as the procession passed. The mourners passed the police station and chain stores in the centre of Roodepoort. The police were taken by surprise at the large turnout of mourners. Roodepoort was brought to a standstill. All Indian businesses in Roodepoort closed as a mark of respect.

Khudeja Choonara (now Pochee) recalls, "Even though I was only eight years old at the time of Ahmed's death, I remember it in all its detail, from the time his body was lifted from the house that he laid in for the last time, to the long trail of schoolchildren behind the hearse walking towards the cemetery, crying at the loss of a great teacher and mentor.

"My earliest memory of Ahmed Timol is one of a tall, young man with jet-black hair, soft spoken and articulate in his speech. Ahmed, whom we called Uncle Ahmed, always had kind words to say to us every time he passed us by. He always laughed and joked and made us feel special. I have memories of a lovely blue tea set that he placed on my lap one Eid morning. Just before being detained he had promised my brother and I that he would be taking us to the zoo that weekend. Fate would have it another way and we never got the opportunity to share that day with him.

"We salute you, Ahmed Timol," Khudeja continues, "you were not only a brave soldier fighting for your country, but you were my neighbour as well as my friend. If you were alive today we know that you would have been playing a role in the reconstruction of our country and you would have done a good job of it too. You taught us what courage in the face of adversity was, and how to stand up to your enemies even if death was standing at your door. You have given up your life so that we today could reap the fruits of freedom."

There was a heavy police presence on the day of the funeral. Family members reported that the police were also present at the cemetery and were even taking photographs of Ahmed's body as it was lowered into the grave. The funeral was so big that as the body arrived at the *qabrastaan* (cemetery), people were still at the flat. It was practically impossible to control the crowds, and loudspeakers were not easily available at that time. The *janaazah* (funeral prayers) were performed on the grass outside the cemetery.

The procession stopped on open ground outside the cemetery for a short prayer. Roodepoort Imam Molvi Osman Poothawala was scheduled to lead the prayer. However, Ahmed's father, Haji Timol, led the congregation in the final prayer before Ahmed was laid to rest.

The *Saturday Star*, dated 30 October 1971, reported the funeral as a mere inconvenience to the whites of Roodepoort: "Impatient motorists leaned on their hooters as a seemingly endless stream of white-capped Indians held up traffic for more than a dozen blocks at a time in Roodepoort. Schoolgirls pressing handkerchiefs to their faces, T-shirted whites engaged in serious talk with immaculately dressed Muslims – they all formed part of the 1 500 mourners following the hearse of Ahmed Timol. After a 3km trek, the green velvet bier with its golden tassels was lifted from the hearse outside the Roodepoort Muslim cemetery. Shoulder-high, hand by hand, it was passed through the crowd. When the congregation broke into mass prayer, loud sobbing rose from the ranks of children whom Mr Timol had taught up to last week." The *Star* article vividly brings out the stark divide between the grief of those who knew Ahmed and the historically privileged who resented that grief for clogging the roads.

The chant of "Allah is great and Muhammad is his Prophet" was heard as

Ahmed Timol's body was laid to rest.

Hamid "Timer" Vally recalls that it was a hot cloudless summer's afternoon when they carried Ahmed's bier from the flat. Timer recalls witnessing a single cloud popping over in the cemetery and following the procession. They proceeded to the *qabrastaan* and the necessary funeral rituals were carried out, the final prayers were performed and then there was a heavy thundershower. Timer was convinced that Almighty Allah had accepted Ahmed as a *shayeed* (martyr) freedom fighter for the oppressed people of this country. "The rain was a blessing as it suddenly came upon us from nowhere and Allah had accepted Ahmed as a martyr. About 1 km away from the *qabrastaan* it was bone dry. Allah had recognised Ahmed's sacrifice and the oppressive government of the day was responsible for taking Ahmed's life. Ahmed deserves to be in Paradise."

AFTERMATH

During the month of Ramadan, Haji Timol sat in *ittikaaf* (the state of seclusion during the last 10 days of Ramadan). The torment of the Security Police would still not cease. They continued to visit Hawa and to pester her and her family. Not satisfied after killing Ahmed, the Security Branch members now wanted to enlist his brother, Mohammed, to work for them.

Aysha would walk from the flat to the mosque followed by the Security Branch members in their car. She refused to sit in the car with them. She would shout out to Haji Timol to come out, as the police attempted to get him to sign papers agreeing to working with the police. Haji Timol responded by saying that he would think about it but obviously they could never submit to their remaining son working for an oppressive system that had already murdered their other son. The police showed utter contempt towards the religion of Islam and the holy month of Ramadan. Eventually, on 14 March, police released Ahmed's younger brother Mohammed.

Yunus Moola (Ahmed's cousin) recalls that as the month of Ramadan came to an end, there was a knock on their door late one evening. "My parents were afraid and hesitant to open the door as they suspected that it was the Security Police. This was the fear and anxiety that the police had caused in the community." Yunus finally opened the door, and it was someone from the community who had come to announce that the moon had been sighted and that it was Eid.

"After Ahmed's funeral, police questioned everyone associated with him," says Timer. "This was a frightening experience and it was the reality of the time. It was difficult to assess how many informers there were in the community." Timer is left with one abiding thought: those responsible for informing on Ahmed, and subsequently for his death, are yet to meet their Creator and account for their deeds. "Ahmed was a good human being who had given his life for humanity. He dedicated his life to a humanitarian cause. His death had a profound impact on my life."

Ebrahim and Choti Choonara, neighbours of the Timol family, narrate that relatives of the Timol family from the rural areas of the Eastern Transvaal would come to the flat to sympathise and provide support to the family. They would break their fasts in the Choonara flat. Ebrahim remembers one of the family members mentioning how helpful the Choonaras were to the Timol family. All the neighbours opened their doors to the Timol family.

The day after Ahmed's funeral, Ebrahim remembers a heavy storm in Roodepoort. The downpour was so heavy that the ceilings caved in at their flat. There were residents who questioned Ahmed's activities and some wanted to know what Ahmed had achieved. How was his death going to assist them? This was unfortunately the attitude of some of the residents of Roodepoort. Choti reminded them that Ahmed could have left the country, but he was prepared to sacrifice his life for the oppressed people of this country and in the long term they would reap the benefits of Ahmed's ultimate sacrifice. Ebrahim and Choti's hearts would cry out to Hawa and the family. What did she as a mother go through? Allah must grant Ahmed paradise and Ebrahim pondered as to what torture Ahmed had to endure before his death.

The Security Branch continued to harass the Timol family. They would visit the flat and search all the dustbins. They would continue to question Hawa and would work on her nerves by asking the silliest of questions. They showed no remorse or sympathy towards the family. Hawa would call upon Choti as a means of support. Rumours would spread that the police were going to be raiding. The family and the community were literally terrorised. It was well known that there were informers in the community.

Ebrahim Choonara recalls, "At a prayer service that was held at the flat after the funeral, people sympathised and showed compassion towards the Timol family. Ahmed was a martyr and had given his life for the betterment of his people."

Ebrahim once mentioned to a white person that the white community of South Africa must be thankful to Comrade Mandela for forgiving them for what they had done. After hearing about Ahmed's death, Ebrahim mentions that if he had obtained a machine-gun, he would have killed any white person he saw.

Beyond terrorised Roodepoort, visible support for the Timol family was overwhelming with the majority of South Africans – irrespective of their race, denomination or political affiliation – demanding a public enquiry. On 28 October 1971 about 200 students at the Transvaal College of Education for Indians in Fordsburg held an hour-long silent sit-in before noon to mourn the death of Ahmed Timol. Students staged a spontaneous walkout of lectures shortly after 10 am. At about 11 am 200 of the 250 students at the college, most wearing black armbands, sat down in the grounds of the college.

Pupils at the Nirvana High School in Lenasia staged a protest sit-in over the death. Ahmed had taught many of them at the Roodepoort Indian High School before they moved to Nirvana School in Lenasia. Ahmed was regarded as a very intelligent man and a popular teacher.

Calls were made by students and academic movements for a commission of inquiry at students' mass meetings at the Johannesburg College of Education and at the University of the Witwatersrand Medical School. A Presbyterian minister, the Reverend Ian Thompson, told the meeting that no reasonable person could any longer doubt that violence was being done to detainees.

Eighty-seven third-year students at Wits Medical School had signed a statement sent to the *Star* protesting against the detention of their colleague, Salim Essop. Five hundred lecturers and staff of the Durban and Maritzburg campuses of the University of Natal had passed a resolution calling on the minister of justice, PC Pelser, "to bring those detained to trial by conventional processes of justice, and to respond to widespread public demand for the appointment of a judicial commission to inquire into the treatment of prisoners held under detention laws".

At a meeting attended by more than 1 500 people in the Great Hall of the University of the Witwatersrand, poet and journalist Don Mattera said: "It is because of the laws of this country that my brothers on Robben Island beat against the battered breast of liberty." Another speaker at the meeting called for the total scrapping of the Terrorism Act and said that the long-term solution to the critical situation on South Africa's borders which was supposed to make the Act necessary was to create "such conditions of life in South Africa that all men, black, brown and white, would be proud to live here in freedom".

The vice-chancellor of Witwatersrand University, Dr GR Bozzoli, and the university's Academic Staff Association also protested against the detention of five of the university's students.

The National Union of Students (NUS) of the United Kingdom sent the following telegram to the family of Ahmed Timol: "We extend our deepest sympathy on the death of Ahmed, victim of a brutal regime. Representing half a million students we honour him and continue the struggle against South African repression."

The annual conference of NUS had sent a telegram to Prime Minister Vorster condemning the detention and death of Ahmed Timol, condemning the detention of other South African students and calling for the release of all political prisoners. The North London Association of the National Union of Teachers, of which Ahmed Timol was a member when he was in Britain, passed the following resolution: "This North London Association of the National Union of Teachers deplores the death of Mr. Ahmed Timol, formerly a member of the NUT, and demands that the South African government make an official public inquiry into the circumstances of his death. It also demands the release of other political detainees in South Africa. Furthermore it recommends that the National Executive of the NUT instructs its members to uphold the academic boycott of South Africa."

Resolutions condemning Ahmed Timol's death were also to be discussed at meetings of the Westminster, Hackney and Wandsworth NUT Associations. The Anti-Apartheid Movement asked individual supporters and sympathetic organisations to send letters and telegrams to Prime Minister Vorster deploring the death of Ahmed Timol and calling for the release of other detainees.

The religious denominations responded to Ahmed's death. More than 3 000 people packed the Juma Mosque in Durban to offer a special prayer on his death.

The Reverend Bernard Wrankmore, who had just ended a 64-day protest fast over the death of the Imam Haron, expressed his shock at the death of Ahmed. The

Anglican priest said: "I am deeply shocked that another life has been lost and naturally hope that the matter will be thoroughly investigated. But there is nothing more that I can do actively anymore as God has removed me from the scene and has now taken over ... It is now up to the public, the newspapers, the churches and all the people who asked that I come off the hill and that they should do something themselves to show their mettle."

The Chief Rabbi of the United Progressive Jewish Congregation in Johannesburg, Dr AS Super, said many rabbis had addressed their congregations on the subject of the detainees at that night's services.

Leading Johannesburg churchmen reiterated their call for a judicial inquiry into deaths of police detainees. They expressed their shock and amazement at news that an Indian detainee had fallen to his death from a 10th floor window at John Vorster Square.

An appeal was made to all denominations to attend a prayer meeting in Johannesburg comemorating Ahmed's death in detention. It stated: "The hour-long meeting will begin at 2pm at the Indian Sports Ground in Vrededorp, near the corner of Krause and 17th streets. We especially appeal to other members of the community to come along – they will be most welcome," said Mrs M Coovadia, a member of the Johannesburg Muslim community. She said that although Muslim men and women did not normally pray together they would do so at this event because of the special nature of the occasion.

In Cape Town, Cardinal Owen McCann, Catholic archbishop of Cape Town, called for an immediate public inquiry into Ahmed's death. He announced that there would be a night vigil prayer in St Mary's Cathedral, Cape Town. The Christian Institute called on all South Africans to observe a day of prayer, penitence and denial to show their concern over detention without trial, and Timol's death.

A special call was made to the people of Pretoria to observe a day of prayer and penitence between 6 pm on Monday and 6 pm on Tuesday. The call was made, after a meeting in Pretoria, by representatives of the Anglican, Roman Catholic, Presbyterian and Methodist churches. The Anglican dean of Pretoria, the Very Reverend Mark Nye, said the meeting had been "very deeply concerned" at the death of Timol and the illness in detention of Salim Essop.

Speaking at a prayer meeting in Johannesburg which 1 200 people attended, Miley Richards, a leader of the Coloured Labour Party, said: "We are all being challenged. It is time for us to stand up and be counted. Are we just going to sit down and pray? God will not answer my prayers if I don't take positive action."

In Durban, a packed meeting of all races called for a national day of mourning which was observed on 10 November, when very large numbers of black-owned shops closed and students and schoolchildren stayed away from schools. The anger of the people was summed up by I Bhagwandeen, an executive member of the Natal Indian Congress, when he told the Durban meeting: "If we have to pay the final penalty that Ahmed Timol paid, let us pay it."

Political parties also responded to Ahmed's death.

The Indian Congress also issued a statement saying that it "abhors beyond belief the death of Ahmed Timol" and calling on Bantustan heads, the Coloured Labour Party, the Federal Party, who were co-operating with the government to display in tangible terms their opposition to the government in power.

The stooge South African Indian Council sent a telegram to Vorster asking for a judicial inquiry into Ahmed Timol's death. It reported that there was "a tremendous amount of unrest" among the Indian community.

The man in the street reached a state of mind where he strongly suspected that detainees were being tortured in dark little rooms and feared that the methods of the Gestapo were being used by the Security Police, Mike Mitchell, the United Party shadow minister of justice, told the *Sunday Times*.

International organisations likewise entered the fray. Amnesty International called upon the minister of justice to order an "impartial" (not a police) inquiry into Timol's death. This would support those in South Africa who were demanding an inquiry into not only Timol's death, but the whole matter of police interrogation and torture of detainees. Amnesty called on people to protest to the South African ambassadors or consuls against detention without trial and demand the release of the detainees presently held and sent a cable to the Secretary-General of the United Nations urging an investigation into the death of Timol.

At the UN, India called on the General Assembly to deplore the deaths of Asians and others while under detention in South Africa and to declare those responsible "criminals". The Soviet Union and Guinea co-sponsored a draft Convention on the Suppression and Punishment of the Crime of Apartheid. The UN Special Committee on Apartheid was to prepare a report on all known cases of "maltreatment and torture of prisoners" in South Africa.

In London the office of the ANC issued a statement saying: "These brave patriots who are challenging the fascists' regime inside South Africa are in dire need of the support and protection of every self-respecting human being throughout the world. The external mission of the ANC therefore urgently calls on all its many supporters and sympathisers to urge their governments through their parliamentary representatives to support our call to the United Nations for:

• The immediate expulsion of South Africa from the United Nations Organisation and all its agencies; and

• The adoption of mandatory sanctions against South Africa until the scourge of apartheid and racial discrimination is wiped out in our country.

Furthermore, we call on all those who detest the white racist regime in South Africa:

• To contribute towards our fighting fund so that our underground machinery and our fighting forces could be maintained and strengthened;

• To get your organisations, trade unions, student unions, political parties, etc., to send messages of protest to the government of South Africa;

• To actively support our call to boycott and isolate white South Africa in every field; and

• To demand the release of all political prisoners.

We for our part pledge to avenge the death of Timol and all the others who have been murdered in order to maintain white supremacy in our Motherland.
We shall not allow these murderers to get away with their crimes and shall re-double our efforts to prosecute our struggle inside South Africa. Vorster and his gang will be destroyed!"

An Urdu poem was composed by Azhar "Jomo" Saloojees's mother in tribute to Ahmed Timol. It was sung by Azhar's late father at many political rallies and the rendering of this poem often brought tears and comfort to the late Ahmed Timol's parents.

TRANSLATION
Hail! O Youth, with such dignity did you give your life
Without doubt, it is the destruction of youth, for the pleasure of the nation.

Thousands of oppression and tyranny did the enemy pour upon,
without just reason,
In spite of many hardships, yet you remained steadfast;

Who is able to achieve such a task as you had achieved?
You have passed away, yet your name lives in the world;
You have achieved the rank of a warrior, O youth!
The earth and the firmament cry tears for you;

You were in your youth but now you have given the great sacrifice;
Alas! The flower withered away even before the arrival of spring;

Your blood letting shall one day achieve great results
The oppressor shall indeed, finally receive his punishment, one day;

This prayer from the heart of Sham'a, O Allah! Grant it,
May the blossom of Mercy shower upon the tomb of the deceased, forever

UNITED NATIONS RESPONSE
In late 1971, Ahmed's close friend Yusuf "Jo Jo" Saloojee was asked by Dr Yusuf Dadoo to address the UN Special Committee on Apartheid on torture and death of political prisoners, arising especially from the death of Ahmed. Yusuf found great difficulty in composing himself to speak about a brother, a friend and a real comrade.

United Nations Official Records of the General Assembly, 26th Session, Special Political Committee, note: "Mr Saloojee said that since it had assumed power in 1948, the South African government had fought any opposition to apartheid with increasingly repressive legislation. He further stated: 'South Africa had a long record of indiscriminate killing of those who opposed its racist laws. Examples were the massacres at Bulhoek and Port Elizabeth in 1920, the Bondelswart massacre in 1921 and more recently the death of the Imam Abdullah Haron, Mr Mayeni Cushela and Mr Ahmed Timol.' He [Mr Saloojee] had known Mr Timol personally, the latter having been a colleague in the teaching profession; he paid homage to a man who had been loved and respected by everyone and whose funeral procession had been joined by his students," the UN records.

The *Star* reported in November 1971 that the majority of Western powers voted with an overwhelming majority of United Nations members in the General Assembly for a resolution expressing "grave indignation and concern" over any and every act of maltreatment and torture of opponents of apartheid.

The resolution, sponsored by 53 states, was prompted by the conviction and sentencing of the Dean of Johannesburg and the death of Ahmed Timol in a fall from a window at Johannesburg police headquarters.

The United States representative, Ernest Grigg, said his delegation was concerned about recent reports from South Africa, particularly the reports on Timol, meaning the continuing controversy as to the circumstances of his death and the defensive response of the apartheid government over this.

The resolution called on all states to do all in their power to promote the cause of justice for all people in South Africa and to use their influence to achieve the repeal of all legislation designed to give effect to apartheid and to persecute and suppress the rights of those opposed to that policy: to achieve the liberation of people imprisoned or detained for their opposition to apartheid, and to achieve the removal of orders against those banned or banished because they oppose apartheid.

It asked the UN's apartheid committee to prepare a special report on all known cases of maltreatment and torture of political prisoners, and requested the Secretary-General to publicise all available information on this subject.

VORSTER'S RESPONSE

Faced with nationwide calls for a judicial inquiry into the death of Ahmed Timol and the whole attitude and activities of the Security Police, the government closed its doors. Prime Minister BJ Vorster said that the procedure prescribed by the law had always been and was still followed whenever a person died, whether in police custody or otherwise, and he therefore saw no reason for the appointment of a special judicial commission to inquire into any case.

"The police have proved abundantly that they do not hesitate themselves to act against any member of the force who makes himself guilty of any contravention."

John Vorster – who was also acting minister of police – responded to a long list of questions by referring repeatedly to clauses of the Terrorism Act, or not answering at all. Asked how many people had been detained that week, who they were and when they would be brought to court, he said: "It is not in the interest of the public and the safety of the state to give the names of persons detained. They will be released or charged as soon as investigations are concluded." To all questions on Timol's death, he referred to the inquest court or did not answer.

What, then, are the precise circumstances surrounding the fall? How many policemen were with him? What measures were in operation to prevent this type of fall? Were the windows covered by bars, shutters or wire mesh? Did Ahmed really just fall? All drew no satisfactory reply.

9

INQUEST

At the time of Timol's death, political repression in South Africa was rising to new heights, especially as there were small but significant signs that resistance activity was beginning to increase, slowly, intermittently, but surely, to break the long lull following the two Rivonia trials in the early Sixties. With the high command of the ANC serving long sentences on Robben Island and other activists in exile, apartheid was in full force and resistance had been crushed for almost a decade. But in the late Sixties, and early Seventies, the Black Consciousness movement began to emerge, forming new organisations to mobilise the oppressed communities, especially students. At the same time, the ANC was beginning to accelerate its covert operations against the apartheid state.

Timol's arrest was part of a crackdown in October 1971, described as the most extensive since 1964. A string of people perceived by the state to be connected to Timol or the ANC were caught up in the net, including Timol's brother Mohammed and fellow detainee Salim Essop's sister Fatima.

On Timol's death, there were calls from a range of groups for a full judicial inquest. Timol's family approached a firm of lawyers who had been recommended to them by members of the Indian community. Cachalia and Loonat were one of very few legal firms in the entire country representing victims of state repression, having represented Winnie Mandela, among others. They also had some experience representing Indian clients challenging the Group Areas Act and other apartheid laws.

Saeed Cachalia and Mia Ahmed Loonat began practising as attorneys in 1967. They set up offices in Becker Street, Ferreirastown, west of the Johannesburg city centre, where many Indian families, including the Pahad family, lived mostly in flats. The firm's premises, formerly dentists' rooms, were situated on the ground floor – not an ideal situation for a legal office, but Becker Street was the area where most community activities gravitated to. There were travel agents, merchants and wholesalers, and cricket was administered from offices in the street.

Cachalia was closely related to an activist family that had been involved in the struggle against colonialism and racism from the early 1900s, and included Molvi Cachalia, his brother Yusuf and his wife Amina Cachalia, who were part of the inner circle of ANC leaders like Nelson Mandela and Walter Sisulu. Molvi Cachalia's father had participated in Gandhi's passive resistance campaign in South Africa.

Loonat was a young lawyer with progressive leanings. His brother-in-law Dr Mohamed Momoniat was one of the people arrested when Timol was detained, but was released a few days after Timol's death. Another brother-in-law was in exile. Timol's family were convinced, as were many in the country at large, that the activist's death was by no means accidental, and certainly not the result of suicide, as had been claimed by the police. GH Bhabha (a prominent member of the Kholvad Madressa) and other members of the Indian community rallied around the Timol family and assisted in the raising of funds for the country's best legal brains to uncover the facts relating to Ahmed's death. The community was aware that the police had got off scot-free for the death of Babla Saloojee.

As Haji Timol was well known to the Indian community in the Transvaal people contributed generously to funding for the case, and only a few days after Ahmed's death, the Timol family approached Cachalia and Loonat. Haji Timol put his faith in Cachalia and Loonat to do whatever was necessary and consulted with them throughout the case.

Cachalia and Loonat's first duty was to communicate with police to advise them that they were the legal representatives for the family. Relevant departments of the South African Police were contacted, as were court officials responsible for the inquest. Most of the communication was conducted through letters addressed to respective officials and responses were given in writing. Arrangements were made by telephone, and the inquest court informed the lawyers with regard to the details of the inquest – the date, venue, etc.

Cachalia and Loonat appointed George Bizos, a well-known figure who had already done some work challenging the state in apartheid-related trials, as well as Issy Maisels, also a well known legal figure, who had represented the treason trialists in the famous Rivonia case. Cachalia and Loonat also enlisted Jonathan Gluckman, a pathologist, to examine the body and determine if his injuries were consistent with the police version of events.

The case took up much of Cachalia and Loonat's time, and despite the coming of the holiday season, Cachalia and Loonat found themselves embroiled in a case that meant they had to forgo their annual breaks. The Muslim fasting month, Ramadan, also fell in October that year, so when Timol died there was much discussion in mosques and the community provided a support system for the Timol family.

The state released Timol's body after it conducted a post-mortem, at which

Gluckman represented the family. Hundreds of members of the community milled around outside the pathology lab at Wits University, where the head of forensic medicine, Dr NJ Scheepers, carried out the post-mortem.

Cachalia and Loonat, although operating in a situation fraught with tension, unstated threats and state vindictiveness, were not intimidated by the authorities, who plainly were not pleased by the challenge. They felt they had to rise to the occasion and pursue the matter. There was no question of dropping the case or shrinking from doing whatever was necessary to pursue the truth.

Cachalia led the charge. The atmosphere at the hearings was very tense but Cachalia and Loonat knew they were well represented by Maisels and Bizos. They felt there was no way any prosecutor would evade the legitimate requests of a powerful legal team.

In the first hearing, held on 24 January 1972, representations were made to get access to all information relating to Timol's death. After legal argument between prosecutor, magistrate and counsel the magistrate ruled that Timol's statements, notes made during the interrogation, medical reports and other relevant documents were not liable to be disclosed to the Cachalia and Loonat team. Maisels took issue with the ruling and advised that he would apply to the Supreme Court for an order to have documents in the state's possession handed to the magistrate.

The Supreme Court ruled against the police and ordered that all relevant documents be released to the inquest magistrate.

In the midst of the inquest Cachalia and Loonat had also been approached by the Essop family to bring an application in the Supreme Court to restrain the police from interrogating and assaulting Salim Essop while in detention. They asked that he be removed from the HF Verwoerd Hospital, where he was being treated for injuries inflicted by his interrogators. Salim Essop's case was also handled by Maisels and Bizos. The Supreme Court granted an interdict restraining police from interrogating, assaulting or exerting pressure on Essop while he was in detention. According to John Dugard, a Wits law professor, this was the first application for an interdict under Section 6 of the Terrorism Act to succeed.

The Timol legal team also held discussions at Jonathan Gluckman's home in Westcliff, regarding Timol's injuries. They spent an entire afternoon on the issue, going over the nature of the bruises and injuries on the body. They were informed by Gluckman that there were bruises on Timol's body not consistent with a fall from the 10th floor of the John Vorster Square building. The injuries pointed to sustained torture. Loonat, not experienced in cases of this sort, remembers being astonished at the forensic discussions.

The matter finally came to court at the end of April 1972, some six months after Timol's death. The application was once again argued by Maisels and Bizos. There were several appearances, including a few postponements.

Eventually it fell to Loonat to appear, as Cachalia was overseas. He accompanied Haji Timol to the Palace of Justice in Pretoria on the day of the inquest hearing. Haji Timol was very upset; he kept saying that the police were responsible for his son's death. Loonat hadn't dealt with the father as much as

Cachalia had but did his best to ease his burden. Haji Timol had to use a walking-stick and found it difficult to climb the steps of the Palace of Justice, climbing slowly, reading verses from the Quran till he reached the top, holding Loonat's hands.

The case was taking a toll on the old man, who was continually having to get the progress reports, meeting lots of people and keeping his emotions in check. He left judicial process in the hands of Cachalia and Loonat, accepted what was decided by counsel, placing his implicit trust in them.

Fanie Cilliers was appearing for the police and the evidence was led by PAJ Kotze, the senior public prosecutor. The magistrate was JL de Villiers.

Inquests are sombre in all instances, but the atmosphere at the Timol hearing was charged by a battle of political wills. It was made clear to the state that there was dissatisfaction with the post-mortem report.

Moreover, the evidence given by the medical experts revealed a picture at odds with the police version. Dr NJ Scheepers, the senior state pathologist, described to the court the extensive bruising and other injuries present on Ahmed's body. He also revealed that "several bruises occurred days before the death and could have been caused by a boot or a blunt instrument".

Dr Gluckman, who attended the post-mortem on behalf of the Timol family, listed the injuries that had been caused before death: "An abrasion on the right collarbone; multiple abrasions on the right thigh; a large bruise and rectangular abrasion on the right elbow and forearm; a few bruises on the right upper arm; an abrasion on the right shoulder blade; two large bruises on the right thigh; an abrasion on the left forearm; multiple bruises on the left side of the chest and a small abrasion on the left side of the neck." Dr Gluckman said that it was clear Timol had sustained injuries either before or after he was brought into custody.

Ahmed's cousin Dr Farouk Dindar states, "I attended the inquest on Ahmed's death. I was particularly interested in the nature of his wounds. I felt that a forensic pathologist would be able to separate wounds inflicted from a fall from those that preceded the fall. The information was not forthcoming from the pathology reports. I still do not know whether Ahmed was killed and thrown out of the window after that, or was dropped accidentally during a torture session.

"Ahmed had wounds on his body which were inflicted during his interrogation. The state pathologist did a microscopic study of these wounds and came to the conclusion that these wounds were old. He quoted a research paper from Australia by an Australian pathologist who had studied wounds and after how many days you will see macrophages in a wound. Ahmed's wounds had a few macrophages and the state pathologist distorted this information to date the wounds to be old and preceding his arrest by four days. I had seen Ahmed's body at his mother's house. The family removed the sheet covering his body and I noted that he had multiple focal wounds all over his trunk. I did not look at Ahmed's nails.

"The state pathologist did a microscopic study of these wounds and came to the conclusion that these wounds were old. Ahmed's skin wounds had many macrophages, which are seen in wounds during the healing stage. The pivotal question was the time when these macrophages would be seen after an injury. The state pathologist concluded that the wounds were over a week old and antedated Ahmed's detention. He then went on to speculate that Ahmed was an alcholic and could have sustained these wounds due to falls following a bout of drinking. He was obviously trying to tarnish Ahmed's reputation amongst the Muslim community.

"It was obvious that the pathologist was covering up. The whole inquest was a farce.

"About three weeks after Ahmed's death his clothes were returned to his mother in a garbage bag. This included a beige sweater and blue jeans that I examined very carefully. The blue jeans had obvious worn out marks on the knee and hip region that I felt could best be explained if a person was dragged on the floor. The beige sweater that belonged to Ahmed's cousin, Iqbal Dindar, had multiple roundish black marks from old blood. These marks would correspond to the wounds on his chest. My guess is that these were multiple puncture wounds inflicted with a sharp object."

Here it is useful to take up the narrative of George Bizos's book *No One To Blame*, in a chapter called "Indians Can't Fly".

The news of Timol's death led to a public outcry and calls for an immediate investigation into the treatment of detainees. As Professor John Dugard commented, "The death of yet another detainee in suspicious circumstances again raises the whole question of the methods of interrogation employed by the security police."

Given the level of public concern, it could be expected that the police would at least attempt to investigate Timol's death with a degree of thoroughness. The task was given to the head of the CID, Major-General Stoffel Buys. The good general did not disappoint his political masters. Before his investigation was complete, Buys told Rapport *that Timol had jumped. The atmosphere in room 1026, the general declared, was the 'most relaxed atmosphere imaginable in such circumstances'. He explained: 'Ahmed Timol was sitting calmly in a chair. There were security men with him. At one stage two of them left the room. Mr Timol suddenly jumped up, aimed at the door. A security man jumped up to intercept him but the Indian then stormed to the window and jumped through it. He was not scared or injured by anybody at any stage.'*

The Sunday Times *noted this peculiar statement by the general, wryly observing, 'One wonders why General Stoffel Buys, head of the CID, bothers to continue with the official inquiry he is conducting into the death of the political detainee Ahmed Timol, considering that he has already given his finding in advance to a Nationalist Sunday newspaper."*

When approached for comment by the Rand Daily Mail, *Buys was less than friendly. 'Why don't you approach me first instead of going off at a tangent and blackening everybody? You have done your damnedest and already thrown dirt,' he told a reporter.*

The magistrate found that the investigation had been impartial, as Buys was not after all a member of the security police. But the vast majority of the people of South Africa and many throughout the world found it difficult to believe that

Timol had died for the reasons given by the security police. Doubts were even expressed by supporters of the apartheid government.

The Timol family was represented [at the inquest] by Issy Maisels and myself; appearing for the police was Fanie Cilliers, who later became an eminent senior counsel; the evidence was led by PAJ Kotze, the senior public prosecutor. He regularly appeared in political trials in the Eastern Cape and the Transvaal, and was later the chosen magistrate to preside over the Neil Aggett inquest. The magistrate, De Villiers, was an official who had done the ordinary run-of-the-mill criminal cases in the district and regional courts. Together with most of his colleagues, he did not enjoy a reputation of tending to disbelieve police officers.

Fanie Cilliers came to Maisels and me to say that he considered it his duty to bring our attention to the fact that the police had handed him a document, with instructions to use it, but he had refused to do so. The document appeared on the face of it to have been issued by the Communist Party. Written in disjointed Marxist jargon, the document advised detained members of the Communist Party to complain of ill treatment and assaults that did not happen and to commit suicide rather than betray their comrades. The last paragraph was even more self-serving for the police propagandists.

It had obviously been drawn up for the purpose of the inquest to explain Essop's supposed malingering and Timol's suicide. It read: 'Rather commit suicide than betray the organization ... Vorster and his murderers will not halt our people when we have comrades like Archbishop Hurley, Rowley Arenstein, Vernon Berrangé, Isie Maisels, MD Naidoo, George Bizos and others who have been fighting with us since the days of Rivonia.'

Given the importance of their catch, the police decided to keep Timol in the security police offices at John Vorster Square. In the past, they explained, communists had escaped from prison or cells, including some whom Van Wyk himself had arrested, such as Harold Wolpe and Arthur Goldreich, the absent main co-conspirators in the Rivonia Trial in which Nelson Mandela and others were sentenced to life imprisonment. Timol was extensively interrogated by a number of police officers, often for over 12 hours each day. Although Van Wyk was in charge of the interrogation, he was assisted by captains Richard Bean, JH Gloy and JZ van Niekerk.

On the night before his death, Timol was guarded by security police sergeants Bouwer and Louw, who testified that he slept well, it was warm and he slept in his underwear. At one point they even gave him some of their coffee while the two of them played cards. They both kept watch while their charge slept, or so they claimed.

Sleep deprivation was common in the security police's interrogation repertoire, and was usually overseen by policemen who were not integral to the questioning process. I thus put it to Bouwer: 'If the intention is that a person should sleep, it seems strange to me that two people should have to guard him ... The office was not a very comfortable place for three persons to spend a night?'

'It is 10 by 18 paces,' he replied.

'It would not even pass municipal regulations. Why was it necessary for two

sergeants to spend the night in the room?'

'It is usual for two guards to guard a prisoner. I think this is a regulation.'

'It is a pity it was not kept when Mr Timol jumped from the window.'

Whether or not Timol had slept, his interrogators found him co-operative the following morning, supplying them with names and addresses. The interrogation session that day, October 27, was the most productive, judging by the notes kept by the police. *'If you compare your notes written on the 27th,'* Maisels put it to Gloy, *'with those of the two previous days, it is incomparably more than the notes written on the two previous days, put together. On this, the last day of his life, he seems to have answered a large number of questions, which you recorded. He seems to have been more co-operative on the Wednesday than ever before.'*

'Judged from the documents it does look that way but is not really the case. On the two previous days we did not take comprehensive notes. He made hundreds of denials.' Gloy's answer confirmed Maisels's question. If Timol was more co-operative, as seemed the case, what had happened that day, or the previous night?

'Even if a man is unco-operative initially he might talk more once we have got his confidence,' Gloy tried to explain. *'This was our aim with Timol.'*

The police had been trying to establish who the three men referred to in Timol's documents as 'Quentin, Martin and Henry' really were. Gloy and Van Niekerk were interrogating Timol on just this point that fateful afternoon. Gloy was happy to declare that it had been an 'intensive interrogation' with regard to Quentin, Henry and Martin. But the interrogator could not remember how long it had endured. Between 10 minutes and an hour, he proffered.

Maisels pointed out that from Gloy's statement it appeared that most of the day was spent on this line of questioning, *'The statement does give that impression,'* Gloy responded, *'but it did not happen like that.'* The interrogation was interrupted by Sergeant João Rodrigues. A clerk at Security Police headquarters in Pretoria, Rodrigues brought the officers some coffee and their pay cheques.

Minutes later there was another visitor to office 1026. Known only as 'Mr X', he declared to Timol that the police knew the identity of Quentin, Martin and Henry.

Timol, the police agreed, was shocked when he heard this. It was, Gloy explained, the 'first and only time' the detainee had expressed this emotion. His eyes were "wild and staring". Or, in the equally expressive words of Rodrigues, "The Indian appeared shocked when he heard the name ... He moved his head from side to side and looked bewildered and shocked." The interrogators hurried to verify the information they had just received, leaving Rodrigues to guard the dangerous communist.

Rodrigues explained what happened next, "The Indian asked me if he could go to the toilet. He was sitting on the chair opposite me. We both stood up and I moved to my left around the table. There was a chair in my way. When I looked up I saw the Indian rushing round the table in the direction of the window. I tried to get round the table but his chair was in the way. Then I tried to get round the other way and another chair was in the way. The Indian already had the window open and was diving through it. When I tried to grab him I fell over the chair. I *could not get at him."*

The 29-year-old schoolteacher lay dead on the southern side of John Vorster Square, 10 floors below the room where he had been interrogated for the past four days. In a matter of seconds Timol had managed to dash across the tiny room, open the window (which was closed because of traffic noise), and hoist himself up and out. It was an incredible story. Rodrigues was vague on details. "How it happened I cannot say precisely, it all happened very quickly," he explained.

"Maisels asked him how Timol had opened the window.

"He opened the catch with his hand," Rodrigues replied.

"Then what did he do?"

"He opened it, and in one movement he dived through, head and arms first." Reconsidering, Rodrigues said Timol had fallen more than dived.

"He must have almost wriggled through the window," Maisels suggested, referring to Timol's height (1,6 m) relative to the window (almost 1m).

Magistrate De Villiers interrupted, "I cannot agree. I stood at the window myself."

"I will argue that point later," Maisels rejoined.

"I will not allow unfair questions to be put to the witness."

"I will ask the witness to say what he saw. What did you see?"

"He opened the window and pushed it and then he fell through," Rodrigues answered.

A strange enough story, made even stranger by the fact that it differed from the one given by General Buys. Buys had claimed that Timol initially made for the door, before jumping through the window. Gloy had also testified that Rodrigues told him that Timol had pretended to be aiming for the door.

"Did Mr Timol ever aim at the door?" Maisels asked Rodrigues.

"No, not that I saw." There must have been a misunderstanding, Rodrigues explained. Rodrigues, it seemed, had given a number of different versions.

Brigadier CW St John Pattle had conducted his own investigation in the wake of the incident. Rodrigues had given him a different version of events, in which he ran round the table in the opposite direction.

Rodrigues gave his version to the court, as did Van Niekerk and Gloy, Pattle and Buys. They all cited Rodrigues as their source, despite the anomalies. Which of the various versions, if any, was the truth?

Buys had taken a statement from Rodrigues two weeks after the incident. 'It seems strange to me,' Maisels observed, 'that the most important person, as far as we can see, should be asked two weeks later to make a statement.'

Although Van Niekerk and Gloy claimed to have made notes at the time, they had destroyed these after making their affidavits.

I put it to Van Niekerk: 'Not even children in standard four would write notes out and then throw them into the wastepaper basket. Why, having wasted your time making notes, did you throw them into the wastepaper basket?'

'I did not think them necessary.'

'I am going to put it to you that between these statements there was a substantial change of front as to how Timol met his death.'

The policeman did not have to answer, as Fanie Cilliers interjected, 'I object – this is a fishing expedition.'

This was a familiar expression whenever we probed into the happenings in the interrogation rooms of the security police. Buys downplayed the significance of the different versions, ascribing discrepancies to 'a matter of interpretation'. His cross-examination was cut short when he collapsed in the witness box and had to leave the court. He was never recalled, allegedly on his doctor's instructions.

Often the body of a dead detainee on the mortuary slab was more compelling evidence on his behalf than the oral testimony he might have given had he survived the ordeal. His release would inevitably have taken place after his injuries had healed; he would have no witnesses to corroborate his story; and a team of security policemen would claim how well they had treated the detainee, even to the point that they had spent their own money to buy him meat pies and cold drinks.

With the assistance of Dr Jonathan Gluckman, the injuries – carefully noted and subjected to scientific examination – often told a story, which could not be controversial, nor easily explained by witnesses whose loyalty to truth and justice was outweighed by their loyalty to the apartheid state, and to their fellow wrongdoers. Such was the case of Ahmed Timol. After he had fallen 10 floors, the fresh injuries on his body could not have been easily attributed to an assault received before he crashed on to the ground.

Gluckman had noticed numerous injuries, which were not fresh; he explained to us that histologists could date the injuries by the length of the macrophage cells. The healing process comes about as healthy cells make themselves longer in order to devour or replace the injured cells. By measuring the length of the macrophagic cells, you could determine whether the injury was inflicted more than two, four, six, eight, 10 or 12 days before.

The scientific evidence showed that the injuries on Timol's body were probably inflicted whilst he was in custody. Three pathologists testified: the state pathologist Dr Scheepers, Dr Gluckman for the family, and Dr Koch for the police. The main difference of opinion related to the timing of pre-death injuries, which Scheepers and Gluckman dated to the time when Timol was in custody, and Koch dated some days earlier.

In concluding, Maisels said he did not want the court to declare whether Timol had been pushed or thrown: 'All I am asking is for the court to find that it is not known how it came about that he left the window.' Indeed, Maisels continued, the police had left many aspects unexplained. One of these was the discrepancy in statements made by Rodrigues on the day of Timol's death and his evidence in court.

'In my day,' Maisels argued, 'one took a statement from a witness as soon as one could. It is quite inexplicable that no written statement was taken from the man on the spot, Rodrigues, before November 11 – a fortnight after the occurrence.'

Maisels also pointed out that the police had not explained how Timol had sustained his pre-death injuries, which threw doubt on the 'whole cotton-wool case'. Timol had had no injuries prior to his arrest, yet was found to have sustained injuries prior to his death. They could only have occurred during his detention.

There was no doubt that Essop sustained such injuries; he was hospitalised because of them.

Ultimately, of course, it was the magistrate who was to decide. In a finding that highlighted his basic assumptions, Magistrate De Villiers stated that it was necessary to determine, in the first instance, if the deceased was murdered; if that was not the case, then he fell out of the window by accident; and if that was not the case, then he jumped out himself and committed suicide. To think of murder, he concluded, was absurd, as Timol was a valuable find to the security police, who desperately wanted to keep him. The possibility that the deceased fell by accident was also absurd, as it was to accept anything other than that he jumped out of the window himself.

Assuming that Timol committed suicide, the magistrate continued, he had to determine, if possible on the available evidence, what the deceased's motive had been. Was it as a result of his torture or mistreatment by the police, or was it self-reproach, or did he dread a lengthy prison sentence or, lastly, was there a political motive, namely that he did it as a result of the communist ideology?

The magistrate rejected Maisels's suggestions that the internal investigation was a 'whitewashing', saying that it was conducted by members of the South African Police, who were not members of the security police. It was difficult for De Villiers to doubt the bona fides of the South African Police.

The magistrate accepted that lesions found on Timol's body may have been caused between one and seven days prior to his death, and the grazes between four and eight days prior to death. If the injuries occurred within four days, then it would have been while in police custody, but all the policemen testified against this, and the court had no reason to doubt their testimony. The medical experts could only speculate that the injuries were inflicted during a 'brawl' when the deceased was pushed around. This, too, was unthinkable. He was a valuable find. He had given valuable information and more was expected.

Although the deceased was interrogated for long hours he was handled in a 'civilised and humane way'. Therefore, the magistrate concluded, one could not find the reason for suicide in torture or mistreatment. Evidence showed that Timol was a communist and was prominent in the Communist Party as leader of the 'Main Unit' in South Africa. It must therefore be accepted that he was conversant with all orders to members, including the one which said, 'Rather commit suicide than betray the organisation.'

Thus the magistrate found that Timol killed himself for a combination of reasons: long jail sentence; giving names and addresses to the police, and the last straw, the revelation of Quentin, Martin and Henry's identity, combined together with the communist ideology. The magistrate concluded that no one was to blame, although he recommended that the district surgeon visit all detainees, especially to look for evidence of assault, which might prevent long inquests and unnecessary embarrassment to the police.

On 22 June, the magistrate found that no-one was to blame for the death and made no finding against the police. The state was thus absolved from any responsibility for the death of Timol while in detention. The court effectively ruled that he had indeed committed suicide but that the suicide was not due to ill-treatment during his detention but rather to his communist ideology – which demanded that he sacrifice himself rather than co-operate with his enemies. The finding was incredible to the family, the community and to everyone opposed to apartheid. A disappointing and sad ending to the inquest. A fine example of the 'independence of the judiciary' during the merciless apartheid years.

THE CASE OF THE FOUR

The following persons were charged with conspiring with the South African Communist Party and or the banned ANC and/or the dead detainee, Ahmed Timol. They were Mohammed Salim Essop (22), Yousuf Hassan Essack (21), Indhrasen Moodley (27) and Amina Desai (51). They all pleaded not guilty to the charges. Today Mohammed Salim Essop is a lecturer in the United Kingdom, Yousuf Hassan Essack – also known as Moe – is a businessman in Durban, Indhrasen Moodley is a professor in the Research Unit School of Family and Public Health at the University of Natal and Amina Desai lives with her daughter in the United Kingdom.

It was only in court that the above accused heard for the first time the details of Ahmed's death.

SALIM ESSOP

Dr Vernon Kemp stated in his affidavit, "I am the Chief District Surgeon of Johannesburg and Senior Lecturer in Forensic Medicine at the University of Witwatersrand. I have been a District Surgeon since 1950.

"During the morning of the 26th of October 1971 at 8.30 am I was called to examine a Mr Essop at John Vorster Square. He appeared to be in an apparent semi-conscious state but further examination led me to believe that he was in a state of severe hysteria. In order to rule out any possible organic disease I arranged for him to be seen by a specialist neuro-surgeon – Dr C W Law. This was done at the Non-European Hospital at about 11.15 am on the same day. I arranged for X-rays and certain blood tests which subsequently proved to be negative.

"At the time of the examinations I noted various injuries which I list as below:
Two small areas of bruising of the right forearm.
Areas of bruising, which showed yellow colour change, below both knees.
• 2cm bruise just below the right eye.
• 2cm bruise of the lobe of the right ear.
• 3,5cm bruise, showing yellow colour change, of the inner aspect of the left arm, just below the axilla.
• There were superficial scratch marks on both anterior chest walls.
"All the injuries that were noted were of a minor nature and did not require any treatment. I did not see Mr Essop again as he was transferred to the HF Verwoerd Hospital in Pretoria."

On 26 October 1971, approximately four days after being arrested, Salim collapsed in detention at John Vorster Square police station and was taken to the HF

Verwoerd Hospital in Pretoria. The state doctors were desperately attempting to revive him.

Before long the news of Ahmed's death had made not only national but international headlines. Concerns were raised about Salim's safety. There was huge publicity in the press about the nationwide arrests that were taking place. A nurse at the HF Verwoerd Hospital worked out that the person lying on the hospital bed was Salim Essop. A newspaper reporter contacted Salim's father, Ismail Essop, and informed him that he had received information that his son was in a critical condition in a Pretoria hospital.

Salim's father rushed to the hospital in Pretoria with a journalist. The hospital initially denied that Salim was a patient, but Ismail Essop succeeded in peering into one of the rooms at the hospital and saw his son lying naked on a bed. In Ismail Essop's affidavit he stated: "At 3 pm I walked into the corridor of the Cassim Adam Ward and saw a bed in the corridor blocking the entrance to room 8. I climbed on the bed and looked through the fanlight above the door. I saw my son lying naked on the far bed in the room. He looked terribly ill. He was hardly breathing and there were bruises and blood clots on his chest. He had a bandage on his stomach just below the navel."

On 29 October 1971 Ismail Essop brought an urgent application against the Commissioner of Police to stop his son being assaulted, interrogated, pressured or tortured during his period of detention. In a landmark judgement, Judge Margo ruled in favour of the Essop family.

Salim has vague memories of his stay at HF Verwoerd Hospital. He says: "I remember seeing some lights. They were pushing things in my nose and I cannot remember what was really going on in a perfect way."

He was then taken to Pretoria Central Prison and kept under 24-hour surveillance in the hospital section of the "black" prison. He remembers: "I was kept in an office that was closed off. This looked like a temporary office that was specifically set up for me. I had no idea what had happened to Ahmed. I had made no contact with any persons from the outside world during my entire stay of detention. I was kept secluded."

Salim was in bed for over a month. He adds: "I literally had to learn to walk again. There was an African prisoner that would feed me. After a month he started taking me to exercise in the yard. This was my recovery process. The prisoner and I could not speak to each other at any time as we were always under the supervision of the prison guards. There were no newspapers or radio and I had no contact with the outside world."

Salim was kept at the Pretoria Central Prison for approximately six months. Despite the Essop family obtaining a court interdict preventing the police from assaulting and torturing Salim, this did not stop them. During the last period of his stay at the prison, Salim went through a very difficult time.

Two high-ranking CID officials once visited Salim. After they displayed their identity cards Salim was escorted to a visitors' room and told that his father had obtained a lawyer to conduct an investigation. The officials had come to establish if Salim had any complaints of torture or if he had suffered any injuries by the

Security Police. Salim had not heard of the court interdict brought by his father against the police and was now confused. "I was trying to work out what were they up to." he said. "How could I trust them after what I had been through?"

That was not the only dangerous encounter. "There were once two security officers accompanied by a so-called 'doctor' in a white coat that visited me one day. I was asked to sit down. My hand was held and I was injected with a 'talking drug'. I felt an immediate rush in my head, I was going high, I felt loose, felt funny, felt as if I was floating. I was elated. Then the questions commenced. Who was working with you? What did you do with Ahmed Timol? Tell us about Amina Desai? Her family? A list of names was shown to me. Some of them were friends, students and some that I did not know." At this stage Salim had no idea that his close friend Ahmed Timol was dead.

Exact dates and times are very difficult to remember for a young man who had virtually come back from the dead. At one stage Salim embarked on a hunger strike for a period of four or five days.

He was finally taken to the Magistrate's Court in Johannesburg to be charged. It was here that he saw a familiar face. Salim recalls: "She looked pale and had aged tremendously. She waved at me and appeared very sad. She had no cosmetics on." As they both proceeded towards the entrance of the courtroom, Amina Desai remarked to Salim: "They think Ahmed was a very big man. They have identified something huge and they believe Ahmed was behind all of this." It was Salim's advocate who informed him that Ahmed had died. Salim says, "I was shocked. This was the first time that I had heard of his death."

Hearing of Ahmed's death made Salim feel empty. Salim recalls, "I felt that I was being charged and that I was taking the rap. I was going to be charged for everything, as Ahmed was dead. I had not fully recovered from the hunger strike. I was weak and had lost a lot of weight and had become very thin and pale. I was now worried and suddenly realised that this was a very big and nightmarish experience. I was now implicated for something that I could not make sense of as I was not responsible for all of this. The person responsible for all of this was not here. I would have liked to see Ahmed on that day and for us to share information. We would be discussing and planning on how to defend us legally. Ahmed would have used the trial as a political platform to convey the message of the oppressed people of South Africa."

Salim was sentenced on 1 November 1972 to five years' imprisonment, following his conviction on a charge under the Terrorism Act. He served his sentence on Robben Island.

YOUSUF HASSAN ESSACK
Hassan Essack, known as Moe, was in Durban when he was picked up by Durban Security Branch members and taken to Fisher Street from where Gloy and another member took him to Johannesburg. In Moe's own words "the trip was terrifying". On route to Johannesburg, they stopped in Pietermaritzburg and he was locked up at the local police station for a few hours. He was in solitary confinement with handcuffs and leg-irons. Later they continued with the journey and he was locked up again in the then Orange Free State for the whole night. Moe relates that the cell

door was opened regularly and he was kicked by the local policemen and repeatedly called a terrorist. In Heidelberg, he was chained to a pole while Gloy and his partner had lunch. In the afternoon when they reached Booysens police station he was locked up in a cell with an African patient that was mentally retarded. The African prisoner shouted and screamed at him in front of the white policemen but never laid a finger on him. This disappointed the policemen when they came to fetch him the next morning and found him intact. He was then taken to John Vorster Square. The police were not sure of his role, as his name was not mentioned by Ahmed or Salim. Moe was sentenced on 1 November 1972 to five years imprisonment following his conviction on a charge under the Terrorism Act. He was released on a legal technicality after serving one year. Moe is currently a businessman in Durban.

AMINA DESAI

When Amina appeared in court in Johannesburg, five months after Ahmed's death, she asked her lawyer why Ahmed could not come and testify. Amina recalls: "The news of his death came as a huge shock to me and I almost collapsed. The state prosecutor was Klaus von Lieres and Justice Snyman heard the case. Klaus von Lieres was a young white prosecutor who wanted a conviction. Justice Snyman, who had at one time been a struggling lawyer in Mayfair, Johannesburg, was on friendly terms with my brother-in-law who had at that time had some professional help from him. Snyman was quite puzzled when I insisted that I was the head of the Shoe Agency and evaluated the business prospects of Indian customers for the firms that they represented."

Amina told the court that she hated apartheid and that the principles of communism were not wrong. She was a pacifist and did not believe in violence as a solution. The state's case against Amina was that she had been assisting Ahmed in terrorist activities. Amina was sentenced to five years' imprisonment on 1 November 1972. The state had found the most ordinary everyday circumstances to be subversive and had succeeded in making Amina appear to be a terrorist and a communist.

Amina spent most of her time at Barberton prison in isolation. She would sit with the cockroaches in her cell. All her personal clothes were taken away from her. She was given a grey flannel gown to wear. Amina was allowed 10 minutes' exercise time daily and she showered in cold water. Amina's brother Mahmood would come and visit her in Barberton with special permission from Pretoria. Only domestic matters like births and deaths could be discussed and there were always at least two warders standing at both sides of the glass. There were visitors from the Red Cross in Switzerland who once visited the Barberton prison; the prison environment changed only for that one day. Amina spent longer than a year at Barberton prison before being transferred to Kroonstad prison.

Correspondence was restricted to receiving and sending only one letter per month. Even at Kroonstad, Amina was kept in isolation. There was no access to the prison library. Amina had enrolled to study at Unisa doing anthropology and English, as she was interested in the cultural backgrounds of various races and people.

Isolation meant no access to radio, magazines and newspapers. "You could not even discuss with visitors," recalls Amina. "I once obtained a copy of the *Reader's Digest*. The outside cover highlighted a story on a Russian who had defected. As I went through the *Reader's Digest*, I noticed that this particular story was cut out, and could verify this by the missing pages. This story did not mean that the defector was anti-communist. It was better for me not to receive any books rather than being subjected to this brazen stupidity," says Amina.

Amina remembers: "I once asked the warder for two aspirins, as I was in the habit of taking one immediately and the other later. I was accused of being a drug addict. This was the sort of meanness displayed by the white warders who had to prove that I was not a 'passive resister'."

Amina adds, "My entire life changed after being arrested. The state knew that I was not involved in any political activities. I had never attended a political meeting my whole life. I had a sick husband, a business and four children to look after." The only women's meeting Amina had ever attended was one called by the first Mrs Dadoo when a discussion with a group of white women was established. "I had vented my feelings that the white women had been given the vote so that it could nullify the very limited vote of the coloured man's in the Cape. My comments were not taken well and I was never asked to attend any meeting again."

In January 1978 Amina was released. She was immediately placed under house arrest. Amina says, "I was not allowed any visitors except immediate family, this also with permission. Only a medical doctor and a priest were allowed to visit me. I could not attend weddings. To attend a funeral, permission had to be obtained two days beforehand – the authorities appeared not to be aware of the Muslim custom for immediate burials. By the time this was done, it was too late for me to attend the funeral. My normal life was completely destroyed."

It was practically impossible for Amina to run her shoe agency. Amina's brother Mahmood would come from Prieska, 800 km from Roodepoort, to meet with the travellers. "I could not even visit people and this was difficult for people to understand. How could I explain my situation to the community? When I met someone in the shop, I had to monitor my actions because if I was reported I would be faced with detention." Amina was under house arrest until 1984.

The attention given by the system to Amina is good evidence of vindictive cruelty. It was clear that she had played no proven active role in Ahmed's activities or any other activities, despite her moral and political solidarity, which never wavered. In fact she herself made no distinction in her own mind between her principled support for the anti-apartheid movement and for Ahmed in particular and the activities for which she was supposedly convicted and punished.

One would never hear her complain that she had been unjustly punished, because such a complaint would have meant some form of distancing herself from the ideals and actions of Ahmed. Such distancing she would never accept. Her admiration for the manner in which he lived and died was and is profound; the price she paid for his activities she refuses to regard as a price at all. Her selflessness and magnanimity make her a true peer of Nelson Mandela and his closest colleagues in our struggle.

INDRES MOODLEY

Indres was in detention at John Vorster Square police station when he was, to his surprise, told that he would be appearing in court the following day. Indres remembers, "My wife had given birth and I had seen my son for the first time. A lawyer had been appointed by my family to represent me. It was in the Johannesburg Magistrate's Court that I met Salim Essop and Yousuf Hassan Essack (known as Moe) for the first time. The case was remanded and we were taken to The Fort in Braamfontein." That would later become the site of the Constitutional Court in the democratic South Africa.

For the first time, after a delay of approximately six months, Indres had an opportunity to discuss the events that had unfolded and redirected his life. "One day after appearing in court, for some reason or other there was no transport available. Salim, Moe and myself were handcuffed and we were made to walk toward the nearby John Vorster Square police station. Only a single warder escorted us. We questioned the motive behind this and realised that this could be a set-up. Maybe the cops expected us to run off and they would shoot us."

Indres, Salim and Moe were then taken from John Vorster to Pretoria Central. "We were placed in a cage outside the court in Pretoria. Visitors and family would talk to us through the cage. It was as if we were in the zoo," recalls Indres.

A Land Rover would normally pick up the three of them from court and take them to the Pretoria prison. Indres recollects, "After our court appearance, we were left outside the court with only one cop. Family and friends had chatted with us and had departed. We waited for hours on end and began wondering that something was not right. We were not handcuffed and were guarded by a small-built cop. We figured out that they expected us to make a run for it. We were alert in our thinking and realised that this saga had been staged. The authorities expected us to attempt to escape and cry out to the world that terrorists had overpowered a guard and escaped."

Like Moe Essack, Indres Moodley was sentenced on 1 November 1972 to five years' imprisonment following their conviction on a charge under the Terrorism Act. They were released on a legal technicality after serving one year.

ﾠ

Today when I see visual images of Palestinians, Iraqis and prisoners at Guantanamo Bay who are handcuffed and have hoods over their heads, the image of Uncle Ahmed walking on the 10th floor of John Vorster Square immediately comes to mind.

The only comforting thought is that Uncle Ahmed had a dignified funeral that was attended by thousands. His body, despite being battered and bruised, came back to his family. What about all the other families who till today don't know what happened to their loved ones? Where are their bodies? It is with this in mind that whenever I go to Uncle Ahmed's grave in Roodepoort I comfort myself.

CONCLUSION

Neither the inquest into Ahmed Timol's death nor the brief hearing called by the Truth and Reconciliation Commission – where the main witnesses to my uncle's death were never subpoenaed – got anywhere near the truth of what actually happened to him. Many questions remain, and cry out for an answer. I have conducted my own investigation and the findings are as follows:

All the indications were that Ahmed was in danger. Why did he not abandon his "operation" and flee the country before his arrest? The book clearly demonstrates Ahmed's tremendous care and affection for those close to him. Ahmed had, prior to his arrest, suggested to his younger brother, Mohammed, that they were under surveillance and that Mohammed should go to Durban. This confirms Ahmed's concern and protection of others.

In Ahmed's statement during his interrogation, he states the following about Amina Desai: "I must point out that my Aunty was at no time approached by me to become a member of the Party or to do any political work for me. It was I who abused the privileges which she bestowed upon me, such as the use of her car and using her house without her knowledge for the efforts I made to further the growth of the Communist Party."

This clearly indicates that Ahmed was taking full responsibility for his actions and not putting the lives of others in danger. Ahmed did not abandon his "operation" because of his dedication and commitment to the ANC, SACP and the liberation struggle. As a true cadre he intended to complete his mission even under the most trying, difficult and dangerous circumstances.

Was the police roadblock a set-up or was it by "accident" that Ahmed was arrested? Policemen based at the Newlands police station reported for "special" duty on the Friday afternoon. According to the police version, the policemen had set-up a roadblock at 10.40 pm and approximately 30 minutes later, at 11.10 pm, they stopped Ahmed and Salim in a yellow Anglia.

Reports indicate that during the early Seventies police were mainly raiding shebeens in the Newclare, Bosmont area and roadblocks of this nature (stopping cars) were unheard of. It was too much of a coincidence for the police to be staging a roadblock and arresting Ahmed and Salim. The police were waiting for them.

Was the secret correspondence material between Ahmed and the Party in the boot of the car when they were arrested? The police had submitted copies of the material as evidence during the inquest. They had re-typed the material, and this is proven by Afrikaans words appearing on the documents such as "*vervolg*" (continued) and "*kodeskrif – keerkant van brief*" (coded writing – other side of the letter). Stephanie Kemp confirms the authenticity of the material.

Why would Ahmed drive with such material in the boot of the car, especially after informing his younger brother that they were under surveillance? According to a friend in Newclare, they had removed most of the leaflets from the boot of the car before Ahmed and Salim were arrested. The friend clearly states that there was no material in the boot of the car.

It also seems quite impossible that, knowing the absolute standard security practices Ahmed had been taught, he would have preserved the secret correspondence "found" in the car. It is more than likely that all or most of the material had been planted in the car.

Policemen claimed during the inquest into Ahmed's death that he was never threatened, assaulted or tortured. John Vorster Square was the new state-of-the-art police headquarters that was supposed to have bars preventing detainees from jumping out of windows and committing suicide. Testimony given by various detainees clearly reveals the methods of torture used by the Security Police. The chilling testimony of Abdulhay Jassat, Hassen Jooma and Salim Essop (told for the first time in this book) proves without any doubt that political detainees were brutally tortured.

George Bizos in his book *No One to Blame* exposed the cover-up by the state of the circumstances of the death of Ahmed Timol. The inquest was a farce.

Magistrate De Villiers, concluding the inquest, remarked: "I would like to make the following recommendation for the future, namely that where people are detained in future in terms of Article 6 of Act 83 of 1967, that is the Act on Terrorism, that as soon as possible after arrest, the detainee must be examined by a District Surgeon in order to ascertain the health condition of the detainee and in particular to determine if there are any signs of assault on the body. It could possibly prevent long investigations like this one and could prevent the police from being embarrassed unnecessarily."

Ahmed was the 22nd person to have died in police custody since 1963 and 50 more were to die up to 1990. How wrong was De Villiers? Detainees continued dying in police custody and the Security Police kept on being protected by the apartheid judiciary.

The findings of the inquest in terms of Article 16 of the Inquest Act 1959 were:

"The deceased died because of serious brain damage and loss of blood sustained when he jumped out of a window of room 1026 at John Vorster Square and fell to the ground on the south side of the building. He committed suicide."

I believe that the findings of the apartheid court must be rectified. Law students in the new South Africa must not remember the legacy of Ahmed Timol with the findings of Magistrate De Villiers.

The police claimed that the information provided by Mr X (prior to Ahmed's alleged suicide) about Quentin, Martin and Henry in room 1026 caused an expression of shock or disappointment in the face of Ahmed. This triggered Ahmed into "committing suicide". Bizos has earlier explained the inconsistencies with the above sequence of events. I believe that there was no Mr X. This was a deliberate ploy by the Security Police to create havoc and sow mistrust in the Indian community. There was no Mr X and the explanation given by the police about the sequence of events was not true.

Magistrate De Villiers stated during the inquest that Ahmed was involved in the distribution of a document that stated: "Harass your enemy by going on hunger strikes, act insane, lodge complaints, whether true or false, resort to civil and criminal actions in courts as often as possible, make sure your complaints and actions the suppressors get the most publicly [sic]. Rather commit suicide than to betray the organisation," issued by the Communist Party of South Africa.

The statement by the magistrate is an insult to the integrity of the members of the South African Communist Party. The statement about committing suicide is obviously a fraud. The language is totally inconsistent with the instruction material issued by the SACP. It reinforces my view that the findings of the inquest must be rectified.

So, what really happened to Ahmed? In the statement given during his interrogation, Ahmed explained the link between the ANC and the SACP and openly declared his membership of the Communist Party. He wrote: "At two meetings of the ANC youth branch which I attended in 1968 (around March and June), the slogan *Amandla Ngewethu* was shouted – this slogan in essence is transformed to that of an oath."

Ahmed went on to explain the manner in which he had received the pamphlets from London and how they were distributed. He made it very clear that the persons that assisted him in the typing and addressing were unaware of the contents of the envelopes. He protected everyone. His statement began with the spurious claim that he personally knew Stephanie Kemp who, in fact, had never met him. This Kemp interprets as a deliberate misstatement, and such deliberate distortion would be consistent with the training as to how one ought to conduct oneself during interrogation.

Protecting those who had worked with him, Ahmed wrote: "Miss Khadija Chotia and Miss Aysha Bulbulia, the two persons I asked to have the envelopes addressed, were in no way made aware for what purpose they were typing the envelopes. They are in no way connected with the attempts made by me to develop the underground organs of the Party."

Ahmed clearly indicated that he had mentioned names of prospective and potential candidates for the Communist Party without having any political discussions with any of them. He had either known them or had come to know them because of a third person. The names mentioned in Ahmed's statement are the same names that appear in his correspondence with London, which he knew to be in the possession of the police.

In his statement Ahmed wrote: "Soon after I arrived from London and my first dispatches to my contact Stephanie, I mentioned some names and referred to them as prospective candidates for the Party. Here I must emphasise that all the names were written without any prior political discussion or soundings with each of them. Most of their political leanings I was not aware of but wrote their names down because I had known them in the past (or come to know them through a third person)."

It is important to note the change in Ahmed's handwriting as he wrote his statement. There is no doubt that this statement was written under duress. On the last page of Ahmed's statement, it was Captain Gloy who wrote the questions and answers posed to Ahmed. Why was Ahmed no longer writing his own statement? It is clear that Ahmed was in no condition to continue writing.

The point at which his own handwriting ended and Gloy's began is precisely the point at which the questioning focused on the identification of those with whom Ahmed was working on leaflet bombs. Ahmed refused to co-operate. He was operating in accordance with his training despite the most intense pressure. He had no reason for remorse or suicidal dismay at having, for instance, betrayed colleagues contrary to his training. It is clear that the police simply were not getting what they wanted from Ahmed.

If they were using systematic and scientific means of torture when interrogating Salim Essop, they no doubt did worse to Ahmed. We know this from the experiences of other detainees, including Jooma, Naik and Essop. One cannot believe the police version that Ahmed was not tortured or threatened in any way. If they could torture Salim to such an extent that he was eventually hospitalised, it is difficult to believe that they were not more brutal in their interrogation of Ahmed. Ahmed most likely died due to the sheer force of torture.

Salim Essop's view is simple: "Ahmed was a 'big fish'. Ahmed was someone the Security Police thought had never existed in South Africa. You need to put into context that the late Sixties and early Seventies was a time of intense political repression. The South African authorities and police believed that they had mopped up the underground structures. They could not believe that ANC/SACP sympathisers could be active in the country. It was highly unlikely that persons could enter the country legally or illegally and set up structures. It was in this context that the police had found Ahmed with documents indicating the setting up of underground structures; communication with the Communist Party abroad; names of persons who were potential recruits for the Party; secret communications; banned leaflets and pamphlets that were distributed throughout the country."

Salim states: "The police must have got frustrated, pushed beyond the limit. In the statement that Ahmed provided during his interrogation he mentioned the work that was carried out in setting up the underground structures. Ahmed was tortured on this basis. They wanted to ensure that they got the maximum out of Ahmed and pushed him to and past the limit. The intention was not to kill either Ahmed or Salim. The use of torture was to get information. If you collapsed, they were trained to revive you and they knew you would survive."

Salim says: "I think that the torture on Ahmed was so severe that he collapsed a number of times and at some point he died. Once Ahmed was dead, the police panicked. They thought they would revive Ahmed as they did with Salim. Ahmed had died under torture and they did not expect this to happen. The South African government of the day would have made more political capital if they had put Ahmed on trial. They would have shown there was this huge conspiracy taking place and Ahmed would have probably confirmed this in court."

There was a witness present when Ahmed fell from the sky to the ground. Mohamed Ali recalls: "It was definitely mid-week. We were having difficulty in obtaining a trading licence and had arrived from Pretoria. It was the month of Ramadan. My cousin and I were filling petrol at Dollars Garage, opposite JV Square (Commissioner and Goch Street). I caught it from the side of my eye as I saw something coming down. I heard a THUD! We heard no screaming, no shouting, saw no hand movement, no nothing.

"In less than a minute the cops were surrounding the place. It was as if the cops were waiting for this body to come down as they were there in a flash. Before we even attempted to get a closer look, we were immediately pushed off and told to move. 'You're not supposed to be here,' they said. As we tried to move, the cops were standing there. We were interested to know what was happening and only found out later who fell. The street was cordoned off so that no traffic could enter."

Ahmed Timol was no more.

A policeman who was based at John Vorster Square informed me in a telephone conversation that he had carried Ahmed's body after it had landed. He refuses to divulge additional details or speak to me. The eyewitness account of Mohamed Ali, who was filling petrol across the road when Ahmed fell, explaining that he heard no screaming or shouting, and less than a minute later there were police surrounding the area where Ahmed had landed, proves that they were waiting for the body to come down.

Here is another account: Mohammed Khan was employed by the Central Islamic Trust in 1969 as the burial and hearse supervisor. He was responsible for making all the necessary funeral arrangements. This included obtaining death certificates from the police liaison with hospitals and the mortuaries. Khan had built up an excellent rapport with state officials to ensure that when a funeral took place, he always received excellent co-operation from them.

According to Khan he received instructions from his office on 26 October 1971 to collect Ahmed Timol's body from the Hillbrow Mortuary and make the necessary funeral arrangements. Khan was not given access to the body, and made contact with Sergeant Fourie, who worked at the Hillbrow Mortuary. Fourie asked him to return to the mortuary later that evening. He had arranged for the security guard to go to the café, and Khan entered the mortuary.

Khan adds: "Upon my arrival at the mortuary I met Sergeant Fourie who took me to the section within the mortuary where the bodies were kept in the fridge. I established that Timol's body was kept in the white section of the mortuary.

"Sergeant Fourie opened the drawer of the fridge where Timol's body was kept. The body was fresh. The place was well lighted and I could see clearly. Fourie mentioned to me that the Security Police told him that this man had jumped from the tenth floor at John Vorster Square. He further questioned as to how this was possible as one of his shoes was found on the ninth floor of the police station."

Khan had seen many bodies involved in car and train accidents, but nothing like Ahmed's. "I noticed that Ahmed's eye was out of the socket, his body had blue marks, his nails were removed, and he had burn marks over the body as a result of shock treatment."

Fourie added that it was not possible for someone who had jumped to have his eye out of his socket and have bruises and burn marks on his body. He made Khan promise that he would keep as a secret what he had seen and that he had been allowed to see the body.

The Timol family was informed on 27 October 1971, late in the evening, about Ahmed's death. Khan's recollection that he was contacted on 26 October is probably faulty as his practice (and Islamic practice more generally) would always be to inform the family immediately.

The answers to the question raised above can be supplied by Gloy and his colleagues. Gloy made it clear to me that it was not necessary for him to have applied for amnesty, and that I must accept the court's findings and continue with my life. This is not so easy for me. The brutal death of my beloved uncle cannot just be forgotten. In the spirit of the Truth and Reconciliation Commission and building a new democratic, non-racist South Africa, one has to let go of the past and build for the future. However, in order for me to do this, I need to know the truth. I need Gloy and his colleagues to make a full disclosure surrounding the death of my uncle. Until they do this, and explain their innocence in detail, they will remain the murderers of Ahmed Timol.

I have informed the National Prosecution Authority about the failure of Gloy and company to apply for amnesty, and also the failure on the part of the TRC to subpoena the policemen involved in the case. They have registered the case and are waiting for me to provide them with more evidence. There is nothing more that I can do, except hope that the South African public will exert pressure on the NPA to re-investigate the Ahmed Timol case. My message to Gloy and his colleagues is that the memory of Ahmed Timol will never be forgotten.

The death of Uncle Ahmed has had a profound impact on my life. The death and shock of losing a loved one was devastating for the family. From a young age, I had formed a tenuous but cherished connection with my beloved uncle, despite spending little time with him. Conducting my research, I have heard of so many positive aspects of his life that he is a presence which is close to me. I found that he was a true comrade, prepared to sacrifice his life for the oppressed people of this country. His life serves as an inspiration and a monument to democratic South Africa.

In a very personal sense, he inspired me to do my share for our land. The political situation has changed. The oppressive racist regime has been defeated, and we have earned our victory. However, different challenges await us. We need no longer conduct an armed struggle, but a struggle to deliver to our people. We must continue the struggle to educate the masses about the legacy of fallen comrades who were unable to witness victory. The heroes and heroines of the struggle need to know that we shall never forget them.

We can contribute. We can make a difference. When comrades forget our history, and forget our responsibilities as citizens, they need reminding. We need to find and develop leaders such as Dr Yusuf Dadoo who was not only responsible for transforming the Indian Congress Movement, but for helping so powerfully to consolidate the oppressed people of this country. It was while researching this book that I came to appreciate the significance of the role Dadoo played. We need to appreciate and ponder the leadership roles of OR Tambo, Walter Sisulu, Nelson Mandela, Govan and Thabo Mbeki, Bram Fischer, Joe Slovo, Chris Hani and others, who saw the need to abandon the dialogue of the dead and to embark on targeted, limited armed struggle.

These were leaders who took the hard decisions and changed the course of our history. Ahmed Timol was a young recruit to this cause. He ennobled us all in his death.

Conducting this research has brought me into contact with people such as the Pahad brothers, Rookaya Saloojee, Ronnie Kasrils, Abdulhay Jassat and others. They are woven into the narrative and have helped to explain and articulate the life of Ahmed Timol. They have confirmed that this, and related, history must be recorded; that we must never lose sight of where we come from. It is the road map to our future.

My uncle, the inspiration of my life, is a cogent reminder that, as they say: *Aluta Continua* – The Struggle Continues.

AHMED'S STATEMENT DURING INTERROGATION
(Rewritten from original)

According to my knowledge there is close co-operation between the Communist Party of South Africa and the African National Congress. Every South African who goes abroad is a potential recruit to the ranks of the African National Congress and the Communist Party irrespective of his race and colour. I joined the Party because of my stay in London at my relatives' place – Mr Essop Pahad and by 1969 I had developed a prior friendship with Stephanie Kemp who was a member of the Central Committee of the Communist Party of South Africa.

Regarding the Radio Peking, Radio Moscow and Radio Tanzania broadcasts – the latter was advertised in one of the pamphlets of the ANC distributed in the country.

The pamphlets are printed in England. To my knowledge the record distributed was also made in Home Studio in London.

At two meetings of the ANC-youth branch which I attended in 1968 (around March and June) the slogan *Amandla Ngewethu* was shouted – this slogan in essence is transformed to that of an oath.

I was given the sum of R500 by Jack Hodgson prior to my departure for South Africa to use the money for the purchase of printing machinery and stationery for distribution purposes. I, however, did not buy any printing machinery but used the school's duplicating machine for the cyclostyling of *Inkululeko*. The draft copy of the newsletter was sent to me by post and I therefore had to print the necessary stencils. The size of the stencil was to be of a uniform motive and it was typed by me with my own Underwood typewriter with a red cover. This machine has been taken into possession by the police.

DISTRIBUTION OF PAMPHLETS BY ME
The first occasion was sometime in August 1970. The posting on this occasion was done by me and Salim Essop from the Jeppe Street Post Office after 8pm. About 400 to 500 were posted by us simultaneously. Soon after the distribution comments of the distribution were being heard and also advertised by the daily papers. I think ANC (CP) headquarters in London sent me a letter of congratulations through Jack Hodgson. The addresses on the first occasion was typed out by Khadija Chotia and was typed onto the envelopes using my typewriter. I gave her R3 for her work. She was given the envelopes and was not told for what purposes they were for. The list of the names was sent with packet containing the pamphlets. The pamphlets were in this occasion sent inside a box containing Darjeeling tea to PO Box 446, Roodepoort in my name. Around 1 000 pamphlets were sent in the box. After having receiving the printed envelopes I then personally put them into the envelopes, bought the stamps and posted about 400 to 500 together with the assistance of Salim Essop. (Salim Essop only assisted in posting.)

The second occasion when I received pamphlets through my father's postbox: 446, Roodepoort was in the early part of 1971. This time the pamphlets were concealed under a box of chocolates and there were about 500. I personally printed some 250 and posted these also from Jeppe Post Office after 8 pm.

On the third occasion I received a draft copy of *Inkululeko* and was directed to cyclostyle this using approximation in size. I typed the text onto the stencils (eight stencils used – learning and typing) and duplicated these one afternoon in late July using the school's duplicating machine. The envelopes were given by me to be addressed to Miss Ayesha Bulbulia of Cajee's Commercial College who was completely not aware of what was to be placed inside the envelope. She typed some 300 to 400 envelopes from the address list sent with the packet. This time two different sized brown envelopes were used and I paid her about R3 for her work. The placing of the newspaper inside the envelopes was done by me at home in the night and posted by me from Jeppe Street Post Office at night. The distribution of the paper was to come out by the end of July 1971. This marking the 50th Anniversary of the birth of the Communist Party of South Africa and I think some were posted by me from Roodepoort.

The first and second batches of leaflets were titled as:
• Son's and Daughters of Africa; and
• What the ANC says to Vorster and his gang.
The third was under the following heading:
Inkululeko – Freedom July 1971
African Organ of the Communist Party of South Africa.

INDRES MOODLEY
Came to know the above person through my cousin Bahiya Desai, who had given to me his phone number at his place of work. I phoned Indres from home after July 1970 and arranged to meet him at the corner of Becker and Market Street in Johannesburg. Thereafter I met him a few times at his place in Lens where we had general discussions on politics. At one of these meetings I had shown him the draft guidelines of the organisational structure of the Party with its main and sub groups operating initially within the country. Soon after this he was to leave Johannesburg. And in the New Year was to settle in Durban. I recommended his name to Headquarters and they later approved. But I did not inform him of any recommendation to Headquarters but took this initiative upon myself. During my visit/holiday to Durban in the first few months of January I contacted Indres by phone and arranged to meet him at his place. I went down to Indres's place and had a general talk with him and offered to give him and Saths Cooper (Indres's friend) a lift to Johannesburg on the day when I was also leaving for home. I had also given him on one of these occasions two books on Marxism – namely *What is Marxism* and *Marxism versus Positivistic Philosophy*. In Durban I had also given Indres my friend Yakoob Varachia's (social friend of mine) flat number in the centre of Durban whom he could contact on a social basis.

By about April I had not heard from him and decided to write to his wife implying very clearly in the letter that he should contact me and questioned him as to why he has not done so. I did not receive a reply from Indres to this letter and did not again hear from him.

YAKOOB VARACHIA

The above person comes from the same town as I do, Roodepoort, thus I know him and his family well. My relationship with him has always been of a non-political nature. During my holiday in Durban I visited Yakoob three to four times purely on a social basis. He studied at the Textile Engineering College in Leicester during the period 1967-1969 and returned to South Africa immediately thereafter. He is at present an engineer of textile hosiery machines in his father's factory, Hosiery Manufacturing Company, Durban.

Soon after I arrived from London and my first dispatches to my contact Stephanie, I mentioned some names and referred to them as prospective candidates for the Party. Here I must emphasise that all the names were written without any prior political discussion or foundings with each of them. Most of their political leanings I was not aware of but wrote their names down because I had known them in the past (or come to know them through a third person). Persons such as Hassen Jooma. I had known him at the Teachers College in 1961 to 1963 but met him once only after I had come back from London. He has to the best of my knowledge had no connections whatsoever with the Communist Party internally and externally. The same can be said of the following persons:

1. Dilshad Jetham
2. Shireen Areff
3. Kantilal Vallabh
4. Kantilal Naik
5. Fatima Wadee
6. Omar Vawda
7. Yusuf (Chubb) Garda
8. Khadija Chotia

The persons that I approached to recruit were the following three:
1. Salim Essop – he was only on one occasion involved with the gradual aspect of our work and that was at the time of the first posting of the pamphlets in August 1970. I did however have theoretical discussions on Marxism with him but there were no organised meetings whatsoever.
2. Indres Moodley showed interest until January 1970 but I lost complete contact with him from that time onwards.
3. Bahiya Vawda Desai had never shown any desire to work as a member of the Party and I dismissed her right from the onset. At present she is abroad with her husband (Omar Vawda) who is on a scientific course sent by the firm JP Coats of Isipingo – the course lasts for three months. They should be returning to South Africa by January.

MY AUNTY MRS AMINA DESAI

I must point out that my Aunty was at no time approached by me to become a member of the Party or to do any political work for me. It was I who abused her privileges which she bestowed upon me, such as the use of her car and using her house without her knowledge for the efforts I made to further the growth of the Communist Party.

I had no documents or stencils relating to the Party left with Salim Essop's sister Fatima Essop.

Miss Khadija Chotia and Miss Ayesha Bulbulia the two persons I asked to have the envelopes addressed were in no way made aware for what purpose they were typing the envelopes. They are in no way connected with the attempts made by me to develop the underground organs of the Party.

I am associated with the Dynamos Soccer Club, and am the acting secretary. The main purpose of my association has been motivated by the desire to exercise influence and control the activities of the club. However, it must be pointed out that my association with this club dates back prior to my departure abroad in 1966.

Gloy's handwriting
Q: Who assisted you to distribute the pamphlets on 3/8/70 in Durban and Cape Town? And in PE on 14/8/70?
A: No one assisted me.
Q: Where is the typewriter that was used on this occasion?
A: My private typewriter was used. In possession of police.
I have no contact men in other centres.

LIST OF PEOPLE WHO DIED IN DETENTION

This list has been compiled from a number of sources and may contain some errors or ommissions.

YEAR	NAME	DATE DIED	PLACE	DAYS HELD	OFFICIAL / ALLEGED CAUSE
1963	NGUDLE, Looksmart	05/09/63	Compol, Pretoria	17	Suicide by hanging
1963	MAMPE, Bellington	??/09/63	Worcester	140	Undisclosed
1964	TYITA, Bellington	24/01/64	Port Elizabeth	?	Suicide by hanging
1964	SALOOJEE, Suliman	09/09/64	Johannesburg	65	Suicide, jumped from 7th floor
1965	GAGA, Ngeni	09/05/65	Transkei	<1	Natural causes
1965	HOYE, Pongolosha	09/05/65	Transkei	<1	Natural causes
1966	HAMAKWAYO, James	09/10/66	Pretoria Prison	13	Suicide by hanging
1966	SHONYEKA, Hangula	09/10/66	Pretoria Prison	40	Suicide
1966	PIN, Leong	19/11/66	Leeukop Prison, Pta	1	Suicide by hanging
1967	YAN, Ah	05/01/67	Silverton Police Sta.	37	Suicide by hanging
1967	MADIBA, Alpheus	09/09/67	Namibia	1	Suicide by hanging
1968	TUBAKWA, Jundea	11/09/68	Pretoria Prison	1	Suicide by hanging
1968	Unknown person	??/??/68	?	?	Reported by Minister of Police
1969	KGOATHE, Nicodemus	04/02/69	Held: Silverton Police Sta. Died: HF Verwoerd Hospital	85	Natural causes: bronchial pneumonia after slipping in the shower
1969	MODIPANE, Solomon	28/02/69	Held: Silverton Police Sta. Died: HF Verwoerd Hospital	3	Natural causes: after slipping on piece of soap, fatal injuries
1969	LENKOE, James	10/03/69	Pretoria Prison	5	Suicide by hanging
1969	MAYEKISO, Caleb	01/06/69	Port Elizabeth police cells	18	Natural causes not specified
1969	SHIVUTE, Michael	17/06/69	Ondangwa police cells	<1	Suicide
1969	MONAKGOTLA, Jacob	10/09/69	Pretoria Prison	222	Natural causes: thrombosis
1969	HARON, Abdullah (Imam)	27/09/69	Maitland Police Station, Cape Town	122	Natural causes: heart trouble caused by fall down stairs
1971	CUTSELA, Mthayeni	21/01/71	Held: Pondoland. Died: Transkei hospital	40	Natural causes. Brain haemorrhage
1971	TIMOL, Ahmed	27/10/71	John Vorster Square, Johannesburg	5	Suicide, jumped from 10th floor
1976	MDLULI, Joseph	19/03/76	Security HQ, Durban	<1	Injury to neck after falling against chair
1976	TSHWANE, William	25/07/76	Modderbee Prison, East Rand	<1	Shot while trying to escape, justifiable homicide
1976	MOHAPI, Mapetla	05/08/76	Kei Road Jail, East London	22	Anoxia and suffocation as a result of hanging
1976	MAZWEMBE, Luke	02/09/76	Caledon Square, Cape Town	<1	Suicide by hanging
1976	MBATHA, Dumisani	25/09/76	Held: Modderbee Prison Died: Far East Rand Hospital	9	Natural causes, extreme sympathetic system activity with avuncular fibrillation of heart
1976	MOGATUSI, Fenuel	28/09/76	Johannesburg Fort	70	Natural causes. Suffocating during an epileptic fit

YEAR	NAME	DATE DIED	PLACE	DAYS HELD	OFFICIAL / ALLEGED CAUSE
1976	MASHABANE, Jacob	05/10/76	Johannesburg Fort	4	Suicide by hanging
1976	Unknown man	05/10/76	Carletonville police cells	?	Undisclosed, police said allegation of assault before death involved
1976	MZOLO, Edward	09/10/76	Johannesburg Fort	8	Undisclosed
1976	MAMASHILA, Ernest	19/11/76	Balfour, Transvaal	3	Suicide by hanging
1976	MOSALA, Thalo	26/11/76	Butterworth, Transkei	87	Natural causes. Internal bleeding
1976	TSHAZIBANE, Wellington	11/12/76	John Vorster Square, Johannesburg	2	Suicide by hanging
1976	BOTHA, George	15/12/76	Sanlam Building, Port Elizabeth	5	Suicide. Jumped 6 floors down a stairwell
1977	NDZANGA, Lawrence	08/01/77	Johannesburg Fort	51	Natural causes: heart failure
1977	NTSHUNTSHA, Nanaoth (Dr)	09/01/77	Leslie Police Station	26	Hanging, probably suicide
1977	MALELE, Elmon	20/01/77	Held: John Vorster Square, Johannesburg, Died: nursing home	13	Natural causes: haemorrhage after hitting head against desk during interrogation
1977	MABALENA, Matthews	15/02/77	John Vorster Square, Johannesburg	25	Accidental, fell from 10th floor
1977	JOYI, Twasifeni	15/02/77	Idutywa, Transkei	?	Post-mortem result not revealed
1977	MALINGA, Samuel	22/02/77	Held: Pietermaritzburg Died: Edenvale Hospital	22	Natural causes. Heart disease and pneumonia
1977	KHOZA, Aaron	26/03/77	Pietermaritzburg Prison	106	Suicide by hanging
1977	MABIJA, Phakamile	07/07/77	Tvl Road Police Station Kimberley	10	Suicide. Jumped from 6th floor
1977	LOZA, Elijah	01/08/77	Held: Victor Verster Prison Paarl. Died: Tygerberg Hospital, Cape Town	65	Natural causes, stroke
1977	HAFFEJEE, Dr Hoosen	03/08/77	Brighton Beach Police Station, Durban	1	Suicide by hanging
1977	MZIZI, Bayempin	13/08/77	Brighton Beach Police Station, Durban	35	Suicide by hanging
1977	BIKO, Steve	12/09/77	Held: Port Elizabeth. Died: Pretoria	24	Brain injury during scuffle with police
1977	MALAZA, Sipho	16/11/77	Krugersdorp police cells	138	Suicide by hanging
1978	TABALAZA, Lungile	10/07/78	Sanlam Building, Port Elizabeth	<1	Suicide. Jumped from 5th floor
1980	NDZUMO, Saul	10/09/80	Umtata, Transkei	9	Natural causes. Heart trouble, diabetes, blood pressure
1981	MGQWETO, Manana	17/09/81	Engcobo, Transkei	?	Unknown

YEAR	NAME	DATE DIED	PLACE	DAYS HELD	OFFICIAL / ALLEGED CAUSE
1981	MUPFHE, Tshifhiwa	12/11/81	Venda	2	Assault by police
1982	AGGETT, Dr Neil	17/09/81	John Vorster Square Police Station	70	Suicide by hanging
1982	DIPALE, Ernest	08/08/82	John Vorster Square Police Station	3	Suicide by hanging
1983	MNDAWE, Simon	08/03/83	Nelspruit Prison	14	Suicide by hanging
1983	MALATJI, Pans	05/07/83	Protea Police Station, Soweto	<1	Culpable homicide: shot in forehead at point-blank range
1984	TSHIKUDO, Samuel	20/01/84	Held: Venda. Died: Tshizidzini Hospital	77	Natural causes
1984	SIPELE, Mxolisi	??/06/84	Sulenkama Hospital, Transkei	±150	Unknown: police claim he died in hospital a month after his release
1984	MTHETHWA, Ephrahim	25/08/84	Durban Central prison	165	Suicide by hanging
1985	RADITSELA, Andries	06/05/85	Baragwanath Hospital, Soweto	2	Fatal head injury, fell from Casspir
1985	NDONDO, Batandwa	24/09/85	Cala, Transkei	<1	Shot by police
1986	KUTUMELA, Makompe	05/04/86	Lebowa	1	Police assault
1986	NCHABELENG, Peter	11/04/86	Lebowa	1	Police assault
1986	JACOBS, Xoliso	22/10/86	Upington	129	Suicide by hanging
1986	MARULE, Simon	23/12/86	Held: Modderbee Prison Died: Boksburg / Benoni Hospital	183	Kidney failure
1987	MASHOKE, Benedict	26/03/87	Burgersfort Police Station	215	Suicide by hanging
1987	MNTONGA, Eric	24/07/87	Mdantsane Cells, Ciskei	1	Police assault
1987	BANI, Nobandla	29/07/87	North End Cells, Port Elizabeth	222	Stroke
1988	ZOKWE, Sithembele	12/01/88	Butterworth, Transkei	<1	Police shooting
1988	MAKALENG, Alfred	26/08/88	Held: Nylstroom, Died: JHB Hospital	804	Natural causes, fluid on the brain
1990	SITHOLE, Clayton Sizwe	30/01/90	John Vorster Square, Johannesburg	4	Suicide by hanging
1990	TLHOTLHOMISANG, Lucas	26/03/90	Klerksdorp	7	Police report: meningitis
1990	MADISHA, Donald Thabela	01/06/90	Potgietersrus Police Station	130	Police report: suicide by hanging

LETTERS TO THE EDITOR

AFRIKANER SPEAKS
I AM an Afrikaner, but I am also a South African. Until recently I was proud of this fact. Now I am ashamed of the country of my birth.

Can you be proud of a country in which patriotism and party politics are inextricably confused: a country in which any opposition to inhumane policy is barely tolerated.

It is not only perversion of justice which has changed my attitude, but the apathy and acquiescence with which my people regard the wrongs in this country.
Rian Malan, Linden
The Star, Tuesday, November 9, 1971

IT MIGHT HAVE BEEN OUR SON
"It might have been our son. You bear a child, you bring him up in joy and hope – and then this happens," said my wife when we heard of the death in detention of Ahmed Timol and the serious unexplained illness of Mr Mohammed Essop. Yes, it might have been our son, or daughter.
Jack Curtis, Westcliff
The Star, Friday, October 29, 1971
Jack Curtis's daughter, Jeanette Schoon, and his granddaughter, Katryn, were murdered by the Security Police in Angola in the late Eighties.

TIMOL'S PARENTS THANK STAR READERS
The loss of our son, Ahmed, has left, as you can well imagine, a very great gap in our hearts. His unfortunate and sudden passing away has only magnified our grief.

We have found the thoughts and wishes of your readers a great comfort. It has helped us beyond description to know that our grief has been felt by many people of all races and denominations.

The fact that so many of your readers took the trouble not only to attend our son's funeral, but also attend prayer meetings, has stirred and encouraged our hearts immensely.

We would sincerely have preferred to meet each one of your readers personally and tell them how very much we appreciate their thoughts and feelings for us.

Naturally, we regret we cannot do this, and hope your readers will not take offence by our thanking them most warmly through your newspaper.
Mr Hajee Yusuf Timol and Mrs Hawa Timol, Roodepoort
The Star

JOHN VORSTER SQUARE DEATH REGISTER Reference No. SAP.183/3991/71

Name	Number	Comments	
Sergeant Leonard Gysbert Kleyns	23123B	Stationed at Newlands Police Station	Was at the police roadblock
Constable S. Le R. Fourie	50182H		Was at the roadblock
Res/A/Off. A. S. Verster	203465		Was at the roadblock
Constable Adam Alexander Cecil Thinnies (Coloured)	152109P	Stationed at Newlands Number 60 District	Was at the police roadblock
Lieutenant Colonel Willem Petrus van Wyk		Stationed at Security Police, Head Office, Pretoria	Read pamphlets as Ahmed was brought to John Vorster Square
Captain Richard Bean (Deceased 21/06/2001)		Stationed at Security Police, John Vorster Square	Interrogated Ahmed
Adjutant Officer Neville Els		Security Branch, Johannesburg	Statement on material found in car
Captain Johannes Zacharia van Niekerk		Stationed at Security Police, Head Office, Pretoria	Interrogated Ahmed
Captain Johannes Hendrik Gloy		Security Police, Head Office, Pretoria	Interrogated Ahmed
Adjutant Officer Jacobus Liebenberg		Security Branch, Johannesburg	Went to the Timol flat
Sergeant Joao Anastacio Rodriques		Sergeant, Security Branch, Pretoria	Guarding Ahmed when he allegedly jumped.
S.A.O. Gabriel Johannes Deysel		Security Branch, John Vorster Square	On duty at John Vorster Square when Ahmed had died. Saw body lying on the floor
Jacob Johannes Schoon	19916P A/O	Security Branch, John Vorster Square	Witness
Speurder-Adjutant Officer CPF J van Rensburg		Security Police John Vorster Square	Went to the Timol flat
Lieutenant Marthinus David Ras		Stationed in Johannesburg	Went to the Timol flat
Detective Sergeant Frederick Robert Bouwer		Security Police Johannesburg	Seen Ahmed in Detention Room
Detective Sergeant Jacob Willem Stefanus Louw		Security Branch, Johannesburg	Seen Ahmed in Detention Room
Brigadier Cecil William St. John Pattle (Deceased 1999)		Stationed at John Vorster Square	Report given to him after fall
Denis Kemp		Statement by District Surgeon	
Jacobus Johannes Mostert		Statement by Assistent Curator at the State Mortuary	

Name	Number	Comments	
Johan Petrus Fourie		Statement by Assistant Curator at the State Mortuary	
Nicolaas Jacobus Schepers		Conducted post mortem	
Adjutant-Officer Petrus van der Merwe	32969T	Assigned to the photographic division	Took photographs of the tree that Ahmed landed on and photographs of room 1026
Major Johannes Frederick Coenraad Fick		Stationed at John Vorster Square	Assisted in the investigation
Captain Jacobus Petrus le Roux		Stationed at John Vorster Square	Went to flat and confiscated typewriter, passport, etc.
Detective-Sergeant Petrus Johannes du Preez		Stationed at Security Branch, Head Office, Pretoria	Statement on usage of typewriter
Captain Frederick Jacobus Fourie		Stationed at SA Criminal Bureau	Handwriting expert
Captain F. J. Fourie		SA Police	Statement on handwriting
Captain Carel Joseph Dirker		Security Branch, Johannesburg	Statement on material found

Death Register in the Timol inquest supplied by Cachalia and Loonat who were the lawyers representing the Timol family at the inquest.

АНКЕТА-"()"

Слушателя *Шестимесячных парткурсов*

1. Фамилия и имя (настоящие)
   Ахмед Эссоп Тимол

(по паспорту)
   то же

(в школе)
   Симонс Поль

2. Пол *муж*   3. Год, месяц и число рождения *1941г. 3 ноября*

4. Место рождения *г. Брейтен, Южно Африканская Республи*

5. Национальность *Южно Африканец* 6. Подданство *ЮАР*

7. Социальное происхождение *из семьи торговца*

8. Партийная принадлежность *член Южно Африканской компартии*
   (с какого года член компартии)
   с 1968г.

9. Выполняемая партийная работа *Партпоручений не имеет*

10. Состояли ли в Союзе молодежи (комсомол, социалистич. и др.) и сколько времени
    Не состоял

11. Состояли ли в других политических партиях (когда и причина выбытия)
    не состоял

12. Членом какого профсоюза состоите и когда были приняты
    Не состоял

13. Привлекались ли к судебной ответственности, в том числе и за политическую деятельность

где, когда   *Не судим*

Ahmed's registration form, written in Russian, for the Lenin School.

Mrs Hawa Timol

P.O. Box. 446
Roodepoort
1725

Dear Mr & Mrs Agget & family,
My deepest sympathies on the loss of your son Neil. I can imagine how you must be feeling beccuse I felt the same when I lost my son also while in detention and also the same age.
Please be brave. God is great and may HE rest his soul in peace.
Yours truly
Mrs Hawa Timol
P.O. Box. 446
Roodepoort
1725.

Tel 699-1762

Letter written to the Aggett family by Hawa Timol on the death in detention of their son Neil.
Source: UCT Library

– 13 –

H24
124

10 AUGUSTUS 1970.

My dearest Ahmed,

Paul has asked me to let you know that he and
Mary have broken up – she has gone to live with Alan.
As you can imagine he has taken a terrible knock and
is quite shattered by events. It really is too bad –
his wife and his best friend.

He is too upset to write to anyone at present and
we are all trying to give him support and succour. I
know how much he would appreciate a letter from you
at this time – even just to know that his friends
are all standing by him.

He can't even imagine, when or how it all began.
They say the partner is always the last to know. Not
that any of us really noticed it happening – what
a sorry mess. I think she has made a terrible mistake, but that is life, I guess.

I am rushing off to the theatre and want to
post this on my way.

Regards to all,

Stephanie.

KODESKRIF : KEERKANT VAN BRIEF :

5/10/7/70.

Under separate cover you will receive a "present"   X
containing 1,000 leaflets. Please post on or after
13th August even if there has already been publicity
about propaganda drive.

The "present" also contains a letter to cover   X
you if the parcel is opened, etc.

The present is a box of fortnum and manson's
darjeeling tea.

ENDS.

——oOo——

Copies of some of the secret correspondence between the Party in London and
Ahmed. Retyped by the police and used as evidence during the inquest.

My dear Ahmed,

Thanks for your last letter. It is good to know you are well, despite the departure of summer.

I must say it is lovely here now that the weather is so much warmer. I go for long walks in the evenings and watch all the beautiful people in their spring clothes. The evenings are so long that it is quite disruptive. And then the light comes pouring in at my window as early as 5 o'clock in the mornings. So I don't get much sleep these days.

I had a lovely trip to Paris. What a beautiful city it is. I don't know why I continue to live in London which is so grey in comparison with Paris. The Seine too is so much more manageable a rive than the Thames. One cannot be in Paris and fail to notice the river and its beauty.

My plans for working in Paris are still in the very early stages but I did have some useful discussions with a couple of the academics there and one in particular who holds quite a senior position seemed very interested in what I had to offer. However it will still be some time before I know whether the wheels have even begun to move. Meanwhile I have a job here at the British Museum just to keep body and soul together. I love going there actually. It is very tranquil.

Write again soon - I do enjoy your letters even though my own leave much to be desired.

Regards to all.

                                        Steph.

KODESKRIF : KEERKANT VAN BRIEF :

  5/5/71 :

Urgently require information as to why you consider your brother should not return to S.A. Mota considers it desirable he should do so in the near future. Reply immediately.

  ENDS.

                    ---oOo---

TRIBUTES

YUSUF "Jo Jo" SALOOJEE

When the news broke out about Ahmed's death, I was in a state of absolute shock. I was convinced that I was in a sleep and someone was telling me this terrible story. If you knew someone like Ahmed, a real human being, you felt such warmth that you can never forget him as long as you live. One of Ahmed's tremendous and remarkable skills was his combination of seriousness with humour. This is unparalleled in most human beings. Ahmed's care and concern for people was real and this quality is scarce in most human beings. If Ahmed was eating a sandwich and he saw someone who was hungry, Ahmed would give his sandwich away. (Yusuf witnessed Ahmed doing this on numerous occasions.) This quality comes from Ahmed's father who had a soft and golden heart. Ahmed's mother would read him very carefully in terms of his manners, who he associated with and not to get involved in anything illegal, such as politics. Hawa would encourage Ahmed to concentrate on his studies and religion. She blamed me for Ahmed's naughtiness, which at times was true. Both of us were naughty. I did tell Hawa that there were so many other influences on Ahmed being politicised. The greatest influence was Ahmed himself. Ahmed had his own mind and it was not politics that Ahmed was about, but rather Ahmed's deep love for humanity, which he acquired from both his parents.

An exceptional and remarkable trait of Ahmed was that if you had developed a friendship with him, it was for life. Ahmed would be absolutely loyal and would do practically anything for you.

You could be Ahmed's best friend, but if you did something wrong, he would take you to task. Ahmed believed very strongly in honesty in friendship. This is a quality that is absolutely rare.

Ahmed always mentioned: "We will be free one day. We will see freedom in our lifetime."

RUTH LONGONI

Ahmed was really an ideological person. I think he had great compassion for people and a sense of justice and injustice and so on. He wasn't dogmatic and I don't think he was particularly ideological either in those kinds of ways.

Ahmed was very compassionate. He also very much wanted to enjoy life. He wanted to savour the freedoms and enjoyments of life in this country. I saw him as a responsible person who cared for other people including members of his family and so on. He was a teacher after all and he liked to teach. That was his job. He was able to do that and to help people. There was a real, real mix to him. There was a side to Ahmed that was hedonistic and ready to enjoy life. He was almost spoilt, but that is not the right word to use. He was living in a nice situation and wanted to enjoy life, but there was also a deeply serious side to him. I think he was a complex individual and he had all sorts of qualities and contradictory qualities as well.

I'd like to remember him as he was when we used to meet up and go to a film.

I remember the night we walked back from Barnet station to where I was living in Arkley and the laughs that we had. I liked the humorous, warm relationship that he and Lesley had as well. Lesley was the companion who I shared my flat with. I liked the way that he could joke with her and the three of us were happy there. If he could stay Lesley was happy to see him as well. So I like to remember the good things. I also remember the intensity of our feeling for one another. Those clichés about times when you're walking on air – actually I remember a particular walk that we went on where I felt that that's what I was doing. We were very happy walking in the countryside, just that sort of love and intensity of feeling for each other. There were some very good times with Ahmed.

I will remember him for his compassion and the values that he believed in. His compassion and empathy for other people, the easy and quick compassion that he had for them. His tenderness and his sensitivity. His lack of dogmatism.

There were sort of emotional values as well to do with politics and struggle that we shared. I think probably I read more after Ahmed left than I did during that time. But we shared a very strong sort of feeling of a sense of justice, a need for change and commitment to revolutionary change.

You have to admire that depth of commitment and intensity of feeling and if he could bring it to bear as he did in the struggle on South Africa he could obviously bring that to bear in relationships as well. Ahmed had a depth of feeling for people and intensity about him and that's an unforgettable quality. His depth of commitment.

NEWSPAPER OF THE ANTI-APARTHEID MOVEMENT, DECEMBER 1971
Ahmed was a teacher who was respected throughout the community for his dedication to his work and for the tremendous effort and sacrifices he made for his students and friends in every aspect of their lives.

From a very young age he involved himself actively in community affairs. He was always in the forefront fighting against the injustices perpetrated by the apartheid system.

Throughout his short life he worked for the ideal of a non-racial South Africa, based on the equality of all the people that lived in it.

Prevented by the system from advancing his studies and learning new educational techniques, Ahmed came to Britain in 1967. He taught in Slough and attended evening classes.

Those that had the opportunity of meeting him for the first time or of renewing old acquaintances, were impressed by his dedication and his abhorrence of injustice, whether it was in the UK or in South Africa.

He was a member of the National Union of Teachers and took an active interest in its activities. In his last year in the UK he worked among the immigrant community in Slough.

The demands of his ageing parents and the strong urge to be with the oppressed peoples of South Africa led him home in 1969. He immediately became involved with the problems of his students and his community.

Within two years of his return he is dead, killed because the vicious system of apartheid cannot tolerate anyone demanding basic human rights.

Ahmed was only 29 years old. He paid the ultimate penalty for his beliefs, but the work he did will not be forgotten; and the spirit of what Ahmed stood for will never die in South Africa.

Once again the regime has taken the life of an individual, whose death is a loss, not only to his family and friends, but to the future of non-racial South Africa. No community, let alone South Africa, can afford to lose such men.

At the moment an unknown number of people are being detained; many have been subjected to torture; and every day new names are added to the list of people that have vanished without trace.

The greatest tribute we could pay to Ahmed would be to resolutely continue our struggle against the apartheid system. We must build a massive movement of solidarity with those detained, the millions of oppressed South Africans.

Our words must be transformed into action and we must give concrete material and other aid to the forces that are fighting the South African regime. It is this that will help ensure that Ahmed did not die in vain.

AMINA DESAI

Ahmed was a very congenial man. He was always good with the neighbours. He was not born an extraordinary figure. He was a diffident man. Ahmed displayed his heroism in the qualities of a very ordinary man. The freedom that we have today did not just come about. Ahmed had showed that an ordinary man could accomplish heroic measures to foster his beliefs. He was always kind and a nice young man.

The apartheid government made Ahmed a hero for the people. They created him. Ahmed gave his life for his people. The statement made by Ahmed during his detention indicates that he was a caring man who was prepared to sacrifice his life.

MEG PAHAD

Ahmed's arrest and death devastated not only his immediate circle in West Kensington, but students from South Africa studying in the UK generally. Many thought: if they can kill Timol and at the same time slander the Communist Party and the ANC as devils and pigs, then I want to join these bodies. The event caused a huge outcry in South Africa, too; but in the internal conditions of repression the government was able, through media manipulation and tyranny, to obscure much of what was happening from the view of the populace at large. The situation abroad was different. The story came through more clearly, in Timol's and other cases. The fact that Timol had spent time in London, getting to know a wide circle of people, sharpened the impact. It is in such crass ways that the white Nationalist government of South Africa played directly into the hands of the liberation movement, acting, as it were, as recruiting agent.

However apolitical people's backgrounds were, Ahmed's fate made them re-think their beliefs. This was particularly so among South Africans abroad. If someone like Ahmed was arrested and killed, it meant that others who suffered a similar fate must have also been good people. It is this ripple effect of the martyrdom of Timol that gave so much to struggle in South Africa. It was a turning point in the allegiances of many people.

Today, in the remarkable conditions of peace and reconciliation that exist now, these factors require adequate articulation and commemoration, as part of the deepening and strengthening of our democracy.

Timol can be seen, in this sense, as a pillar of non-racial, democratic South Africa.

SPEECH BY NELSON MANDELA – RENAMING OF SCHOOL
(29 March 1999)

Master of ceremonies
Ladies and gentlemen
Friends

I am very glad to be able to spend even this short while with you. It is always a special pleasure to be with teachers, parents and my favourite kind of people, the youth. Few things in life are as painful as losing one's child. Anyone who doubted that, had only to listen to the testimony of Ahmed Timol's mother as she told her story to the Truth and Reconciliation Commission. The memory of the suffering, frail woman, like thousands of other mothers who appeared before the Truth Commission, still brings us as much pain as the inhumanity of her son's death. Like most of you, I did not know Timol personally. But all of us, I'm sure, wonder who he would be if he were alive today.

Would he have been a father and a teacher himself and perhaps have taught at this very school? What we can say with certainty is that Timol was a brave young man who believed in freedom and justice, and who fought for non-racialism and democracy. Timol would have been proud to be citizen of a democratic South Africa, where all our cultures and religions are guaranteed by the constitution. He would have rejoiced in the fact that we are on the eve of our second democratic elections. He would surely have been amongst the first to register and to mobilise others to do so, so that they can make their voice heard in the elections on 2 June.

Living in Azaadville he would have been proud of a community that is a thread in the rich tapestry of South Africa's diversity; of this school with its large enrolment of students from underprivileged areas; and of a community that played a role in relief for the residents of Swanieville in times of distress. He would have encouraged the community to be active in the building of the new South Africa, and not to sit back and wait for government to do everything. Democracy brings us the opportunity to have a say over our lives, and we should do everything possible in partnership with government to tackle the problems of crime, poverty and injustice that still prevail. Timol would have encouraged those with skills to share them with the less privileged. Timol the teacher would have approved of our new education system, which provides education for all children equally. But he would have also wanted those who have opportunities his generation never had, to study hard in order to become productive members of society.

There are also things that he would have fought against, such as corruption, theft and unaccountable leaders. Many youngsters today know little or nothing of the proud legacy left by our heroes. He would have wanted the youth, all of you, to be firm in your knowledge of where you come from.

Few of today's young people have experienced first-hand the cruelty of apartheid repression. We hope that renaming this school after Ahmed Timol will help you understand the courage of those who opened the way for all of us who are free today.

We hope too that what you learn today about Timol will lead you to find out about others like him, like Looksmart Ngudle, Imam Haron, Neil Aggett and many more who died because they dared to challenge the inhumanity of apartheid. They sacrificed careers and livelihoods, and sometimes even life, so that we all could one day live with dignity. They would want you to learn about the strong alliances, since the time of Gandhi and Dr Xuma, between the different sectors of the oppressed – African, Indian and coloured – and the support of democrats from the white community.

They would want you to know that our democracy is a product of all the people of South Africa who reached out to one another across the divisions of centuries.

That tradition is alive today in the rebuilding of our country, as men, women and youth from every community and political party are increasingly joining hands to work for the objective of a better life for all that Timol fought for.

Ladies and gentlemen, we thank all those who persevered in this project: friends, family, the school governing body, teachers and the community. Ahmed Timol's mother asked that a school be named after her son. Had she lived to see the bright young faces I see now, she would perhaps have felt that her son did not die in vain. I am sure that all the children at this school, knowing that, will strive to live up to the memory of Ahmed Timol. The best way that we can honour his memory is by ensuring that our democracy remains strong and that it does bring a better life for all. As a nation, we are already bringing down the walls that keep us from this goal. Each of us must do whatever we can to bring delivery of services to those who were denied to them before. Each of us should make our contribution to creating jobs and to reconciling our nation. It is a great privilege to have the task of unveiling the plaque that bears the new name of this school. Let us remember Ahmed Timol in our striving.

INDEX

Homekillers 58
Huddlestone, Father Trevor
Naught For Your Comfort 45
Hurley, Archbishop Dennis 137, 152
Hutchinson, Alfred 39
hydroquinone 119

I

Iftaar 127-128
used for fast-breaking time
Immigration School at Slough 74-75
Indian Congress Movement 35-36, 45, 56, 169
  establishment of the Central Indian High School 39
  recruitment into 92-93
Indian Cricket Union (ICU) 56
Indian people co-operate with African people
  declaration in 1918, Indians part of population 32
  Three Doctors' Pact, 1947 35
Indian Training College 43
Inkululeko-Freedom 102-103
inquest into Ahmed Timol's death 147-162
International Lenin School 80
Israeli Defence Force 115
ittikaaf 140
  used for the state of seclusion during Ramadan

J

Jacobsen, Quentin 99, 117, 135-136
Jameson Raid, 1896 32
janaazah 139-140
  used for funeral prayers
Jan Smuts Airport 59-60, 106
  used for Johannesburg International Airport
Jassat, Abdulhay 69, 114-115
Jassat, Checker 58
Jeppe Street Post Office 98, 100
Jhetham, Dilshad 116, 119-120
Jina, Sadique 74
Johannesburg College of Education 50, 141
Johannesburg Indian High School (JIHS)
  education at, Ahmed Timol 38
  matric, Ahmed Timol, 1959 40
Johannesburg International Airport
  see Jan Smuts Airport
Johannesburg Training Institute for Indian

Teachers 41, 46-51
John Vorster Square 105, 112-117, 152, 154, 164
Jooma, Hassen 49-51, 105, 116, 166
  detained at John Vorster Square 121-122
  interrogation of 127-131
  Nirvana High School, at 51
Joubert, Staff Sgt 116
JP Coats 104

K

kaffan 138
  used for burial shroud
Kaka, Ahmed Suliman (Ronnie) 77-78
Kallicharan, Alvin 57
Kasrils, Ronnie 86, 93, 101-102
Kathrada, Ahmed 44, 69, 85
Katz, Max 117
Kemp, Stephanie 92, 94, 100, 102, 106, 165
Kemp, Dr Vernon Dennis 136, 157-158
Khan, Mohammed 167-168
Kholvad 28-30
Kholvad House/Hostel 29, 46, 88, 109
Kholvad Madressa 35-36, 47, 71-72, 148
  see also Madressa Anjuman Islamia of Kholvad
Kholvad Welfare Society 36
Khota, Ahmed (Quarter) 88, 95
Khota, Goolaam Mohamed Ahmed (Goramota) 46-47
Khota, Naeema 71
Khota, Rafique 63-64
Kleyns, Sgt Leonard Gilbert 111, 134-135
Kliptown 58
Kloppers, Maj JM 111
Koch, Dr 155
Kosi, Humphrey 65
Kotane, Moses 69, 80
Kotze, PAJ 150, 152
kurma 88
  used for cooked lamb that is fried

L

Labour Monthly 75, 84
Lappies
  see Durban Deep Gold Mine Compound
Lawrence College, Rawalpindi, Pakistan 90
Lekhogale, Cornelius Tebogo 117
Lenasia 96-97, 100
Lenasia Indian High School 41

AUTHOR'S NOTE

I was five years old when my uncle was murdered. The bulk of the information collected for this book is based on interviews done with family and friends. I apologise for any factual errors that may appear in this book. I have to the best of my ability attempted to reflect the life of my uncle as correctly as possible.

The author

SPONSORS

Thanks to the following people whose generous donations made the publication of this book possible.

GAUTENG
Congress of Business & Economics
Setar Motani & Family
Jabbar Mia Patel
Zaheed Faqui-Dawood
Jay Pema
Akhar Seedat
Rooknudeen Cajee
Ebrahim Terajia
Khalil Sayed
Shahid Sharif
Ashwin Mancha
Moosa Teba
Ameer Amod
Ahmed Asvat
Mohammed Khota

WESTERN CAPE
AK Peer, Chairman of the LA Group
Shaheen Ebrahim, Chairman of
Oasis Group Holdings

NATAL
Abdul Saccoor
Ashwin Beosumbar
Chris Naidoo
Anant Singh
Vivian Reddy
Deen Letchmiah
Desmond Chetty
Dr Adam Mahomed
Nirode Bramdaw
Harish Mehta
Jay Patel
Robbie Naidoo
Moosa Moosa
Morgan Nadesan
MS Paruk
Ruben Reddy
Saantha Naidu
AK Paruk
Abdul Patel
Suresh Naidoo
AK Lockhat
Willy Govender
Yacoob Paruk